CHRISTY MATHEWSON, THE CHRISTIAN GENTLEMAN

CHRISTY MATHEWSON, THE CHRISTIAN GENTLEMAN

How One Man's Faith and Fastball Forever Changed Baseball

Bob Gaines

ROWMAN & LITTLEFIELD
Lanham • Boulder • New York • London

Published by Rowman & Littlefield
A wholly owned subsidiary of The Rowman & Littlefield Publishing Group, Inc.
4501 Forbes Boulevard, Suite 200, Lanham, Maryland 20706
www.rowman.com

16 Carlisle Street, London W1D 3BT, United Kingdom

British Library Cataloguing in Publication Information Available

Library of Congress Cataloging-in-Publication Data

Gaines, Bob.
Christy Mathewson, the Christian gentleman : how one man's faith and fastball forever changed baseball / Bob Gaines.
p. cm.
Includes bibliographical references and index.
ISBN 978-1-4422-3314-0 (cloth : alk. paper) – ISBN 978-1-4422-3315-7 (ebook)
1. Mathewson, Christy, 1880–1925. 2. Pitchers (Baseball)–United States–Biography. 3. Baseball players–United States–Biography. 4. Christian athletes–United States–Biography. 5. Christian athletes–Religious life. 6. New York Giants (Baseball team) I. Title.
GV865.M327G35 2015
796.357092–dc23
[B] 2014026165

CONTENTS

ACKNOWLEDGMENTS

Jean McCasland (Escondido, California), the daughter of the great Giants' shortstop Art Fletcher, who invited me to view his wondrous scrapbook.

Betty Cook (Lewisburg, Pennsylvania), the teenage girl who accompanied Jane Mathewson to numerous Hall of Fame events in Cooperstown in the 1950s and 1960s, who provided splendid stories about the Mathewson family.

Terry Wise (Factoryville, Pennsylvania), an associate professor of sports and recreation management at Keystone College, who graciously let me explore the school's vault of Mathewson memorabilia and provided insight about Christy's hometown.

Jon Terry (Lewisburg, Pennsylvania), the director of sports information at Bucknell, who uncovered a few old clippings from Christy's college days and pointed me to the university archives.

Ryan Whitfield (Virginia Beach, Virginia), a chaplain in the U.S. Navy and my son-in-law, who provided keen insight and great discussions about religious history.

To the great folks who work at the Baseball Hall of Fame (Cooperstown, New York).

To the old newspaper writers of long ago—Grantland Rice, Damon Runyon, Sam Crane, Bozeman Bulger, Arthur Daley, Ring Lardner, Dan Carr, Sturdy Pexton . . .

To my daughter, Megan, and son, Robbie, for their spiritual advice and never ending love.

INTRODUCTION

It was an old scrapbook, thick with hundreds of stained, brown newspaper articles and crumbling photos, housing the life of Art Fletcher—absolutely beautiful.

Fletcher had played for the New York Giants in the early 1900s, a fiery infielder built in the mold of pugnacious manager John "Muggsy" McGraw. "There was fighting everywhere they went," wrote Giants' historian Frank Graham back in the day, "and Fletcher always was in the thick of it. He fought enemy players, umpires, and fans."[1] As a player and later coach for the Yankees, Fletcher would earn checks from fourteen World Series, with the *Sporting News* naming him the best third-base coach of the first half-century of baseball.

As a sports columnist for a daily newspaper in San Diego, I received a call in 1988 from Art Fletcher's daughter . . . she had a scrapbook.

Reading through the pages of this true baseball treasure, I was struck at how sportswriters of the era referred to one of Fletcher's teammates, Christy Mathewson. Most of the players were simply called by their last name—Fletcher, Doyle, Merkle, Snodgrass, Meyers, McGinnity. But Mathewson was continually treated as some sort of baseball god—Matty, Big Six, The Christian Gentleman, The Great Mathewson.

A century later, the details of Matty's phenomenal life have, in many ways, been blurred by history. Not that most everyone hasn't heard the name of the great Hall of Fame pitcher from the Deadball Era. But here's the deal. Baseball folks tend to mark the historical progress of the game as beginning at the precise point of their personal awareness during childhood. For me, that would be a five-year-old boy sitting in a huge movie theater watching a black-and-white newsreel of the 1950 World Series between the Phillies and Yankees, stunned that "Whiz Kids" played baseball. From that point forward, I was a student of the game. Before the 1950s, not so much.

Eight years after writing the column about Fletcher, I happened to land a job at Bucknell University in Lewisburg, Pennsylvania. Strong academics, a pristine campus, storied athletics . . . and on the wall of the Bucknell Sports Hall of Fame, a photo of Christy Mathewson, Class of 1902. Turns out that Christy, Jane, and their son were all Bucknellians, now buried on a hill next to the school.

Call it curiosity, but the Bucknell archives led me to visit Christy's boyhood home in Factoryville to explore the vault at Keystone College. Don't forget the Baseball Hall of Fame in Cooperstown. Intrigue became an obsession, soon creating multimedia presentations for alumni and local churches, even putting together a book for the 2012 reunion. From those seeds comes *Christy Mathewson, the Christian Gentleman*.

Yes, it happened long before our own childhoods, but Big Six was the greatest pitcher in baseball history, the first All-American hero, credited with forever changing the face of a tainted and brutal game . . . loved for his athletic prowess, idolized for his unique character . . . a man who quietly lived within the word of God, never once to falter.

I

THE BOY WONDER FROM BUCKNELL
(1901)

Christy Mathewson sat alone in the Giants' dugout, the vast expanse of the outfield seemingly stretching to another universe . . . a view that could be highly deceptive.

There were the players, of course, a puzzling array of wondrous talent and crude defiance. And the rooters, mostly intoxicated men out for a late afternoon escape, the old wooden stands constantly rocking between their pleasure and rage.

There was nothing small about the mighty Polo Grounds, except that the stadium was a mere pocket to the world beyond—Gotham, with its pace and possibilities, triumph and pain, beauty and ruin.

A small town kid with big dreams, Matty loved God, family, and baseball. He sheltered no doubts that he would thrive within the Grand Design; he was just not quite sure where his place might be.

Probably not with the New York Giants. An outcast on a band of fools, Christy's station had been relegated to the far end of the bench, the dugout floor covered with an irritating mixture of dirt, sweat, and tobacco juice.

❄ ❄ ❄

It was no secret that the 1901 New York Giants were loaded with "knockers, shirkers, and loafers."[1] While harmoniously accepting defeat, the inner circle openly complained that Christy Mathewson was purposely trying to show them up . . . by winning. Just as annoying was that the twenty-year-old college kid owned a $1,500 contract, more than most of the veterans.

Not everyone on the team disliked Christy, just enough to fuel an uncomfortable environment. Kip Selbach and Mike Grady refused to even speak to the youngster. Piano Legs Hickman, who set a major league record with ninety-one errors at third base in 1900, made no secret of his resentment, always addressing Matty as "Sis."

"There could be no justifiable reason for the older players' mysterious dislike of Christy," wrote Blanche McGraw in her biography of her husband, John McGraw. "They were somehow encouraged not to like him."[2]

It didn't matter that Matty won his first eight games or twirled a no-hitter in St. Louis. They didn't seem to care that a team that had reached the top of the National League back on the Fourth of July—the day Matty went twelve innings to beat the Pirates—was now plummeting toward the cellar. A few seemed bitter that attendance was booming, jealous that rooters were anxious to see Christy Mathewson, the handsome rookie, the "Boy Wonder from Bucknell." Even women and children were starting to attend games when Matty was pitching.

"He was the toast of New York," recalled sportswriter Fred Lieb.[3]

But disliked and ridiculed by a clique of veterans in the dugout, branded an outcast on a team of misfits, he couldn't wait for the season to end.

✿ ✿ ✿

Through the turmoil, Christy's mentor was a friend with absolutely no advice about throwing a baseball, but tons regarding life and the wonders of God.

John Howard Harris was the president of Bucknell, a small Baptist college in central Pennsylvania. He had also been Christy's boyhood pastor. Harris was energetic, physically fit, a dynamic orator who mixed a powerful intellect with a resounding faith.

"Honesty, because it is essentially mighty, needs no hiding," Harris had preached to the Factoryville First Baptist Church. "It is the moral and spiritual developments that distinguish the complete man."[4]

As a child, Christy had always sat in the front row, eagerly listening to every word from the pulpit. Now that he was an honor student, class president, and college football star, Matty sat front and center for the required morning worship at Bucknell Hall.

"We often paint Jesus as a passive sufferer in the hands of the ungodly," President Harris told the college students. "But do not forget the moral energy of his nature. "Steady against evil, His love has compassion. For even those who feast on swine have unmeasured worth. Like Jesus, let your anger be without sin."[5]

Matty had always lived the words of his preacher, but how did it translate to Gotham? The world of the New York Giants rotated around drinking, fighting, and trying to hit a baseball . . . a chamber of hateful teammates routinely pounding his ego and emotions.

"Adversity can only make us stronger," President Harris had said. "Character alone shines by its own light."[6]

But in the summer of 1901, Matty's light seemed rather dim, his station relegated to the far corner of the dugout. The idiots mocked him, so he ignored them.

✿ ✿ ✿

In the summer of 1901, his journey still uncharted, Christy Mathewson had no idea that he would soon become the greatest pitcher in baseball history. Forget the early animosity of teammates, Matty was but a couple of seasons from being proclaimed the nation's first All-American idol, the perfect role model, a man of moral integrity and a stinging fastball. Proclaimed by the masses as almost single-handedly erasing professional baseball's rough and tarnished image, the Christian Gentleman would ride a legend from which he would never fall.

"He brought something to baseball that no one else had ever given the game," wrote famed sportswriter Grantland Rice. "He handed the game a certain touch of class, an indefinable lift in culture, brains, and personality. He is the only man I ever met who in spirit and inspiration was greater than his game."[7]

✿ ✿ ✿

Statistically, Christy Mathewson was from another planet. In a seventeen-year career, he would register a National League record 373 victories. In thirteen of those seasons, he busted the twenty-win barrier; four times passing thirty victories. In 1905, he would lead the Giants to their first World Series title by pitching three shutouts in six days, still considered the greatest pitching exploit in postseason history. In 1908, Matty compiled a 37-11 record. Actually, season after season carried a ton of magical moments. There would be 2 no-hitters, 80 shutouts, and 2,502 strikeouts. He would go the distance in 435 of 551 starts, averaging but one walk per game.

In 1936, Matty would join Ty Cobb, Babe Ruth, Honus Wagner, and Walter Johnson as the charter class of the Baseball Hall of Fame. Years later, his name would grace Major League Baseball's All-Century Team.

But Matty's story would become far greater than an extraordinary archive of records and honors. He would change the very image of the game, his virtue and character capturing the nation's admiration.

"He set a high moral code," said Connie Mack, who managed the Philadelphia Athletics for fifty years. "He was lauded by the churches, ministers used his career as sermon topics, he gave dignity and character to baseball . . . he was the greatest pitcher who ever lived."[8]

"He came into the sport when it was populated by rowdies," said sportswriter Arthur Daley. "He didn't descend to their level. Such was his force of character and example that he lifted them up to his."[9]

America was searching for a hero; baseball needed a savior. The timing was perfect.

* * *

As the summer of 1901 began to fade and Christy turned twenty-one years old, he was obviously blessed with some solid options. In two semesters he'd have a college degree, hopefully land a job with the forestry service, marry Jenny Stoughton, and raise a family. Perhaps baseball was not his best path.

Then again, John Howard Harris had always said that every man should "rise as far as his ability and energy will carry him."[10]

Okay, baseball was filled with shady characters, but Christy had a gift.

Christy Mathewson changed the image of professional baseball. Courtesy of the National Baseball Hall of Fame

"Whatever may be your vocation, regard it as a calling of God," President Harris suggested.[11]

Armed with faith and a fastball, Christy Mathewson was glory bound.

2

A NEAR PERFECT BOYHOOD (1889)

The words were eloquent, powerful.

"Happy the child who is born in a family of wealth in all things spiritual," Pastor John Howard Harris would tell the faithful gathering at the Factoryville First Baptist Church.[1]

A captivating presence, the pastor was tall, handsome, and physically fit. His near perfect voice and diction revealed a profound and piercing intellect that could transform doubters into believers. He was dynamic, energetic, compassionate, and fun. With a rock-solid ethical compass as his flag, John Harris was the very definition of muscular Christianity.

"Jesus had iron in His blood, and upon occasion, flaming indignation in His soul and scathing rebukes upon his lips," Pastor Harris avidly declared. "But only let the anger be without sin. The love of Jesus, while on the one hand manifests itself as wrath against evil, on the other appears as passion."[2]

It was never hard for Pastor Harris to find the Mathewson family, together in the front row, the oldest son wearing his Sunday best, sitting upright with undeniable interest . . . Christy Mathewson was rather unique for an eight-year-old boy.

The pastor also realized that the Sabbath was never a day of rest for young Christy, what with chores at dawn and the usual exploration of the backwoods that surrounded his home. What amazed Pastor Harris was not that the boy was never late for church, but that he was always so cleanly scrubbed—truly an act of God.

Actually, that would be an act of Christy's mother, Minerva, who claimed she was "always particular about regular hours of sleep and plenty of plain, wholesome food, good milk, fresh air, and the Golden Rule."[3]

If character is formed in childhood, Christy Mathewson was created for stardom.

* * *

In 1878, many of the folks in Factoryville were a bit miffed that Minerva Capwell had accepted a marriage proposal from Gilbert Mathewson. After all, she was a Capwell—one of the most upstanding families in the area. As a youngster, she was nicknamed "Nervy" for her ability to break the wildest of horses. Now twenty-three, she was beautiful, charming, and vibrant—and knew exactly what she wanted in life. And this, at first glance, would seem to be a rather peculiar match.

Not that there was anything wrong with Gilbert. A veteran of the Civil War, "Gib" was tall, handsome, and humbly quiet. He had been a postal worker and barkeeper with an eye on someday becoming a land developer. Goodness, he was thirty-one years old and didn't quite seem to know what he wanted.

For certain, his barkeeping days were over, Minerva being a staunch supporter of the Woman's Christian Temperance Union.

Bottom line was that she was determined to raise a family with a wealth of love, education, and religion. Turns out that's precisely what Gilbert wanted.

* * *

Their first of six children, Christopher, was born on August 12, 1880. He was healthy and curious, blessed with affection from a village filled with relatives and friends.

True, Factoryville seemed an odd name for paradise, but it provided a near perfect environment. Christy's youthful years were enhanced by a picturesque environment dotted with streams, apple orchards, corn-fields, and forest. Fishing and hunting were plentiful, the air pure and healthy. A small and inviting town with about 650 residents, Factoryville rested within a long valley skirted by adventurous hills. There had

Christy was born in the rural hills of northeast Pennsylvania. Courtesy of the National Baseball Hall of Fame

once been a cotton mill, but never a factory. Folks were neighborly and content, and the three churches were always bustling. And if there was a need to keep tabs on the outside world, there were newspapers from as far away as Scranton and magazines from New York City. Plus, the

Delaware, Lackawanna & Western Railroad line was a daily reminder of high-speed modern transportation.

Scranton, with its big city bustle and scent of coal dust, was sixteen miles to the southeast, still a major trip by horse and buggy. To many, particularly the three-quarters of the country living in rural areas, old ways best be left alone.

But make no mistake, in 1880 there were rapid changes in a nation of thirty-eight states and fifty million residents. James Garfield would become the nation's twentieth president, but Thomas Edison was its genius. His phonograph may have been a monumental invention, but now his electric lights covered the entire main street of Wabash, Indiana, and a good stretch of Broadway in New York City. Railroads, stretching from coast to coast, were the nation's largest industry. It had been four years since the Battle of the Little Big Horn and the Wild West seemed a bit tamer, particularly with Pat Garrett chasing Billy the Kid and Wyatt Earp becoming the new deputy sheriff of Tombstone.

In Detroit, a seventeen-year-old apprentice machinist with a knack for tinkering with timepieces, Henry Ford, proved that modernity was truly an eclectic mix of old and new.

Few in 1880 noticed the births of Helen Keller (Alabama), Douglas MacArthur (Arkansas), Damon Runyon (Kansas), or Grantland Rice (Tennessee).

Out in Southern California, John Tortes Meyers of the Cahuilla tribe was born on the Santa Rosa Reservation, about the time William Claude Dukenfield was starting to crawl in Darby, Pennsylvania. John Meyers—who would be called "Chief" by baseball fans—would become one of baseball's greatest catchers, teaming with Christy Mathewson on the New York Giants. Dukenfield would someday watch Matty and Meyers work their magic at the Polo Grounds, having personally changed his name to W. C. Fields.

❊ ❊ ❊

The first hint that Christy had baseball in his blood was at the age of two when he playfully hurled his mother's dishes out the kitchen window. After a stern lesson from his mother, all was forgiven until he taught his older Aunt Jessie, age four, the art of throwing stones, the unfortunate target being the rump of Grandpa's favorite carriage horse, Dandy.

Hearing panic in his stable, Grandpa rushed furiously from the house and seized a horsewhip.

"He spoke to the now frightened children in no gentle tones," recalled Christy's mother. "Jessie made a bee-line for the house, but Christy stood stock-still. 'Wait just a minute, grandpa, and let's talk it over first.'"[4]

Bravery worked—Grandpa dropped the whip—but another lesson had been learned. No tossing inside the house or at the horse. But nothing was said about throwing balls over the roof, particularly when he could impress the older kids who didn't believe he was strong enough. Always big for his age, Christy's mind somehow calculated that size equaled maturity. Although his arm was powerful, it was not yet accurate, with the ball clearing the roof only to shatter the neighbor's window.

Minerva told her anguished four-year-old that he would need to confess to Mrs. Reynolds and pay for the repairs.

"It had taken Christy a long time to save the dollar the broken window cost," recalled Minerva, "but it taught him a sense of responsibility."[5]

But it didn't hinder his thirst for playing with the older boys. Demanding entry into the baseball games, Christy continually applied to pitch. The assignment was usually right field, a position he held throughout the 1880s.

"I was pretty good at chasing the balls that got away from me," said Christy.[6]

Fishing, swimming, exploring . . . there seemed no finer place in the world than Factoryville. In 1886, when the Mathewsons moved to a modest two-story house on the eastern hill above town, Christy was given permission to throw against a knothole in the barn, away from the house. From persistent practice, he found uncanny control. It also helped to have a passion for throwing rocks, a thousand trees acting as targets. As he grew, Christy learned to skip flat stones on the stream and collected round ones for hunting expeditions.

"When I was nine years old, I could throw a stone farther than any of the boys who were my chums," said Christy. "Then I used to go out in the woods and throw at squirrels and blackbirds, and even sparrows; and many a bagful of game I got with stones."[7]

An avid reader with a retentive mind, Christy excelled in school. In the evenings or down by the summer swimming hole, he would play checkers for hours against the young or old.

What he didn't particularly cherish were his chores—working in the apple orchard, milking the cows, hoeing the potato garden, or gathering eggs from the hens. Although he loved keeping the beehive, he had always had other places to be . . . especially the ballfield.

From wooded hills to rock-skipping streams, he enjoyed an amazing boyhood centered upon a wonderful home with parents who provided guidance, protection, and love. Nervy and Gib were frugal, hard-working, and well-liked. They possessed unbounding faith . . . prayers at the kitchen table, stories by the fire, reading the family Bible, Sundays at First Baptist.

Noting Christy's attraction to religion, Minerva was certain that her son was destined to become a preacher.

"To the best of my recollection, I never gave the matter serious thought," said Christy. "Certainly as far back as that age when every boy contrasts the advantages of being a pirate or an Indian hunter, and tries to determine in which particular profession he would be most likely to shine, I chose the profession of baseball player."[8]

Don't blame the adults for giggling when Christy, age eight, made the official announcement that he indeed planned to pitch in the major leagues. Christy was far too nice a boy for professional baseball, a wicked amusement reserved for hoodlums, ruffians, and squanderers. Real baseball was the amateur game, played in thousands of towns with deep-rooted rivalries like Factoryville versus Mill City.

Nobody said that a kid couldn't dream. Although Christy had never seen a big league game, his picture of playing ball on a smooth, rock-free field inside a big city stadium seemed magical.

✸ ✸ ✸

It should be no surprise that John Howard Harris would become Christy's friend and role model. They had much in common, beginning with similar childhoods.

The same age as Christy's father, John Howard Harris was born in Indiana County, Pennsylvania, on April 24, 1847. Raised on a farm with his fair share of chores, he enjoyed a full schedule of hunting, fishing, hiking, and education. Industrious and ambitious, he was physically and mentally ahead of his peers, his great intellect enhanced by outstanding schooling.

"I have never known anyone who wasted less time," recalled Mary Harris, his only daughter.[9]

He was a tireless reader of biographies, history, horticulture, and the Bible; preferring to study on the hilltops near his home.

Even as a child, the future college president developed an amazing ability to memorize lengthy passages from the Bible, along with a constructive probing of God's intentions.

"The Bible we were expected to read as a duty," he said, "but I soon learned to read it as a pleasure, and I committed to memory large portions of it, which I have found invaluable in all my life."[10]

His mind was fertile, and his wide-ranging facts precise. He also was blessed with a moral integrity that would never falter.

If that sounds like Christy Mathewson, there would be one major difference. Although both loved center stage, Christy was extremely uncomfortable speaking in front of even the smallest of audiences. Harris thrived as an orator.

"He is the most powerful preacher to whom I have ever listened," said Dr. Milton Evans, president of Crozer Theological Seminary.[11]

Warren Davis, a good friend of Pastor Harris, added, "He stirred the hearts and minds and consciences of those who listened to him to their deepest depths."[12]

Harris's resume was stunning.

A certified schoolteacher at the age of fifteen, Harris would leave the classroom at the outbreak of the Civil War. By 1864, he was a sergeant in the 206th Pennsylvania Volunteers, reaching the front line in Richmond, Virginia. Even in the midst of war, he continued to learn and explore, finding comfort at the Christian Association, a tent where soldiers gathered to read, write, and debate. After the war, he entered Bucknell (then known as the University at Lewisburg), presumably to study law. But after graduating with honors in 1869, he was given a commission by the college president, Reverend Justin Loomis, to found a Baptist secondary school in northeast Pennsylvania.

"He had no funds and very little backing," said Mary Harris. "But he had unlimited courage, a great vision, and abounding faith."[13]

Factoryville's Keystone Academy would flourish, with the twenty-two-year-old Harris becoming the first principal, teacher, and builder. What began as the only high school between Scranton and the New York border, originally serving sixteen students at the Factoryville First Baptist Church, soon had its own four-story building with a booming enrollment. As if he had any spare time, Harris earned his doctorate, became an ordained minister, was named church pastor, and oversaw the construction of a second building. In 1889, he was named Bucknell University's eighth president, a post he would hold for the next thirty years, a tenure that remains the longest in school history.

John and Lucy Harris—close friends to Gib and Nervy Mathewson—would raise eight boys and one girl. As children, the two oldest boys—Herbert and Reese—were Christy's playmates. Lucy Harris, like her good friend Minerva Mathewson, was deeply involved in church, charity, and the temperance movement.

❂ ❂ ❂

In 1890, Christy caught his first big break as "second catcher" for the Factoryville men's ball club. His job was to chase foul balls and fetch water for the players.

"I became a known factor in the baseball circles of Factoryville," Christy wrote, "and might be said to have started my career." [14]

The pitcher even taught him how to throw a curve, which Christy relentlessly practiced. Someone should have shown him how to properly hold the bat. Christy insisted on hitting cross-handed, a habit he blamed on all that hoeing he had to do in the potato garden.

"Once in a while, I would connect with the ball, in my awkward, cross-handed style," said Christy, "and it would always be a long wallop, because I was a big, husky, country boy; but more often I ignominiously struck out." [15]

He refused to be deterred.

"Even then," he said, "I would rather play baseball than eat." [16]

And this boy loved his mother's cooking. In fact, he was now so big that the older kids nicknamed him "Husk." And then sent him to right field.

❂ ❂ ❂

Being "second catcher" was fun, but in the summer of 1894, Christy Mathewson stepped it up a notch. The day of the big rivalry game against nearby Mill City, Factoryville surprisingly found itself without its two twirlers. Hearing that fourteen-year-old Christy Mathewson could pitch, the team captain ordered a makeshift tryout with half the town gathered on Main Street the very morning of the game.

"I put everything I had on the ball," Christy said of the two-hour tryout.[17]

Christy's friends—including all the older boys—stood in awe as he boarded the carriage and rode away with the men.

"That, I am sure, was the proudest day of my life," said Christy.[18]

The bad news was that Christy, his arm heavy from the morning workout, was punished by Mill City for seventeen runs. The good news was that the youngster became the hitting hero with an eventual game-winning blast that sailed over the leftfielder's head. Factoryville would win 19-17.

Before any coronation as the Factoryville ace, he would first need to attend high school. Ernest Sterling, who lived sixteen miles to the north, boarded with the Mathewson family, the two boys walking down the hill to Keystone Academy. The same age as Matty, the two quickly became best friends, sharing many of the same interests, from athletics and checkers to academics and faith.

A sharp memory, profound mathematical capacity, and crisp handwriting were but a taste of what made Christy an outstanding student. He buried himself in study, and still left time for athletics as captain of the baseball team and a promising force in football.

In August 1897, a month before his senior year, Matty was invited to pitch for Mill City. Almost seventeen years old, Matty was now a veteran star for Factoryville, but the hometown club had already finished its season.

Here was the kicker: Mill City would pay Matty a dollar per game. The youngster was stunned, ecstatic. Getting paid for having fun seemed beyond his wildest dreams.

Two decades later, he would quip that, apparently, the good people of Mill City were "determined to have a winning ball team at all costs."[19]

In February 1898, during Christy's senior year at Keystone, the outbreak of the Spanish-American War had his full interest. The family plan was that Christy, on his way to becoming a pastor, would attend college. However, reading about Colonel Teddy Roosevelt's volunteer Rough Riders charging up San Juan Hill and Admiral George Dewey's victory at the Battle of Manila Bay, Christy's impulse was to enlist. But the United States dominated the tide of war, erasing Spain's once formidable colonial rule in the Americas and western Pacific. By August it was over, and Christy was busy with baseball and preparing for college.

Plus, it had been a good summer for baseball. After graduation, he had decided to visit Scranton—a huge city in his eyes—to watch the powerful YMCA team. Sitting in the stands munching on a bag of peanuts, he was recognized by one of the YMCA players. Turns out their pitcher was absent that day and they asked Christy if he'd help.

Sure he did, excitedly jumping from his seat and "leaving quite three cents worth of peanuts on the seat, which was no compliment to my natural country thrift."[20]

In a uniform that was several sizes too large, the seventeen-year-old took to the biggest venue of his life and beat the Pittston Reds with fourteen strikeouts. The next week he was pitching for the YMCA at Easton, traveling a personal record eighty miles from home and winning yet another game.

By midsummer, the Honesdale Eagles offered Christy a contract for $20 per month plus room and board, money he could save for college.

"It was a princely salary," said Christy, "and I began to speak of 'J.P. Morgan and me.'"[21]

What proved most valuable to Christy was that he dumped the cross-handed hitting style and learned a strange new pitch that broke the exact opposite way from a traditional curve. According to Christy, a lefty named Dave Williams would sometimes practice a "freak delivery over which he had no control."[22]

Christy also learned a nifty drop to go with his fastball and roundhouse curve. He figured he would never master the "freak" pitch, but he'd have fun trying.

After the Eagles captured the championship of the Wayne and Orange County League, Christy went home for a few days before heading to Bucknell. His intention was to play football, earn a degree, and embark on a solid career. Baseball had been a fun summer job.

✿ ✿ ✿

At a time when barely 6 percent of the nation earned high school diplomas, the surprise around Factoryville was that Christy would not be attending the University of Pennsylvania. A powerful runner with extraordinary kicking abilities—not to mention high intelligence—Christy seemed a perfect fit for Penn. The Ivy League school had the best football program in the nation, with the Quakers winning the national championship in 1897 with a 15-0 record. The 1898 squad was captained by All-America senior John Outland, a man of dubious principles and faith. Same for the Penn coach, George Woodruff, who had already compiled an 82-5 record that included three undefeated seasons.

There were several reasons Christy selected Bucknell. Great academics. Ernest Sterling, his best friend from Keystone, would be his roommate. And his first pastor was the university's president.

That also excited his parents. John Howard Harris would be a brilliant role model for their son, the summertime baseball player and unceasing dreamer.

"I thought baseball would last a little while," said Minerva, "and that then my hope of his being a preacher would be realized."[23]

In late September 1898, Christy was finally on his way to college. He'd never been to Bucknell, or Central Pennsylvania for that matter, but heard the campus was beautiful, with stately brick buildings on the shores of the Susquehanna River. The college was noted for tough academics, and Christy knew his schedule would include algebra, trigonometry, geometry, French, German, and Latin. The required reading list for freshmen was *Paradise Lost*, *The Last of the Mohicans*, *Silas Marner*, *The House of the Seven Gables*, *Ivanhoe*, and *Macbeth*. He couldn't wait.

He also was excited about the eleven-game football schedule, particularly looking forward to road trips against Navy, Lehigh, Penn State, Lafayette, and Buffalo. Too bad they wouldn't be heading for Philadelphia to inflict some bad news on the Penn Quakers. Again, Christy had a very active mind.

In fact, Bucknell was hardly a powerhouse, even though the Bison always seemed to win one or two more than they lost.

To Christy, the hundred-mile trip from Factoryville to Lewisburg by train and carriage could not end fast enough. Academics, athletics . . . he was primed for every challenge.

He was eighteen years old with the glory days just ahead.

✺ ✺ ✺

Founded by Baptists in 1846, Bucknell had a reputation for producing Christian leaders. It was not cheap—tuition, room, and board costing $140 per year. Christy felt blessed to have some spending cash from summer baseball.

With seventy-five members, the Class of 1902 would be hailed as the largest first-year contingent in the school's history. Christy hit campus at full speed, meeting with the football coach, buying his books, and finding a local church. That first Sunday, classmates Christy, Ernest Sterling, and Frank Stanton walked downtown to the First Baptist Church, enjoying the service with the Harris family. Afterward, the three incoming freshmen were invited to dinner at the president's house—quite the honor.

"We were dressed in our best," said Stanton, who would star with Christy in football and basketball. "They really made us feel at home."[24]

Because the Harris family included nine children, the atmosphere was more than comfortable. For Christy, it was good to see old friends, particularly the two oldest Harris kids—Herbert would be starting his sophomore year at Bucknell and Reese was a senior at Lewisburg High School.

Stanton enjoyed President Harris's stories about the Factoryville Baptist Church.

"He recalled Christy at the age of eight sitting in the front seat, very straight, with well-combed hair and a white collar, paying strict attention," said Stanton. "The doctor seemed to think it was a bit unusual."[25]

Although President Harris took interest in all of Bucknell's 269 students, Christy was special to the old pastor. They often spoke about campus life and Factoryville, but even more important were their conversations on faith, moral integrity, and maturity. Christy had always lived within God's word, but he still had a lot of growing up to do.

Academics proved no problem as the youngster notched an average grade of ninety-five with nothing below ninety.

As for football, the six-foot-two-inch, 180-pound fullback was big, strong, and fast, contributing two touchdowns, two field goals, and a bundle of spectacular punts as the Bison finished 4-4-3. At a time when each field goal counted for five points, Matty was quickly regarded as a major weapon.

❖ ❖ ❖

In 1898, students did not leave Bucknell without a full plate of religion; Christy's faith was both secure and inquisitive. President Harris knew Christy would be in the front row at Bucknell Hall for the ten-minute religious service each day before classes. Students were "required" to attend, but there was no penalty for absence. Harris believed that everyone should want to be there.

Often presenting the invocation, Harris had plenty to say, particularly regarding the engagement of moral character.

"The student must aim at the highest manhood," he preached, "act from the highest motive, and pursue right ends by right means."[26]

He didn't need to convince Christy.

"Moral energy is wasted not only by vice and crime," Harris told the faithful gathering, "but even more by inertia, idleness."[27]

Idleness was not in Christy's vocabulary—he was too intelligent, driven, and inquisitive. He loved challenges and competition, with his highly-charged brain able to solve nearly any puzzle. Throughout college, he would be a magnificent student-athlete, a star in three sports. His academic prowess was just as impressive, a continual honor student earning induction into two literary societies.

Even so, the Big Man on Campus constantly battled a touch of immaturity, an awkward shyness that was often viewed by classmates as arrogance. It was a strange dilemma in that he never lacked self-confidence, he always believed he was undoubtedly a step above his peers . . . yet he was hurt that some might brand him a snob. He just was not comfortable in social settings.

Ernest Sterling, the top distance runner on the Bucknell track and field squad, suggested that his best friend face and fight his anxieties. Isn't that how President Harris, as a boy, overcame a speech impediment? Christy agreed—throw off the mask and learn to relax in crowds, around strangers, when people seem too close. With that in mind,

Christy plunged into social activities, including drama, poetry, and the Christian Association. He played bass horn in the Bucknell band, joined the Phi Gamma Delta fraternity, and became active in student politics, ultimately being voted junior class president. To pad the résumé, he also was on the Junior Ball Committee.

As freshman class historian, Christy penned a whimsical account of the war between his class and the evil sophomores.

"One morning," he wrote in the Bucknell yearbook, "we overtook the sophs, who were hastening from chapel, and we proceeded to roll them about in the snow. It was a shame to so misuse the pure, clean snow, but it left the defeated sophs with cleaner faces and a clearer perception of right and wrong."[28]

Bucknell baseball, however, proved a major disappointment to the young pitcher. Although the team finished with a 9-5 record, its best player and captain had issues.

"No pitcher can win games when his men don't field well behind him," said Christy, "or when they refuse to bat in any runs."[29]

Matty, second from right in the back row, and the 1899 Bucknell baseball team. Courtesy of Bucknell University

John Howard Harris taught moral candor—Christy's interpretation apparently included brutal honesty.

❋ ❋ ❋

If college life changed Christy, it did not dent his Christian values, healthy lifestyle, and work ethic. He thrived on competition with a passion for all he loved—from checkers and chess to schoolwork and athletics.

Nicknamed "Rubber Leg" by his classmates, Christy always carried his football on campus, ever looking for an opportunity to practice his kicking.

He had work to do.

❋ ❋ ❋

The summer of 1899 held big possibilities for Christy. After a short visit home to undoubtedly brag about his grades, he returned to Honesdale. Baseball was fun again, still only eighteen and twirling for a strong team with that rent-free $20 per month.

In mid-July it appeared to Christy that he had struck gold when he received his first call from professional baseball, the Taunton Herrings, offering $90 a month for him to pitch in the Class F New England League.

The folks of Honesdale were impressed, with the local newspaper calling Christy "a young man of good habits and we expect to hear well of him in Massachusetts."[30]

Before reporting to the Herrings, Christy visited Boston to see his first major league game as Kid Nichols twirled the Beaneaters past the Cleveland Spiders.

After that, things quickly fell apart. On July 21 at Manchester, the attendance recorded at 200, Christy lost his minor league debut, 6-5. It didn't take long to realize he was stuck on a dismal team. He pitched well enough, completing all of his fifteen starts, but finished with a 2-13 record. The other starter, Tom Brady, yielded 137 runs in 120 innings as the hapless Herrings finished in last place.

"This team makes enough errors of commission and omission to send it to Hades," wrote Christy in a letter to his parents. "I pitched in one game where we had 10 errors, beside half a dozen passed balls by the catcher who does not seem able to hold me."[31]

To complicate the situation, the club ownership was not meeting its payroll and officially went out of business in the final week of the season. Seven weeks after being drawn to professional baseball for big money, Christy was $200 in the hole.

"I had about come to the conclusion that I would have to walk home," said Christy.[32]

Fortunately, the players were bailed out by the owner of the Newport club, who offered to share the gate of a Labor Day double-header in Rhode Island. They accepted, lost both games, and happily split the proceeds. Christy immediately bought a train ticket to Factoryville.

"I felt rather discouraged," he said. "My summer had been a financial failure and baseball prospects were none too bright."[33]

Even so, he had already decided that his future career would be somewhere in the field of forestry. He was anxious to get back to school.

* * *

On October 4, 1899, at Franklin Field in Philadelphia, nobody pretended that Bucknell could pull off an earth-toppling upset of the University of Pennsylvania. In four previous meetings, the Quakers had outscored the Bison 130-0.

"We were their dog," said Matty.[34]

But this year was different—Penn's John Outland had graduated and the Bison were 2-0 for the young season. Okay, the unbeaten Quakers had disposed of their first two opponents by a combined score of 76-0.

Sensing his team might be a touch jittery, Bucknell's new football coach and athletic trainer, George "Doc" Hoskins, pledged a new pair of $7 shoes if someone could just score against Penn. And if the Bison scored again, the second player would get a new raincoat. Bribery or desperation, it worked, the Bison stunning the sellout crowd of 20,000 spectators—not to mention the Quakers—by trailing only 11-10 at the half.

The *New York Times* would call it "twenty minutes that startled the football world."[35]

Bucknell's points were the result of two drop-kick field goals, the "kicking of Mathewson was the finest seen here in a long time."[36]

Penn coach George Woodruff was furious as his squad headed to the locker room, charging that poor officiating was favoring Bucknell. According to the *New York Times*, "Penn protested against the partiality shown by G.W. Hoskins of State College and who, by the way, is Bucknell's coach."[37]

True, George Hoskins was the umpire, but only because he had signed a contract to officiate before accepting the coaching job at Bucknell. Because he was going to be in Philadelphia anyway, why back out?

Just twenty-nine years old, Doc Hoskins was an accomplished athletic trainer who had already spent four seasons as the first football coach at Penn State, going 17-4-4 in four seasons, with three of his losses suffered at Penn. Doc was an honest man, but on this day not particularly wise.

In the second half, John Minds of Philadelphia took over the duties of umpire and Hoskins was relegated to referee. It barely mattered as Penn scored the final thirty-six points to win 47-10, which the *New York Times* pointed out "did not detract from the brilliant work of Mathewson."[38]

Despite the loss, it was actually a bountiful day for Matty . . . and not just the new pair of shoes and raincoat. Before the game, he had been approached by "Phenom John" Smith, a veteran ballplayer and coach who had managed the Portland Phenoms to the top of the New England League. For good measure, the former big league twirler turned outfielder hit .382 for Portland, several of those knocks against Christy and his wayward Herrings.

Smith was moving up to Norfolk of the Class D Virginia League and wanted Matty to pitch for him at $80 a month. When he mentioned that he had a bigger contract at Taunton, Matty was cheerfully reminded by Phenom John that this time he would actually be paid "real money." During the football game, Smith had sat with Connie Mack, the manager of the Milwaukee Brewers in the new Western League. Impressed by Matty's performance, Phenom John took out the baseball contract, drew a line through the signed amount, and raised it $10 a month.

Matty had never been to Virginia . . . summer employment was getting serious.

❖ ❖ ❖

Matty would have a great sophomore season with seven touchdowns and six field goals, including game winners against Lehigh and Penn State. In a 45-0 victory over Susquehanna, he accounted for three touchdowns and nearly had a fourth when he returned a kickoff ninety yards, only to be finally tackled by two Crusaders after shaking loose from another. The Bison would complete the 1899 season at 6-4.

Continuing to notch honor roll status in academics, he made time to play center on the basketball team, Bucknell going 6-3 with big wins against Penn State and Cornell.

Although there was heavy pressure to play baseball, Christy wanted to save his arm for Norfolk . . . and he wanted to free some time to spend with his new girlfriend.

A student at Bucknell's Female Institute, Jane Stoughton was a perfect match for Christy. She was beautiful, comfortable in social circles, and taught Sunday school at the Lewisburg Presbyterian Church.

Jenny, as she was often called, was the second oldest of Frank and Julia Stoughton's seven children. Born on January 9, 1880, in Millersburg, a small Pennsylvania borough next to the Susquehanna River, her family moved forty miles north to Lewisburg eight years later and purchased a three-story brick house at 129 Market Street, two blocks from the river and only one from the Presbyterian Church. Julia Stoughton maintained a beautiful home, even with the constant movement of five girls and two boys. Frank Stoughton, the superintendent of the L & T Railroad—an eighty-mile line from Lewisburg west to Tyrone—was a tireless worker with wealth and influence. He had a hard time hiding his concerns about his daughter's choice for a serious boyfriend. Sure, the Mathewson kid was handsome, athletic, and a good student . . . but he played baseball for money? To Frank, baseball was a stupid child's game.

3

BREATHING IN THE SMOKER (1900)

Opening Day 1900 was a disaster, Christy Mathewson of the Norfolk Phenoms with a bad case of first-inning nerves, was unable to find the plate. After Christy walked the bases loaded with no outs, the Portsmouth cleanup hitter promptly cleared them with a triple. By the time the inning ended, Norfolk was five runs in the hole. From his position in right field, Phenoms' coacher John Smith was hardly fazed. In the dugout, he discussed the calamity with calm assurance. To Phenom John's thinking, talent grows best with patience.

He was right, Christy following with eight shutout innings as Norfolk stormed back for a 6-5 victory.

✿ ✿ ✿

In the early 1880s, back in New Hampshire, teenage twirler John Smith struck out sixteen batters in a game with the ball never escaping the infield. He was tagged "Phenomenal" and made sure the nickname stuck. By 1884, Phenom John was pitching in the majors, compiling a 54-74 career record over eight seasons. By 1900, he had successfully settled into the role of Minor League outfielder and coacher. In fact, Smith was such a popular figure that his teams in Portland and Norfolk were both nicknamed "Phenoms."

"Phenom John Smith did a great deal toward developing me as a pitcher," said Matty. "He pointed out my weaknesses as he saw them and gave me a great deal of valuable advice."[1]

Including how to cope with life in the Class D Virginia League. Remember, Christy was a country boy who had never smoked, cussed, or even tasted beer . . . and now he traveled with a gang of rowdies in the cheap seats of the train smoker.

"The air in this smoker used to get so thick you could plow furrows in it with a baseball bat," said Christy. "I finally solved the difficulty by puffing a cigar myself. I would do this until it made me sick, and then I would endeavor to sleep."[2]

But he survived in style, notching a 20-2 record with four shutouts and a 1-0 no-hitter against Hampton. After much debate and prayer, he made a huge decision.

"It was there that I determined to make baseball my permanent work," he said, "and took my preparatory course in the mastery of the professional game."[3]

Matty's thinking was solidified in July as two Major League teams— the Giants and Phillies—each offered the Norfolk club $2,000 to buy his contract. Phenom John gave Christy the choice of where he wanted to play, and he initially preferred Philadelphia because it was closer to home. However, the Phillies also had the deepest pitching staff.

"I reasoned as a young, untried pitcher," said Christy, "I would stand a better chance of getting a good workout with the inferior twirling staff that then represented the New York Club."[4]

The sale to the Giants called for Matty to still earn $90 a month until he could prove his worth. Otherwise, he would be returned to the minors for more seasoning.

* * *

To Andrew Freedman, the Giants were nothing more than a tidy revenue stream, his main focus was on a hoard of other unscrupulous business and political endeavors. Widely considered the greediest owner in baseball, Freedman once fined his best player $200 for the audacity of requesting a raise. While other franchises headed south for spring training, Freedman had the Giants conduct camp in the winter thaw at the Polo Grounds. He loved his yacht, the opera, and firing managers.

The current coacher was George Davis, an outstanding infielder who had just replaced Buck Ewing in midseason. Ten years older than Christy, Davis had become a Gotham hero three months earlier when he saved the lives of three people, including a child, from a burning building. Davis would have been an outstanding coach on a decent team. The last-place Giants, however, were horrible.

Welcoming Matty to the Polo Grounds, Davis grabbed his bat to personally test the youngster's pitching arsenal. Davis was impressed with the fastball and drop, but belted Matty's roundhouse curve over the fence.

"Put that in cold storage," he yelled to the pitcher's box. "That ain't any good in this company. A man with paralysis in both arms could get himself set in time to hit that one. You got anything else?"

Well, there was that stupid freak pitch with which Matty had been experimenting.

"I will never forget how Davis' eyes bulged," wrote Matty as the manager whiffed at the outside-in breaking ball.

Davis demanded a replay and missed it again.

"That's a good one," he yelled. "Sort of a fallaway or fadeaway."

"And there," Christy would later write, "in the morning practice at the Polo Grounds in 1900, the *fadeaway* was born and christened by George Davis. He called some left-handers to bat against it. Nearly all of them missed it and were loud in their praise."[5]

✿ ✿ ✿

It was unseasonably hot when Christy joined the Giants, and it would soon get worse, scorching weather blanketing New York City and smothering the multitude of congested tenements. Lasting but a few days, the heat would steal the lives of thirty-nine people, including thirty-three children under the age of five. The most modern city in the world could be deadly.

Pardon Christy for being overwhelmed. The distance between Factoryville and Manhattan was a long day on the train, but to first-time passengers, the New York skyline looked like the other side of the universe, a strange and powerful wonderland. British author H. G. Wells called it "the strangest crown that ever a city wore."[6]

New York City was prosperous; a vast market of commerce, industry, and finance. In the early 1900s, the nation's largest city controlled one-third of America's exports and two-thirds of its imports. Titanic banks and insurance companies abundantly gathered assets, and Wells admitted that the metropolis "was lavish of everything, full of the sense of spending from an inexhaustible supply."[7]

It was modern; loaded with just about everything. By the time the subway system opened in 1904, many of the streets had already been paved. In 1908, *Harper's Monthly* quipped, "the motorist whirs through the intersecting streets and round the corners, bent on suicide or homicide."[8]

The city was electric; one visitor likened the lights of Broadway to "fabulous glow worms crawling up and down." It was a cultural and intellectual mecca with theater, nightclubs, cinema palaces, libraries, bookstores, art galleries, and colleges.

New York was elegant, graced with grand architectural monuments, horse carriages trotting through Central Park, and the upper crust of society parading the most expensive fashions at luxurious restaurants.

It was hopeful; on the final day of 1899, the *New York Times* boldly predicted "a brighter dawn for human civilization."[9]

New York was colossal, blazing past the capitals of the Old World to become the largest city on the planet by 1910. Seeking a better life, immigrants began arriving mostly from Russia, Italy, Ireland, and Germany. In the century's first decade, more than nine million immigrants were processed at Ellis Island.

And it was energetic—a constant stream of people, ideas, and change.

No, it was crazy—the constant clatter, the chronic construction, the urgent rush. "Noise and human hurry," charged Wells, "the blindly furious energy of growth that must go on."[10]

And it was horrid—poverty, crime, corruption, racism, congested slums, fire hazards, and disease. Women and children were packed into sweatshops and factories, susceptible to disease, particularly tuberculosis. The average work week was fifty-nine hours for $10 in wages (seventeen cents an hour). A new worker in the textile business made $1 for a ten-hour day. Workers in the garment industry made about $200 a year. In the dark and stuffy confines of Frederick B. Gordon's mill, children worked sixty hours a week for $3. Gordon called it "charity."

It wasn't just New York. In 1900, more than 1.7 million American children under the age of sixteen were working thirteen hours a day; one-seventh of the population living in poverty.

But New York was by far the worst, with Wells lamenting that "individuals count for nothing."[11]

Although industry needed cheap labor, immigrants streamed into New York City, searching for the better life. That notion would usually die early as they rushed to the nearest ghetto for safety—drawn by the heritage, language, and culture of the world they had so desperately left behind. In the forty years before 1900, nearly fourteen million immigrants came to America. That number would be topped within the first fifteen years of the twentieth century. One million immigrants would pass through Ellis Island in 1907 alone at the rate of 5,000 each day.[12] Business and industry soared, a few gained riches beyond imagination, and most spent their days trying to survive.

New York was good, bad, and all things in between.

✿ ✿ ✿

On July 17, 1900, at Brooklyn's Washington Park, temperatures in the high nineties, Christy would get his first call into a Major League game. In the fifth inning, with the Giants trailing Joe "Iron Man" McGinnity and the league-leading Superbas, Davis pulled starter Ed Doheny. Matty, again, was nervous. As luck would have it, the first man he would face was the great Joe Kelley, in the midst of hitting over .300 for twelve straight seasons. Matty's first pitch was a ball, outside and high. He was undoubtedly saving his best stuff for two other future Hall of Famers on the Superbas, Wee Willie Keeler and Hughie Jennings. In four innings, Matty would hit three batters, walk two, and allow six runs.

Fortunately, Matty might be able to redeem himself with the bat. Having dropped the embarrassing cross-handed style, he now prided himself on being a good hitter. At Norfolk, he had a .280 batting average and played some outfield when he wasn't pitching. Still, he would have to face the great Iron Man McGinnity and his notorious underhanded upshot that he called "Old Sal."

Christy would take three hefty swings and sit down.

On his way to a 28-8 record, McGinnity notched the victory. Doheny, who would finish 4-14 for the season, was charged with the loss. Less than impressive, Matty was not making new friends on the Giants.

After getting shelled by the Pirates, he faced the Cardinals, and was tagged with his first Major League loss, none other than John McGraw

Only twenty years old, Christy had already played in the major league when this Bucknell yearbook picture was taken. Courtesy of Bucknell University

scoring the winning run for St. Louis. In all, Matty would go 0-3, allowing thirty-two runs over thirty-three innings and getting drop-kicked back to Norfolk. Fortunately, it was legal at the turn of the century for athletes to get paid for playing summer baseball and still participate in college sports. Matty was thrilled to be moving back to Lewisburg. Hey, he was president of the Bucknell junior class.

✿ ✿ ✿

Late in the 1900 football season, the Bison nearly upset powerful Army at West Point. During an 18-10 loss, Christy nailed a pair of spectacular field goals. One was a drop-kick hit from forty-eight yards at a near impossible angle, impressing Walter Camp to proclaim that Mathewson was "the finest drop kicker in intercollegiate competition." Camp also added that Matty was by far the best punter.

This was major news. After all, Camp was "the father of American football." A legendary player at Yale when Christy was a baby, he coached his alma mater to three national championships. By the time he ended his career at Stanford, Camp had amassed a 79-5-3 coaching record. Now a sportswriter, he was charged with selecting the annual All-America team.

Although Christy missed several games due to injury, the Orange and Blue finished 4-4-1 for the year, including another big win against Penn State. Christy had performed brilliantly, but his biggest fan was not Walter Camp, John Howard Harris, or even his parents . . . it was Jane "Jenny" Stoughton.

"I can still see this tall, athletic body plowing through the Penn State line," Jane recalled many years later. "Football was rough in those days and every time I would see Christy down, my heart would be in my mouth. But he would come up again, always charging forward."[13]

Okay, Christy and Jenny were a good-looking couple, but it went far beyond a physical attraction. What developed was a relationship based on faith, interests, and love. Although her amiable social skills could run circles around his shyness, the difference proved an advantage for both. Christy would always view Jane as his lighthouse, his rock. Naturally, it would work both ways.

On quiet walks by the Susquehanna or through Victorian downtown Lewisburg, they began to talk of marriage. Both were deeply in love. The dream had but one hurdle . . . would Christy be brave enough to face Jane's dad?

✿ ✿ ✿

Christy, second row left, and the Bison football team. Courtesy of Bucknell University

Certainly the Bison basketball five had few concerns in the winter of 1900–1901, constructing a 12-1 record that included a 32-9 trouncing of Penn. With Christy at center, Bucknell's remarkable average of twenty-six points per game would have been higher had it not been for an ice-cold performance up north, losing 8-5 to the Williamsport YMCA.

To Christy, the young sport of basketball—invented ten years earlier by James Naismith—was an enjoyable way to exercise during the winter. Then again, he was rather curious where he might land once the baseball season started.

Christy was not necessarily shocked, but his pride was definitely hurt when his name was not included on the Giants' 1901 reserve list. Sure, he had gone 0-3 during one month with a lousy team, but the new American League would open a lot of pitching spots. Christy knew his math; there had to be a need.

Phenomenal John Smith had told him to have patience and faith.

In late winter, Christy received a letter from Connie Mack, manager of the Philadelphia Athletics. Mack was a keen student of baseball with high moral integrity. Pitching for Mack in the clean, family-friendly American League seemed perfect, not to mention the proposed contract of $1,200. Considering himself to be a free agent, Christy signed the new contract and happily accepted a $50 advance.

There was one big problem.

"This unintentional blunder," said Matty, "got me in the worst trouble of my life."[14]

Giants' owner Andrew Freedman and Cincinnati's John T. Brush had collaborated on a shady deal that had the Reds purchase the rights to Matty for $300, then trade him back to New York for Amos "The Indiana Thunderbolt" Rusie, who had won 245 Major League games with nearly 2,000 strikeouts but had not pitched in two years.

It is still considered one of the worst trades in baseball history. Rusie would never win another game, and Matty, of course, would become the game's greatest pitcher. What gave the deal a foul odor was that Freedman considered his obligation to pay Norfolk for Matty was now the responsibility of Cincinnati . . . and even more suspect was that Brush, while acting for Cincinnati, was a stockholder with the Giants and was negotiating with Freedman to become majority owner.

"Apparently there were considerable shenanigans afoot," said sportswriter Fred Lieb.[15]

But sportswriters had little time to investigate one questionable move, the loud and outrageous war between the two leagues creating a glut of scandal. In all, the American League would steal eighty-two players from the National League, many of the players signing dual contracts.

Busy with college life at Bucknell, which included plenty of studying, Christy received a train ticket from the Giants' owner and an order to report to the New York office. Freedman threatened to sue Matty should he jump to the treasonous and certain-to-fail American League.

"Freedman would blacklist me for life," Christy reported of the conversation. "He would put me out of baseball forever."[16]

Christy relented to Freedman's command, but admitted that he had already spent the $50 advance from Mack. Freedman told the youngster that he would return the money, but he never did. When Christy realized Mack had not been repaid, he sent the money himself.

Whatever the drama, when Christy Mathewson left Lewisburg in March 1901 for the Giants' spring training camp in New York City, he had every intention of returning to Bucknell for his senior year. There was football, basketball, and, most important, Jenny Stoughton.

✿ ✿ ✿

Despite the hazing from Piano Legs and company, Matty had some big moments in his first full season as a major leaguer. The topper was the no-hitter at St. Louis in mid-July. According to a St. Louis newspaper, the crowd of 5,000 Cardinal rooters turned their cheers for Christy in the final innings, rushed onto the field to hoist him onto their shoulders, and chanted "Tiger" as he headed to the team carriage.[17]

Although the Giants would crash to seventh place in 1901, Matty would finish the season 20-17 with a 2.41 earned run average, including five shutouts and the no-hitter, causing the press to trumpet his worth. At the end of the season, the headline of the *New York Evening World* proclaimed "Mathewson a Money-Maker," noting that even women and children were braving the National League danger zone to get a glimpse of "the twirling wonder." It was the same on the road, where Matty had become "the greatest drawing card baseball ever knew . . . worth fully $100,000 to the National League this year."[18]

Certain that he deserved a raise, Matty bravely marched into Freedman's office.

"I opened my mouth to say $5,000, but the words refused to come," said Matty. "When it came to a show-down, I felt in my soul that no such sum of money existed."[19]

Matty requested $3,500, and Freedman agreed without hesitation. He also must have read the "Money-Maker" article.

After a long and deep evaluation of his future, Christy decided not to return for his senior year at Bucknell, figuring he could finish his education after baseball. Still, he might as well have gone back to college, considering the amount of time he spent in Lewisburg visiting Jane. There no longer seemed any reason to mask their intentions, although her father was furious that Christy had dropped out of school.

John Howard Harris was concerned, but never expressed disappointment. As a university president, it was his goal that every student graduate and find a successful life on every level. But his nature had always been to hold the advice unless requested. Besides, Christy was following his gift.

Up in Factoryville, Gilbert and Minerva Mathewson were shocked. They had always known Christy had baseball in his blood, but he was so academically talented that they always suspected he would graduate at the top of his class . . . mainly because he was too competitive to finish second. But they couldn't argue against a dream.

Christy's gallant attempt to explain his reasoning to Frank Stoughton was not quite as smooth. Yes, he would like to earn a degree, but because he was now receiving such a lucrative salary, he needed to concentrate entirely on baseball, spending the off-season thinking about the strengths and weaknesses of the players he had pitched against. Although not a common practice, it seemed reasonable to Christy that he prepare his energetic mind to capture every possible advantage. Because Jane's father still did not consider baseball a productive occupation, Frank was not convinced, even though he was slowly becoming fond of the man his daughter so strongly loved.

Certainly it had not been an easy decision for Matty. Always blessed with an intellectual drive, he loved Bucknell and the college life. However, now twenty-one, he was no longer preparing for a career, he had found it—and was both stubborn and smart enough to realize the importance of mastering his profession. He also was busy constructing the idea that one of the keys to a successful baseball career was an intriguing concept of strategic pitching. He knew he had great athletic ability—throwing a baseball was easy. Why not add one of his unique strengths to the equation—outsmart the opposing hitters. With dedication and brains, Matty would turn twirling into an art.

o o o

New York offered a thousand distractions, but Christy held strong to the values of his childhood. He was a thinker, a gentleman, and a kid with moral values. The owner of a busy and retentive mind, he carried his own Bible, could quote William James, and had read *Les Miserables* three times. He read books on horticulture for fun. He could fashion without hesitation a hundred different moves in checkers and chess. On the road, while teammates explored the nightlife, Christy hit the art museums, libraries, and local YMCA. He was far above the fray.

There were two things Christy read every day: his Bible and a newspaper. He strived to stay within the word of God, but kept an eye on a robust world. Harvard and Michigan recorded unbeaten football seasons in 1901, J. P. Morgan's U.S. Steel was the first billion dollar corporation, and New York became the first state to require automobiles to have license plates. World news spotlighted the death of Queen Victoria in England, the Boxer Rebellion in China, and the Boer War in South Africa.

On September 2 at the Minnesota State Fair, Vice President Theodore Roosevelt suggested that America should "speak softly and carry a big stick." Four days later, at the Pan-American Exposition in Buffalo, President William McKinley was shot twice in the abdomen at close range. Death would arrive on September 14, and Teddy Roosevelt immediately was sworn in as the nation's twenty-sixth president. Only forty-two years old, Roosevelt was the youngest president in U.S. history. Although he was obsessed with sports and outdoor activity, he was never in love with baseball, most likely for the best, because the former New York City police commissioner would have probably had to cheer for the Giants. And that was brutal, because the team was once again a disaster in 1902. The Giants were both bad and complacent, with the players actually "singing and whistling merrily in the clubhouse after losing games."[20]

It would be a tough season for Matty. He started strong, blanking the Phillies on Opening Day before 24,000 rooters at the Polo Grounds and causing the *New York Times* to call him "the champion pitcher of America."[21] Five weeks later, the *New York Times* would dub Matty "the fading idol."[22]

June 16 was a particularly unhappy day, not just because he lost to Cincinnati or that the Giants were in seventh place and fading fast, but because he should have been in Lewisburg accepting his degree at graduation. President Harris, in his commencement address, talked about the apostle Paul and "the good fight." Harris also must have felt a twinge of pain when he glanced at the front row.

In New York, Matty's patience had reached its limit.

"I cannot win with them behind me," he charged, a statement that would increase the turmoil.[23]

New York also had a parade of new coaches in 1902, beginning with Horace Fogel and Heinie Smith. Both crumbled to the team's lethargic mentality as it slid deeper into the National League cellar. When Fogel played Matty at first base for a spell, shortstop Joe Bean purposely tried to make him look bad with throws into the dirt. Meanwhile, the *New York Times* issued yet another delightful quote regarding Matty's ability. The newspaper that had called him the "champion pitcher" in April and a "fading idol" in May now dubbed him "the former pitcher" at the end of June.[24]

Although it would later become imbedded in baseball lore that Fogel somehow believed that Christy would make a better infielder than pitcher, it was hardly true.

"I managed the club for only a few weeks," said Fogel. "I had a terrible team, my first baseman was hurt and Matty was a strong, husky kid who could hit. So I put him on first when he wasn't pitching. This never was intended to be other than an emergency measure."[25]

Matty was fair with a bat, hitting .200 for the season with two homers, three doubles, and two stolen bases. Overall, he would log a .215 career average with seven homers. What mattered was pitching.

4

DUMPING ON THE YANNIGAN (1901)

Adjusting to major league baseball, let alone New York City, was not easy for a God-loving country boy. But he was certainly not the first rookie (called "yannigans" at the turn of the century) to be hazed.

Veterans would remove the laces from a newcomer's glove, hide his bats, dump his clothes in the shower, whisper crude insults, fire spit wads across the hotel dining room . . . when his shoes weren't nailed to the floor, they might be filled with rotten fruit or worse . . . anything the perpetrators might consider hilariously demeaning. Most yannigans took the heat, waiting for that happy day when it would be their turn to dish out the pain.

Of course, a few rookies refused to be intimidated. Ty Cobb bought a gun.

"Every rookie gets a little hazing, but most of them just take it and laugh," recalled Tigers' teammate Sam Crawford, who added that the tightly wound Cobb "turned any little razzing into a life-or-death struggle."[1]

"I was catching hell by the handful," argued Cobb, furious with the 1905 Detroit Tigers. "That gun was forced on me."[2]

Baseball in the early years of the twentieth century was an adventure.

"We had stupid guys, smart guys, tough guys, mild guys, crazy guys, college men, slickers from the city, and hicks from the country," said Davy Jones.[3]

Manners were rough, speech was crude, and education was minimal . . . gladiators cheered for their talent, but never invited for dinner. Road accommodations were limited to fleabag hotels with the stipulation that they "not mingle with the guests."[4]

When Christy was a boy, professional baseball was nearly lawless.

"At the time the game was thought, by solid respectable people," said Connie Mack, "to be only one degree above grand larceny, arson and mayhem."[5]

Baseball certainly had an abundance of against-the-grain characters, but none could rival John J. McGraw. Brilliant in every aspect of the game, the volatile third sacker played with such skill and rage that he could rock an entire stadium.

"His very walk across the field in a hostile town is a challenge to the multitudes," wrote Grantland Rice.[6]

In sixteen seasons, McGraw would fashion a .344 career batting average, but that was just window dressing. At five-foot-seven-inches, he had the look of a bulldog, but the bite of a pit bull. Opposing fans, at least the ones who could yell and quickly hide, called him "Muggsy," a nickname he furiously detested.

He was contemptuous, fiery, and continually one tick away from explosion, mixing violence and vulgarity with a relentless zeal that bordered on insanity. In his younger days McGraw starred for the best and nastiest team in baseball, the Baltimore Orioles, then of the National League. The *Baltimore Morning Herald* described McGraw as "a whole team and a dog under the wagon."[7]

Arlie Latham of the Giants quipped, "McGraw eats gunpowder every morning and washes it down with warm blood."[8]

In the days when only one umpire covered the entire field, McGraw would often trip runners and routinely hindered anyone who attempted to tag up from third by grabbing his belt. One cagey opponent unbuckled his belt, leaving the surprised McGraw standing at third with the belt but no runner.

McGraw knew every rule in the book, breaking them with delight. What the opposition called dirty, he defined as winning.

"Sportsmanship and easy-going methods are all right," said McGraw, "but it is the prospect of a good fight that brings the fans out. I hate to lose and I never feel myself beaten until the last man is out."[9]

✿ ✿ ✿

By the turn of the century, professional baseball was stepping into a new and modern age, even though it did drag along a barge of old traditions. The "Deadball Era" (1901–1919) was loaded with speed, strategy, and daring. Games may have been low scoring, but hits and excitement were in abundance.

"It was as much a battle of wits as a trial of strength," said Johnny Evers of the Chicago Cubs. "Everyone was trying to outguess the other fellow."[10]

Although the basic dimensions of a diamond were the same as today, the rest of the landscape would scarcely be recognized.

It was baseball played in the daytime on fields that were barely groomed. Despite small gloves and erratic bounces, games were quick, usually done within ninety minutes. When the bare-bones wooden stadiums were filled to capacity, fans (known as rooters, cranks, and bugs) crowded behind the catcher and down the base paths. Makeshift ropes were used as barriers, but a huge gathering of bugs often meant that the outfielders had to position themselves almost to the edge of the infield. The atmosphere was always loud and sometimes ugly, especially for the lone umpire working the game.

"Fans were just about as rough as the men on the field," said McGraw. "An attack on the umpire often was a genuine treat for them."[11]

Managers in the early 1900s were called coachers, and many would direct the action while playing in the field. Pitchers were twirlers, working their magic not from a mound, but from the pitching box.

In an age when political correctness did not exist, any difference was fair game to be callously exploited. Insults and chaos were a fixture at the ballpark, with theatrical threats and dirty play leading to fights and brawls. Fans often joined the fisticuffs to attack umpires and opposing players. Women, children, and anyone with a fear of flying beer bottles did not attend.

The rubber-core baseball could be just as dangerous. With all methods of scuffing perfectly legal, the ball resembled a dark and mushy onion by the late innings. The twirlers would scratch and cut, shave the ball with an emery board, rub it with talcum powder, or spit a nice splotch of tobacco juice. Chewed coffee beans made a nice additive because the sap settled between the seams. The ball looked horrid, and the poor catchers began to look like they had been dipped in muck.

Plus, it was custom to use only one baseball per game. When an occasional spectator ran away with a foul ball, only then would a new one be introduced by the umpire, the shine lasting but a moment.

"All the infielders were chewing tobacco or licorice, and spitting into their gloves, and they'd give that ball a good going over before it ever got to the pitcher," recalled outfielder Fred Snodgrass. "Believe me, that dark ball was hard to see coming out of the shadows of the stands."[12]

❉ ❉ ❉

In the summer of 1888, Walt Whitman wrote that he believed "in baseball, in picnics, in freedom." The great American poet must have been talking about town ball—the real version of the game, where hot rivalries within carriage distance sparked the summers of ten thousand communities across the land.

Something was dreadfully wrong.

How could the highest level of the American pastime be operating like some cheap circus sideshow? Professional baseball was a wart that refused to heal, a smudge on the nation's old-fashioned Christian values. The Baltimore Orioles of the 1890s may have won a lot of baseball games, but attendance was in a free fall.

Professional baseball needed reform, and some were ready to act.

At the turn of the century, what cannot be ignored was the rapid and complex frenzy of change tugging at America from a hundred different directions.

On the main stage, the United States looked splendid—a young country flexing its muscles as a new world power with a booming economic base producing one-half of the earth's oil and a third of its steel. Although most of the seventy-five million Americans still relied on the horse and buggy for transportation, profound changes were occurring, from the light bulb and telephone to the automobile and beyond.

Out west, Utah was the nation's forty-fifth state and Hawaii would soon be annexed. As people left the farms and immigrants arrived from across the sea, New York with a population of 3.5 million, was bigger than Chicago and Philadelphia combined. With roughly 102,000 residents, Los Angeles was the same size as Scranton. This was truly the land of opportunity. It all seemed perfect.

Behind the curtain, however, there were massive problems. Brutal working conditions, child labor, women's rights, racism, immigration, corruption, the splintering shift from rural to urban, an ever-widening gulf between the rich and poor, and disease, one in seven Americans dying from tuberculosis. The problem of professional baseball was trivial compared to the reality of an America beaming on its shores, yet screaming from within.

Even religion was experiencing the weight of change.

✧ ✧ ✧

In the 1890s, Walter Rauschenbusch was the pastor of the Second Baptist Church in New York City, located in the West Side section known as "Hell's Kitchen." The church was old, weathered, falling apart; a ragged structure within the slum of overcrowded and badly ventilated tenements. There was poverty, malnutrition, disease, crime, insecurity, and despair. Children had no playgrounds, lack of proper sanitation had gotten out of control, and a single street might have 4,000 residents . . . battered masses in a world of misery. Rauschenbusch believed in the Social Gospel, a liberal and modernist view that Jesus had great concern for the needs of the poor.

"When I saw how men toiled all their life long, hard, toilsome lives," wrote Rauschenbusch, "and at the end had almost nothing to show for it; how strong men begged for work and could not get it in hard times; how little children died—oh the children's funerals! They gripped my heart."[13]

The Social Gospel was spreading throughout the nation, particularly in the north and east. The rural lands were more conservative.

In 1895, a noted group of evangelical Christian leaders created a list of five fundamentals. First was the inerrancy of scripture, followed by the divinity of Jesus, the virgin birth, and that Jesus died on the cross as a substitute for man's sins. The fifth fundamental was that Jesus was physically resurrected and that he will return. To the conservative theologians—known as fundamentalists or traditionalists—the focus of Christianity should be salvation. Involvement in the cultural affairs of society—such as social reform—was impractical because it had nothing to do with the path to heaven. Some argued that the social service programs and modernist teachings of well-meaning people like Rauschenbusch were "a threat to the very core of the Christian faith."[14]

One point that everyone agreed upon was that America was a Christian nation. The census of 1890 listed 145 denominations with 142,487 churches serving 21.7 million members.[15]

Theological differences of opinion between conservatives and liberals were not new, but as the nation's demographics shifted from rural to urban, they became more acute. What made the rift unique was that most fundamentalists and modernists shared the same basic beliefs, causing opinions and responses to continually overlap. Thus, the modernists who followed the Social Gospel also believed in the same five fundamentals as traditionalists, many of whom jumped to the front lines in helping society's downtrodden.

Christy Mathewson and John Howard Harris certainly fell into that category. They staunchly believed that the Bible was authentic, it had no flaws, and Jesus helped the poor. They also had a sense that God was quite aware of the United States of America.

Yes, the list of problems was long, and John Howard Harris was asking his circle of faithful to work to their highest capacity. Christy's gift seemed to be baseball, a field where America was fast losing patience.

* * *

It may have been the public perception, but it would be wildly incorrect to suggest that all players were hooligans before Matty joined the Giants; just as inaccurate to claim that the Christian Gentleman ushered in a complete turnaround of well-mannered batsmen.

The most pronounced change in manners was the rise of the American League, born with the principle of clean baseball. In 1901, plunging into its highly advertised inaugural Major League season, the American League would feature good sportsmanship, friendly stadiums, honest organization . . . an atmosphere conducive to the safety of even women and children . . . the exact opposite of the lunatic ball found in the National League.

With strong financial backing and an energetic president, Ban Johnson, the American League began with eight franchises with three invad-

Bucknell president John Howard Harris. Courtesy of Bucknell University

ing National League marketplaces—Boston, Chicago, and Philadelphia. It also placed teams in Baltimore, Cleveland, Detroit, Milwaukee, and Washington, D.C. What everyone knew was that Ban Johnson was a bulldog with an obsessive drive for success; his future agenda aimed at placing an American League franchise in New York City.

To Andrew Freedman, the grizzly owner of the Giants, the nation's largest metropolis was his private property. Freedman hated Johnson and everything about the American League, viewing the upstart league as absolute heresy.

Johnson didn't blink, his group of owners blatantly raiding the established league for its players, even Christy Mathewson. How enlightening it would be to jump to the new circuit of gentleman athletes to play clean and honest baseball.

How clean? Well, the player/manager for the new Baltimore franchise would be a superstar third baseman from the old National League Orioles, John J. McGraw.

Strange world . . .

5

HIT THE ROAD, SLACKER (1902)

The uncertainty was sudden, dramatic . . . John J. McGraw, "Little Napoleon," walked into the Polo Grounds as if he ruled the world. Even the veterans gulped, feeling the shake of once-plush jobs slipping away.

On July 17, 1902, Andrew Freedman would hire his third manager of the season. This one arrived with a warning that nothing would ever be the same.

For the next three decades, McGraw would manage, control, and command the New York Giants. He would fashion team upon team in his own image—fast, fearless, and feisty. Only the brave need apply.

"Any mental error, any failure to think, and McGraw would be all over you," said outfielder Fred Snodgrass. "And I do believe he had the most vicious tongue of any man who ever lived. Sometimes that wasn't very easy to take, you know. However, he'd never get on you for a mechanical mistake, a fielding error, or failure to get a hit."[1]

Change was immediate, McGraw looking over the twenty-three-man roster and drawing lines through the names of nine players to be released. Joe Bean, a Matty detractor who had committed thirty-two errors in fifty games, was unceremoniously dismissed, as was Jack Hendricks, the yannigan with a smooth glove but weak bat.

"There is a story that McGraw fired me off the team the moment he saw me swing," Hendricks would tell sportswriter Frank Graham. "Fired me off the Giants the first day. That is a lie. I hid in the clubhouse the first day. McGraw never fired me until the second day."[2]

Once the inquisition started, several news reports predicted Matty would be traded. After all, Mathewson and McGraw were polar opposites on seemingly every level.

Essentially, it was good versus evil. Matty the cerebral, well-mannered country boy and McGraw the vulgar bully from the city. The extremes included size, looks, character, and noise level. Christy had the idyllic childhood and Johnny McGraw ran away from an abusive father. Matty was Protestant, Muggsy McGraw Irish Catholic. Matty was the All-American hero and the egomaniac McGraw a "venomous viper." One was fair and square, the other despicably cunning. One would be known as the Great Mathewson, Big Six, the Christian Gentleman . . . the other Little Napoleon, Little Round Man, and Muggsy. One spoke softly, the other was constant thunder.

Christy had a hundred intriguing interests, McGraw only one—baseball. Which is precisely the point at which one of the world's most impossible friendships was born. To McGraw, there were three elements that made Matty perfect—potential, intelligence, and a blistering desire to win . . . pick your order. Although most would paint Matty as the tall, handsome ballplayer with impeccable manners and a great fastball, McGraw simply saw him as a brilliant star drenched in competitive juices. From that foundation, they would build a lasting respect and admiration that at times seemed oblivious to the fact that one was sunshine and the other a hurricane.

Okay, their concept of winning was a touch different. If it were football, Matty would tackle his worthy opponent, then help him off the ground. McGraw would pulverize the chump, then step on his hand.

It was a strange brew all right.

Most of the baseball world realized that Matty already was an exceptional pitcher before McGraw arrived in July 1902.

"The finest pitching motion I ever saw," said McGraw.[3]

But Little Napoleon was never shy to take credit in developing the greatest pitcher in history.

"Careless management had allowed him to drift along," said McGraw. "By constant efforts at speed, he had become wild. He simply knew nothing about pitching at all. His wonderful equipment was being wasted."[4]

Only twenty-nine years old, McGraw managed the same way he played—ferocious, strategic, the wind within a firestorm.

John J. McGraw of the New York Giants. Courtesy of the National Baseball Hall of Fame

"When he and his team took the field," said his wife, Blanche, "everyone on the other side, including the batboy, was his mortal enemy."[5]

McGraw loved to instigate turmoil, especially in Pittsburgh. Since Exposition Park did not have a visitors' locker room, the Giants would put on their uniforms at the famous Monongahela House hotel, which was located downtown. They would then ride in open carriages over the river bridge to the ballpark in Allegheny City. On the Pittsburgh side was a public marketplace, and the players would taunt the Pirates' fans, who in turn would heave fruit and vegetables back at them.

Iron Man McGinnity once took a direct hit of four ripe tomatoes on the seat of his pants, the stain lasting the entire road trip. While razzing some rooters on another trip, Sammy Strang was beaned by a mushy cantaloupe, which landed like a tight-fitting hat.

"I suppose we did antagonize them too much, but it certainly was a lot of fun," said McGraw. "There were hot doings anytime the Giants arrived. We were roundly hated."[6]

They would catch it from both sides of the bridge, before and after the game.

"They'd throw rocks and trash and pieces of brick on the Allegheny side," said McGraw, "potatoes, onions, tomatoes, cantaloupe on the other . . . we loved to lick the Pirates and then drive by the market."[7]

It wasn't always fun, particularly the day in Philadelphia when Roger Bresnahan got nailed in the head by a brick, the price you pay to enhance ticket sales.

In Cincinnati, McGraw once notified the newspapers that he had asked for police protection.

"The public couldn't understand what it was all about, but for fear something might happen and they would miss it, they filled the park."[8]

McGraw was passionately hated everywhere but New York, where he was loved for his energy, his drama, and his absolute refusal to lose.

If he didn't agree with an umpire's decision, the entire ballpark was included in the conversation. In 1901, it was widely considered insane that Ban Johnson had given the okay for McGraw to manage the Baltimore Orioles in the newly formed American League, which was founded, remember, as an alternative to the lunatic brand of baseball in the National League. But McGraw had been Baltimore's most popular player back when it was in the National League, so if Muggsy would agree to behave himself, perhaps the inevitable explosion would be avoided. Surprise, it didn't work. There were fines, suspensions, more fines, and more suspensions.

As the two leagues battled for dominance, there was often more fighting in the board rooms than on the field. Slapped with an indefinite suspension by American League president Ban Johnson, McGraw leveraged $7,000 that he was owed by the Orioles to win his release and then signed an $11,000 contract with the Giants, making him the highest paid man in baseball, player or coach. McGraw promised that he would not attempt to lure any of the Baltimore players to New York, which apparently was valid for about a week. With new majority owner John T. Brush giving him complete control to rebuild the Giants, McGraw immediately ripped the heart from the Orioles, stealing four players and the groundskeeper.

Little Napoleon was instantly a prominent celebrity in New York City, although his club was in such poor condition that it could only be repaired by a genius. To build for the future, McGraw decided to tank the 1902 season. Accordingly, the Giants finished dead last at 48-88, with Pittsburgh coasting to the crown with a 103-36 record. McGraw was not alarmed. After signing four of his favorites from Baltimore— Roger Bresnahan, Jack Cronin, Dan McGann, and Joe McGinnity—he took off on a scouting trip for undiscovered talent. He had the pitching staff in Mathewson, McGinnity, and Luther "Dummy" Taylor—he just needed a dominant team behind them.

Although he respected McGraw's long-range ambitions, Matty was bothered by the 1902 season. He led the league with eight shutouts, had a crisp 2.12 earned run average, and the *Sporting News* called him the game's greatest pitcher. His anxiety was being slapped by a dismal 14-17 record. Imagine his talents on a decent club. What would life be like in the American League?

✿ ✿ ✿

In late August 1902, the Giants were in St. Louis—the nation's fourth-largest city—for a series against the Cardinals. To Christy's surprise, he was contacted by Robert Hedges, the owner of the American League's cross-town Browns. The war between the two leagues was just heating up, and Hedges offered Christy a lucrative contract, twice what he was receiving from the Giants.

Matty was immediately drawn to the personable Hedges, who truly exemplified Christian manners and sportsmanship. At every ballgame, "Uncle Bob" Hedges personally greeted customers at the entrance to Sportsman's Park, occasionally working the ticket booth—a practice Christy would someday follow. Hedges did not allow alcohol in the stadium and even hired security guards to maintain a family environment. Known for his contagious smile, Hedges was "a wonderful mixer, an excellent entertainer and a club owner whose first consideration was his public."[9]

His players also realized his expectations.

"I will not stand for any rowdyism on the part of my players," said Hedges. "I will have it suppressed if I have to set down every member of my team."[10]

Christy weighed his options. The American League was thriving, he loved St. Louis, and the Browns had the foundation for a powerhouse, looking as if they just might knock off the Athletics for the 1902 pennant.

He also hated losing. Christy wanted to play for a proven winner, not the floundering Giants. He noticed that the stadiums were packed and the fans exuberant wherever he pitched. He was twenty-two years old, a valuable commodity who now understood the business side of baseball.

Christy signed the new contract, thrilled to be joining next year's Browns.

Yes, there was the matter of two contracts. The Giants would probably be perturbed, but the American and National League's "salary wars" had created a deserving windfall, the newspapers expecting that half the National League players might jump.

"It will not be long before every star player in the country will carry a lawyer around with him," predicted *Sporting Life*. "This business of a player changing his mind every day, a sort of 'contracts fresh every hour' is growing very ridiculous."[11]

To Matty, it seemed like the perfect time to play in the brand new National Football League (no relation to the modern NFL). The 1902 baseball season in the books, he headed west to the Steel City to play fullback and kicker for the Pittsburgh Stars. There were three teams in the Saturday league with two located in Philadelphia, the Athletics and Phillies, run by the baseball organizations. Playing in the North Shore Coliseum, the Stars would go 3-2-1 and claim the world championship with an 11-0 victory over the Athletics. The first NFL would then go out of business forever.

It didn't matter to Matty, who returned to Lewisburg to ask Jane for her hand in marriage. All the parents were excited, although Jane's father was still skeptical, particularly after Matty arrived with two baseball contracts.

If anyone understood the art of jumping teams, it was McGraw, who immediately tracked down his wayward hurler and asked him to double-jump back to the Giants. But Christy had been burned before and, to his stubbornly calculated thinking, it was all business.

"I like New York, but McGraw has got to show me that he is going to have a winning aggregation, and then offer me a fat contract if he wants to sign me," said Matty. "I would be foolish if I didn't get all the money I can. A pitcher's professional career is short at the best, and it behooves him to look out for himself."[12]

Then again, McGraw would make a compelling argument. Knowing it would be unwise to threaten or hoodwink, the new King of the Giants instead played to Christy's intellect and competitive drive, painting a portrait of what they could do together to build this franchise into a contender. It would be hard work, a challenge, but the two of them could pull it off. Oh, McGraw may have danced lightly, but he knew Christy's mind.

Still, the overall picture of professional baseball could not have looked more insane, every day an explosion of fresh controversy.

"Reports of dealings and double dealings, leads and counters, cross and double cross," wrote the *St. Louis Post-Dispatch*. "It is a merry war of rumors . . . ricocheting through the baseball world."[13]

At the same time, it was obvious that the American League was scorching the senior circuit, not only stealing a good number of its stars, but outdrawing it by 32 percent. The most lopsided situation was Philadelphia, where the Athletics were drawing four times as many fans as the Phillies. The American public wanted clean baseball, period.

The two leagues agreed to a peace settlement, if for nothing else than to diffuse the massive pay scales. The *Sporting News* reported that the compromise was essentially "horse-trading"—some players were sent back to their original teams, some stayed. But the underlying carrot was that a new American League franchise would be placed in New York City. Not wanting a new neighbor, John T. Brush vehemently opposed the move, but found no sympathy from any other owner. It was decided that the old Baltimore club would become the New York Highlanders (the original Yankees). While Brush fumed, Robert Hedges made a peace offering by giving Mathewson's contract back to the Giants.

"My individual and club interests were of comparatively minor importance when the future of baseball was at stake," said the owner of the Browns. "Somebody had to make concessions."[14]

Including Brush, who gave Matty a new $4,000 contract with a $1,000 bonus.

Years down the road—his franchise languished in the cellar— Hedges looked back at what could have been if Matty had jumped to the Browns.

"I lost a pennant for St. Louis in that deal, but I brought about peace in the baseball world."[15]

* * *

Christy and Jane really didn't care where they lived—they were in love and ready to tie the knot. Their original plan was to wait until they had financial security before getting married. But at that time, the average worker was making twenty cents an hour, and Christy was passing that with each pitch.

Christy first had to sit down with Jane's father, the sometimes grumpy railroad supervisor. Undoubtedly knowing that this moment would arrive, Frank Stoughton firmly lectured Christy about eternal commitment and sound financial planning. There was one more jab about baseball, of course, but apparently the stupid game was paying big money. Shaking Christy's hand, Frank grudgingly gave his blessing.

Jane and Christy also had to work out a few personal differences. In a premarriage trade, they agreed that he would become a Presbyterian and she a Republican. Fair enough.

Christy and Jane were married on March 5, 1903, at her home on Market Street, with the Rev. Wellington Thomas of the First Presbyterian Church conducting the ceremony before 150 guests. Ernest Sterling was the best man, Jane's sister Margaret was the maid of honor.

The Lewisburg newspaper—delivered weekly for $1 per year, in advance—carried a front-page article noting that Jane was "a young lady of charming disposition and an energetic church worker."[16]

The wedding party would conclude across the river at the Milton train station, the newlyweds catching the Buffalo Flyer for a southern honeymoon. At the depot, Christy's college friends passed out flyers to boarding passengers that read, "Christy Mathewson, New York's great baseball pitcher, and newly wedded wife are on this train. Make them feel at home as there may be 'something doing.' Note: He will be easily recognized by his boyish countenance and Apollo-like form."[17]

The honeymoon was set for the romantic city of Savannah, Georgia, where the Giants just happened to be holding spring training, McGraw and Brush preferring warm weather over Freedman's penny-pinching March workouts in New York City.

Like their husbands, Jane Mathewson and Blanche McGraw also matched the definition of an odd couple. Although both were personable and attractive, they definitely hailed from different sides of the tracks. Jane was the straight-laced Sunday school teacher from Central Pennsylvania. Blanche was a high-society girl from the big city of Baltimore, a fashionable dresser with a sparkling wedding ring that appeared far too gigantic for her petite finger.

The only two wives at spring training, they spent a good portion of an afternoon trying to avoid one another in the lobby of the DeSoto Hotel.

"For hours, days it seemed," said Blanche, "each staring when the other wasn't looking. She had gray eyes and dark brown hair. She was dressed rather nicely, I thought . . . I caught her staring at me a few times, thinking narrow thoughts, perhaps."[18]

Jane probably had plenty of concerns. What kind of woman could be married to John J. McGraw? How old is Mrs. McGraw? She looks rather young. And why the overload of sequins on her dress? Is that the style in New York City? And what about that ring?[19]

Blanche knew it.

"It was the dazzling engagement ring that reflected my husband's pride and affection," she said. "It represented something else to the bride across the lobby. She actually thought, 'only a hussy would wear a ring like that.'"[20]

A funny thing happened—Jane and Blanche became instant friends.

"She and I just seemed to be drawn towards each other," said Jane. "She is so wonderful and fun."[21]

They walked past the southern live oak and Spanish moss of Savannah, laughing and jabbering about their earlier suspicions of each other.

"While the men were practicing," Blanche wrote, "we would stroll down Bull Street to Forsyth Park where the early spring azaleas were budding and all of life seemed green and new and full of hope."[22]

Blanche Sindall had been born to Baltimore wealth in 1882, making her two years younger than both Jane and Christy. She met John McGraw—nine years her senior—while attending Mount Saint Agnes College.

That evening, after telling John about her new friendship with Jane, Blanche asked what he thought of Christy.

"I knew he was big and bulky, blond, and with big blue eyes," recalled Blanche. "John replied, 'Looks like he can pitch with his head as well as his arm,' and he honestly believed that answered my question."[23]

When the team headed north for the new season, the McGraws asked the Mathewsons to share a home. The two couples moved into a seven-room furnished apartment at West 85th Street and Columbus Avenue, just a block from Central Park. The McGraws paid the $50 rent and the Mathewsons bought the food.

It is important to note that John McGraw at home was the exact opposite of the ruthless coacher he played every afternoon.

"He was always kind, considerate, and affectionate," said Blanche.[24]

McGraw was night and day on and off the field," said Hall of Fame infielder Frankie Frisch.[25] "Quiet-spoken," added Branch Rickey, "almost disarmingly so."[26]

Certainly, the early development of the friendship between Matty and his manager must have been interesting—like slow-dancing in the moonlight with a werewolf, careful not to step on any toes, both sizing up the other until realizing, probably like a bolt from the heavens, that their opposite personalities were somehow a textbook fit. Forget establishing any ground rules, they truly liked each other—a closeness that would forever be blind to their obvious differences. Both admired the other's talents and intellect. Both respected the other's turf, accepting long-cemented personality traits with an understanding usually reserved for the closest of families. Muggsy became both best friend and father, Matty both pupil and son. Muggsy could puff out his chest and rage into battle, while Matty was quietly content to observe from afar.

"It is the prospect of a good fight," Little Napoleon would proclaim, "that brings out the crowds."[27]

"I have seen McGraw go onto ball fields where he is as welcome as the Black Plague," said Mathewson. "He doesn't know what fear is."[28]

But what really made the alliance work was that both were extremely intelligent and zealous competitors, obsessed with winning baseball games, with an absolute hatred for losing. Of course, Christy was a bit more philosophical about defeat, confessing he would make up an alibi so as not to damage his self-confidence. McGraw considered defeat a mortal enemy.

No matter the outcome, both were ready for another nine innings. It was always about the challenge, the game.

With the beginning of the 1903 season, the relationship between the Mathewsons and McGraws was already quite comfortable. The women cooked the meals and often played cards while the men talked baseball. When the men could be pulled from their work, the four best friends settled in for a relaxing game of bridge.

✿ ✿ ✿

McGraw was an infielder, but he did appreciate the skill and science of throwing, always willing to discuss ideas. Theirs was a journey of strategy and discovery, two artists working their passion, kindred spirits from opposite sides of everything but baseball. And the admiration was genuinely sincere, neither questioning nor attempting to manipulate the other's character or beliefs . . . poster boys for harmony.

They could chatter late into the night, both maintaining a mental sharpness that often pushed past the border of genius. To them, the subject and dialogue were riveting.

The Giants' coacher found that the youngster possessed a hunger to learn with an intelligence ranging far above the average ballplayer.

"I never had to tell Mathewson anything a second time. From that first day, it seemed, Matty carefully studied all opposing batters. Once he learned what they could hit and what they couldn't, he never forgot."[29]

"Anytime someone got a hit off me, I made a mental note of the pitch," said Matty. "He'd never see that one again."[30]

Mathewson, of course, possessed a busy and brilliant mind that enjoyed most any topic.

"He had an unusual mind, a quick mind, and the stubbornness of a person with a trained mind," recalled Blanche. "He had the ego of a great competitor and a deep-rooted belief that every opponent was his inferior."[31]

Add to that the windfall of a photographic memory.

"When he played checkers, his response to a move was drawn from his memory of the proper defense," said Blanche. "It wasn't even necessary for him to see the board at checkers or chess, which enabled him to defeat eight or ten really good players while blindfolded . . . and he would talk about the most common opening, Old 14th, or its countless variations as long as you would listen."[32]

Little Napoleon also had a fabulous memory, but only concerning baseball. As a player, he had carefully studied the strengths and weaknesses of every pitcher. He knew habits and quirks, the ability to recall every pitch of a ballgame. And absolutely no one better understood the tactics of the game.

"They were happy in their scheming, because the Giants were a winning team," said Blanche. "We couldn't realize, of course, that they were making baseball history by sheer force of personality and determination. Nothing else, in my opinion, can account for the Polo Grounds miracle of 1903 and 1904."[33]

McGraw had promised it would be hard work and challenging . . . it also turned out to be amazing fun.

6

MATTY AND THE IRON MAN (1903)

Several months earlier, when Matty was considering a move to St. Louis, the picture John McGraw painted for him was that, together, they would build a championship team. Part of the challenge, of course, was that it would not be easy—there would be bumps.

It didn't take long. In the 1903 season opener, the Polo Grounds was packed with 20,000 rooters, anxious to see Matty and the new-look Giants about which McGraw had been busily bragging to any sportswriter wanting an inside scoop. By the way, he would inform them that Mathewson would soon be the best pitcher in the majors.

No pressure for a twenty-two-year-old kid coming off a 14-17 season who was plagued by an inconsistency usually involving wildness; a hardworking youngster who, really, was still searching for an elusive self-confidence that seemed content to pop in for a brief visit before scuffling off to the land of doubt.

Sure, Matty received tons of encouragement from the likes of John Howard Harris, Phenom John Smith, John J. McGraw, his mother . . . they all believed in him, so he must be good. Then again, there would be that first game, Brooklyn pounding him with four runs in the top of the first inning.

It was shades of Matty's opener three years earlier in Norfolk, which he came back and won. Not today, as the Giants would commit six errors, Christy contributing to the mess with five walks and a pair of wild pitches in a 9-7 thumping.

McGraw was right—it would be a challenge.

❀ ❀ ❀

Four days later, the rivalry moved to Washington Park in Brooklyn, with Matty hurling a three-hitter for a 2-1 victory. That was just the beginning as the Giants barreled into first place, Matty besting Honus Wagner and the defending champion Pirates three straight times in May. By June, the Giants had a six-game lead, with their growing fan base near delirious. Hey, the previous season New York had finished 53.5 games to the rear of Pittsburgh.

After Matty embarrassed the Bucs again, 10-2 in Pittsburgh, the usually quiet Wagner ordered his teammates to spit on their bats and hit the ball.

Apparently, Wagner's motivational speech would be a turning point as the Pirates regained their misplaced supremacy and eventually

The legendary Honus Wagner of the Pittsburgh Pirates. Courtesy of the National Baseball Hall of Fame

grabbed a third straight National League title, outdistancing the second-place Giants by 6.5 games. The season would have been a lot easier for Pittsburgh had Matty not gone 8-0 against them in securing his first thirty-win season.

If anyone had considered McGraw's confidence in Mathewson to be slapdash speculation, they were dreadfully wrong.

Matty would finish 30-13 with thirty-seven complete games and a 2.26 earned run average. Meanwhile, "Hans" Wagner would win his second of eight batting crowns with a .355 average, the two building a mutual respect seeded by talent and character.

In 1903, McGraw's first full season as manager, attendance at the Polo Grounds nearly doubled to 579,530 and then to 609,826 the following season. Although the American League Highlanders would put together a fairly strong club, they were no match when it came to the hearts of New Yorkers.

The Giants had a contender, the cranks invading the Polo Grounds in droves. It didn't matter that the new subway was still under construction; they rode the elevated train, or arrived by horse-drawn carriages or a day boat up the Harlem River. General admission was seventy-five cents with box seats going for fifty cents more. For those who enjoyed a full afternoon of sun, bleacher tickets cost forty cents with the first 100 fans paying only a quarter. If that was too pricey, a free partial view was available on Coogan's Bluff, with the bravest rooters climbing trees.

With McGraw as guide, Mathewson was now studying every hitter. Outfielder Roger Bresnahan, who would be moved to catcher in 1905, continually traded strategic notes with the young pitcher, as did the Giants' old backstop, Frank Bowerman. Now there was another strange relationship!

"A sourpuss rock-head of a catcher named Bowerman," wrote Frank Graham. "Kind of classic, the upper-class gentleman picks for his friend a dead end character."[1]

Well, they both were avid hunters . . . and loved baseball.

"Mathewson would instinctively rise to surrender his seat to a lady in the subway or streetcar," said Blanche McGraw. "Bowerman once raced a lady for a campstool on a Brooklyn-New York ferryboat and got there first. When she slapped his face in anger, he called her a bum sport and had her arrested for assault."[2]

Yet another mentor was Joe "Iron Man" McGinnity, who taught Matty a devastating change-up along with a wealth of pitching secrets. Iron Man just might have been the toughest man in baseball. The future Hall of Famer had been a miner and a muleskinner and had worked in a foundry. At one time he owned a saloon, employing himself as the only bouncer. Twenty-eight years old when he hit the majors, Iron Man had a vicious side-armed curve he called "Old Sal" and a seemingly indestructible arm. In August, he would pitch both ends of three doubleheaders and win all six games while displaying "no signs of fatigue."[3]

McGinnity would notch a league-best thirty-one wins in 1903, pitching a record 434 innings while combining with Matty for three-fourths of the Giants' victories.

"It was difficult for a batter to get McGinnity's measure," said Connie Mack. "Sometimes his fingers would almost scrape the ground as he hurled the ball. He knew all the tricks for putting a batter on the spot."[4]

Like Matty, Iron Man feasted on individual weaknesses.

"I had to do the remembering for most of my clubs," said McGraw. "It is rare that a man comes along like McGinnity or Mathewson, who will remember with me."[5]

Matty and McGinnity were the best one-two punch in baseball for seven seasons, one or the other always leading the league in victories. But even though they were equal in strategy and stats, Christy was clearly the crowd favorite.

"He won every heart in town," recalled Blanche McGraw. "He was nearly six feet two inches with two hundred pounds of well-conditioned body. He read a lot."[6]

One other important piece of business was that McGraw immediately established a new clubhouse environment, making it quite clear that the days of hassling or bullying the club's young ace had ended. In fact, friendship throughout the team was now a requirement, lest the perpetrator care to test the wrath of McGraw. Of course, Little Napoleon had already fired most of Matty's old tormenters.

Amazingly, Christy was rapidly becoming the most respected player in the Giants' dugout. It helped that he had rapidly matured, the once-conceived condescension replaced by a dry and genuine sense of humor. To Matty, it didn't matter that half the team had never finished elementary school or may not attend church. He communicated,

Matty (left), McGraw (center), and Iron Man McGinnity (right). Courtesy of the National Baseball Hall of Fame

showed respect, listened, and joked. Okay, he was different, but his teammates soon discovered that he was amazingly interesting. He opened up to them, they opened up to him . . . and suddenly he was one of the boys. Now respected for his talent and brains, Matty sincerely enjoyed the hard-earned status.

"Matty never thought he was better than anybody else," said team-mate Rube Marquard. "It was just the way he carried himself. But it was okay, because when you came to it, Matty *was* different."[7]

If McGraw ever instructed Matty on the talent of making friends, it is unlikely. It was certainly a bonus that Mathewson was amiable to the newly established team camaraderie. But the bottom line was that McGraw had made it possible for Matty to be himself. It was long overdue, but what a relief.

In all things baseball, McGraw relished authority.

"I am absolute czar," he boasted. "My men know it. I order plays and they obey."[8]

In those horrid hours of defeat, Little Napoleon's decisions were not to be questioned. But when his team pulled out a victory, John J. McGraw was a master of self-praise.

"We'll win," he told sportswriters, "so long as my brains hold out."

* * *

The 1904 season opened with mechanical splendor as Superbas owner Charles Ebbets and John Brush rode in large "gasoline-powered" auto-mobiles, leading a grand parade down Fifth Avenue and over the Brooklyn Bridge, thousands of New Yorkers cheering both teams. In what would be the largest crowd ever to pack Washington Park, Christy would hurl a three-hitter, the Giants winning 7-1 in what would be a taste of genius.

McGraw's construction of a powerhouse was brisk, New York win-ning the 1904 championship, their 106-47 record besting the runner-up Cubs by thirteen games. Matty *improved* to 33-12 with a 2.03 earned run average and a team-leading 212 strikeouts, but he was not the ace of the staff. Iron Man McGinnity, a decade older than Christy, had a career-best 35-8 mark with a 1.61 earned run average. Matty and McGinnity were primed to chalk up even more victories in the postsea-son. Winners of the first World Series—at the expense of the Pirates—Boston had repeated as American League champions. Led by veteran pitcher Cy Young, the Americans, and all Bostonians, were excited for a showdown with the Giants.

And now for the old change of pace . . .

As noted by John McGraw, there was nothing in the rule book ordering a postseason series between the winners of each league. So, sorry, the Giants were not interested. McGraw reminded the baseball world that his club had already won the only legitimate championship—the National League pennant. Owner John T. Brush added that the Giants did not need to prove themselves to an inferior product and, oh by the way, Boston is a "minor league" town.

McGraw agreed. "It is a minor league," he said, "and the Giants would outclass them."[9]

Bostonians were outraged. Even the *New York Evening World* called the remarks by Brush and McGraw "so stupid it will not even deceive the bat boys at the Polo Grounds."[10]

What Brush and McGraw were not saying was that they both hated everything about the American League. McGraw despised American League president Ban Johnson for repeatedly suspending him during the 1901 season in Baltimore.

"No man likes to be ordered off the face of the earth like a dog," grumbled McGraw. "Ballplayers are not a lot of cattle to have the whip cracked over them."[11]

Brush detested Johnson and the American League for inserting the New York Highlanders into what he considered his private territory.

Whatever their excuse, McGraw and Brush were universally lambasted in the press and on the street. What also angered baseball fans in Boston, New York, and across America was the cancellation of a championship series that might have presented a pitching matchup between Matty, the young idol, and Young, the aging legend.

The owners of both leagues, with none other than Brush at the helm, promptly agreed on rules for a World Series beginning the next season. Cy Young would be thirty-eight years old by then and still six years from retirement, but his team was beginning to tumble. And McGraw, with his ace not yet twenty-five, had a juggernaut. Of course, anyone who had not heard of Christy Mathewson by 1905 was simply not paying attention, for the legend was beginning to take a life of its own.

7

A BUSY MIND (1905)

According to Jane Mathewson, her husband loved to make lists. Christy kept a catalog of plants and flowers he had discovered while hiking in various parts of the country, a record of books he had read, a journal filled with checkers and chess moves, and self-help thoughts on maturity and control. He annotated notes in his Bible and kept a chronicle of scriptures, prayers, and personal spiritual thoughts. There also was his baseball catalog, complete with tendencies for every hitter he had ever faced, from what was thrown to what was missed and what was hit.

Blessed with a retentive memory, he possessed the uncanny ability to search through the index of his mind to find the exact information he needed. Like John Howard Harris, he could recite hundreds of passages from the Bible, breaking down the words with meanings and thoughts. It was never a repetition, but a genuine understanding.

The same was true with baseball—all the knowledge he had written in notebooks was filed within his brain.

"One of the most remarkable memories I have ever encountered," wrote John McGraw in his autobiography. "Baseball pitching was as fascinating a science to him as playing checkers. He loved the art of it."[1]

Life was a puzzle that Christy constantly studied.

"He had the perfect temperament," added McGraw. "Always he sought to learn something new, and he never forgot what he had learned in the past."[2]

In the summer of 1905, as Matty approached his twenty-fifth birthday, his list of personal successes no doubt included pitching, marriage, lifestyle . . . and, of course, staying within the word of God. To the public, Matty was the young idol of all things perfect—looks, intelligence, faith, character, and talent.

Then again, there was another side of Christy's private ledger, that irritating list of flaws, unfinished issues he was bent on conquering. He was winning the battle against immaturity, but was still working on how to be smart and humble at the same time. He realized that personality traits are never easily shaken, but that didn't hinder him from constantly attempting to improve. And there was always that awkward shyness.

"He disliked having people, even teammates, close in on him," wrote Fred Lieb.[3]

Teammate Fred Snodgrass would second that opinion.

"He was a wonderful, wonderful man," said Snodgrass during an interview with Lawrence S. Ritter for *The Glory of Their Times.* "A reserved sort of fellow, a little hard to get close to. But once you got to know him, he was a truly good friend."[4]

Christy had no problem with celebrity; he just wanted space, respect, and the right to disappear.

"A cold and distant personality until you knew him well," said Damon Runyon. "No hand shaker. No seeker of the limelight of publicity. But he had a character that would have made him great in any calling."[5]

Christy's backpack was filled with possibilities—from writing to horticulture to playing professional checkers (sorry, there was no league). Except when in the pitching box and completely engulfed within his craft, his mind was always churning at what seemed to be a million miles an hour . . . he simply had no time for mundane chit-chat.

"Matty was not given to loose talk and it was that characteristic that gave some the impression that he was cold," said Bozeman Bulger. "As a matter of fact his sympathy was intense. He looked on life just as he did on pitching . . . the details had to be just so."[6]

He was constantly caught on a pendulum between the public spotlight and a personal need for privacy. There was no escape, particularly since it was against his nature to be rude.

"I remember how fans would constantly rush up to him and pester him with questions," said Laughing Larry Doyle. "He hated it, but he was always courteous. I never saw a man who could shake off those bugs so slick without hurting their feelings."[7]

* * *

If the fans had heard that Matty was aloof, they did not seem to care. What they saw was a tall, handsome athlete with still uncharted potential. What they read about was his character—moral Christian values, honesty, work ethic, intelligence—the newspapers built him up as a "Greek God in flannels" and the readership could not get enough.

It was remarkable how it all was woven together. Professional baseball was saddled with the rowdy image of uneducated thugs bashing one another over the head on a warm summer afternoon. At the same time, as rapid societal change seemed to be grinding cherished values, America longed for a hero, a champion, an idol.

And so the legend of the Boy Wonder began to percolate. Here was a college kid who embraced sportsmanship and moral strength, a new breed of ballplayer, the Christian Gentleman . . . and coached by Muggsy McGraw, of all people.

Stories spread in newspapers and magazines from the big cities to the farmlands. Who was this tall, good-looking kid with grit and brains and manners?

Of course, sportswriters helped fuel and enhance this legend in early bloom—the Great Matty was part super hero, part ordinary guy trying his best in a wicked world, and a nice dose of myth. Even a bad decision in the midst of a free-swinging brawl against the Phillies in Philadelphia could not derail Christy from his golden track. It seems that a fight between players was joined, in the middle of the diamond, by a party of drunken rooters. Protecting himself against an onrushing teenaged lemonade hawker, Christy decked the kid. Strangely, the Philadelphia newspapers blamed the lemonade punch on McGraw, charging that Little Napoleon's "venom had rubbed off on even Matty."[8]

Christy could do no wrong—not in the eyes of the public.

Certainly the newspapers and the public might not have paid much attention to a good, clean-living American boy with rural values if he hadn't also been a phenomenal pitcher. Plus, just two seasons removed from the pits of the National League, The Christian Gentleman had become the leader of a legitimate powerhouse.

In his autobiography, John McGraw would call the 1905 Giants the "greatest ball club I have managed."[9] They led the league in hitting, stolen bases, doubles, and home runs. Their 105-48 record was nine games superior to second-place Pittsburgh.

In early May, at the near-frozen South End Grounds in Boston, Christy notched his 100th career victory, 8-2 over the Beaneaters. On June 13 at Chicago, Matty became the first pitcher of the century to record two no-hitters, blanking Three Finger Brown and the Chicago Zephyrs 1-0. "Neither run, nor hit, nor base on balls did Mathewson allow," reported the *Chicago Daily Tribune*, adding that the soon-to-be-renamed Cubs were "made to look like automatons of putty, so completely did Mathewson have them fooled."[10]

For the season, Turkey Mike Donlin led New York with a .356 batting average; Joe McGinnity and Red Ames each captured twenty-win seasons. Matty was even better, cracking thirty victories for the third straight year while leading the National League in wins (31-9), earned run average (1.28), strikeouts (206), and shutouts (8). He completed 32 of 37 starts and only allowed 64 walks in 339 innings.

Plus, Matty's record should have been 32-8. On August 5 in Pittsburgh, umpire George Bausewine awarded the Pirates a forfeit because the Giants spent too much time arguing a controversial safe call as the sun was setting in the ninth inning. It didn't matter that the game was tied; Matty was officially tagged with the loss. Strangely, three days later in Chicago, he was not credited with a win despite entering a one-run game in the fourth inning and blanking the Cubs the rest of the way. According to modern rules, a starting pitcher needs to pitch five innings to earn a victory, and Giants starter Dummy Taylor had only gone four. Matty didn't care; but the next two games he hurled consecutive shutouts—just so there was no doubt.

Christy's popularity was now undeniable. He was the good guy, the role model for seemingly every kid in the land . . . and best of all, he would be pitching in the World Series.

Yes, the new rules were in place; McGraw's Giants were ready and willing to meet Connie Mack's Philadelphia Athletics of the American League. Although the Athletics compiled a 92-56 record—thirteen wins less than New York in the National League—the sportswriters were near unanimous in their predictions favoring Philadelphia.

McGraw would come prepared, outfitting his Giants in stunning new uniforms—completely black except for a large NY on the chest. Philadelphia also had new threads, their shirts adorned with a clever new "elephant" logo. A few years earlier, when the American League was forming, John McGraw had told the press that the Athletics were spending far too much money on players, that it was likely they would end up with a "bunch of white elephants." Connie Mack may have looked stoic, but he had a sense of humor . . . and a thunderous pitching staff.

What Mack didn't have was the service of his ace pitcher Rube Waddell, yet another of the era's most colorful personalities. A left-handed marvel, the gangly and lovable Waddell was truly a kid at heart. Early in his career, playing for the Pirates, Rube was supposed to be pitching but had disappeared from the dugout. Players began the hunt, finding him playing "miggles" (marbles) with a group of twelve-year-old boys under the stands. Rube didn't want to leave the fun, but his team-mates finally prevailed, escorting him to the pitcher's box where he hurled a three-hit shutout. Rube Waddell wrestled alligators, didn't give a hoot for money, preferred fishing over baseball, joined a fire depart-ment, and once missed a game because he was leading a parade.

"When Rube trotted to the pitcher's box, it was as if he were walking over a plowed field," said Mack, "the fans would greet him vociferously with: 'Hey Rube!' He always acknowledged the salutations with a court-ly bow."[11]

In 1905, Waddell led the American League with a 27-10 record, a league-high 287 strikeouts, and a 1.48 earned run average. In a Fourth of July marathon victory over Cy Young and the Boston Red Sox, Wad-dell pitched the entire twenty innings. Unfortunately for Philadelphia, his season would end one game short of the World Series, injuring his left shoulder after playfully instigating a wrestling match with teammate Andy Coakley at the train station in Boston. Applying his own method of therapy, Rube slept on the ride to New York with his pitching arm hanging out the train window. It didn't work.

But at least the Athletics had plenty of pitching strength with Eddie Plank (24-12) and Albert "Chief" Bender (18-11).

Four years younger than Matty, Bender had graduated from Carlisle College in 1902, his first baseball coach was Pop Warner. In sixteen Major League seasons, he would win 212 games and eventually be voted into the Baseball Hall of Fame, but his finest World Series was still down the line. This one would belong to Christy Mathewson.

Game one was played at Philadelphia's Columbia Park, Matty besting Plank with a 3-0 four-hitter.

"I was so proud of my young husband," said Jane. "He then was twenty-five and already a nation's idol, but to me, he still was that big, good-looking boy from Bucknell."[12]

Perhaps not so attractive to Connie Mack.

"He was the greatest pitcher who ever lived," Mack would write many years later. "Matty had knowledge, judgment, perfect control, and form. It was wonderful to watch him pitch when he wasn't pitching against you."[13]

Unfortunately for Mack and his Athletics, Matty would be back in the Columbia Park pitcher's box three days later. In the second game, played at the Polo Grounds, the Athletics had tied the series, Bender contributing his own 3-0 four-hitter at the expense of Iron Man McGinnity.

Game three would follow the pattern, The Christian Gentleman with yet another four-hit shutout, the only difference being the Giants scored nine times off Andy Coakley as the usually slick-fielding Athletics committed five errors.

After Iron Man McGinnity won an incredible 1-0 pitcher's duel over Plank, the Giants were one game from the crown.

The Polo Grounds was humming, the outfield partitioned at 275 feet to allow room for the overflow crowd of 25,000 rooters. Despite Christy having only two days of rest, McGraw selected his ace to face Bender for a classic showdown. Bender would pitch a phenomenal game, but Matty would be even better, the Giants capturing a 2-0 victory and their first World Series championship.

Afterward, as a band marched around the field, most of the crowd gathered at the entrance to the Giants' clubhouse in centerfield, chanting for their heroes to emerge. McGraw was first with a rousing speech followed by euphoric jubilation as Matty and Roger Bresnahan unfurled a large banner that had just been created by several of the more artistic players. "THE GIANTS, WORLD'S CHAMPIONS, 1905." Even the usually quiet Mathewson spoke to the crowd, mostly about how it was a team effort and he simply tried to do his best . . . an excellent job on his quest to be humble.

The *New York Evening World* wasn't buying it, running two banner headlines on the front page of its sold-out October 14 edition—"Giants

In the 1905 World Series, Matty threw three shutouts in six days. Courtesy of the National Baseball Hall of Fame

Champions of World" followed by "Final Game is a Triumph for Great Pitcher."

That was a major understatement—"The Great Mathewson" had secured three shutout victories in six days—that's twenty-seven score-less innings with eighteen strikeouts, fourteen hits, and only one base on balls. It is still considered the greatest pitching feat in baseball history.

"Philadelphia tried its best, but it was only a shadow reflecting the masterful Mathewson's will," boasted the front page story of the *New York Times*. "He bestrode the field like a mighty Colossus, and the Athletics peeped about the diamond like pigmies who struggled gallantly for their lives, but in vain. Christie Mathewson, the giant slabman, may be legitimately designated as the pitching marvel of the century."[14]

All five games had been shutouts. In his two games, Bender chalked up a 1.06 earned run average. Poor Eddie Plank lost twice, even though his earned run average was 1.59. But how can you top Mathewson's 0.00 earned run average?

Every Giants player would receive a winner's share of $1,141 and a diamond-studded gold button. Well, that was fine, but there was a much bigger picture—the game of professional baseball was suddenly being hailed as honest, respectable, and loved.

The American pastime had found its moral center, its hero. For there, in the belly of the monster stood Christy Mathewson, sword and shield a glimmer.

* * *

It would be a mistake to think Matty had completely forgotten about football. He loved the sport, missed it, and closely followed the news from Bucknell, still coached by Doc Hoskins.

Christy was four years past his playing days, but one thing had not changed in the least—football was rough and wild.

According to President Theodore Roosevelt, living a noble life was a lot like playing football: "don't flinch, don't foul, but hit the line hard."[15]

Roosevelt heartily believed in the "strenuous life" and that exercise builds character. In a perfect world, every American would be consumed by an energetic work ethic of pure intentions with a sound body and mind. Sports, by definition, was an ideal arena for muscular Christianity.

It should be no surprise that most of football's greatest coaches were devout Christians—Amos Alonzo Stagg, Pop Warner, Walter Camp, John Outland, Fielding "Hurry Up" Yost, John Heisman . . . the list is extensive. They led their teams in prayer, mentored wholesome character, and sought spiritual guidance for victory and defeat. Most didn't smoke, drink, or curse. And none—this is that perfect world again—would ever cheat.

In forty-four years of coaching, most at Carlisle College, Pop Warner insisted that football would never be great if its tactics were dirty. Amos Alonzo Stagg had been a tremendous baseball pitcher during his college days at Yale, but refused to play the professional game because alcohol was sold at the stadiums. Instead, Stagg would become Mister Football, the legendary coach for the University of Chicago.

The University of Michigan's Hurry Up Yost argued that football was a "sanctified instrument for good" and that his position was a "pulpit for moral and religious teachings."[16] Yost also taught his team to crush the opposition. In fact, in the fall of 1905, some wondered if Michigan would ever lose again. By late November, Yost's "Point-a-Minute" Wolverines had amassed a fifty-six-game unbeaten streak, averaging fifty points a game and yielding less than one. Going into the "national championship" against Stagg's unbeaten Chicago Maroons, the Wolverines had not allowed a single point all season. That would all end in one of the greatest upsets in football history, the University of Chicago toppling mighty Michigan 2-0. Hold the celebration—football fans in the east were busy saluting Yale (10-0) as the national champs. With no national regulatory body, the argument was open for discussion.

But college football had bigger problems than a dispute about which school was king. With mass momentum plays that were based on brute strength, the game was violent and chaotic. Kicking, slugging, maiming—life on the gridiron was dangerous.

Georgia Tech coach John Heisman, now fourteen years past his playing days at Penn, had a vivid recollection of plowing through heavy traffic: "Sometimes two enemy tacklers would be clinging to the runner's legs, and trying to hold him back, while several teammates of the runner had hold of his arms, head, hair, or whatever they could attach themselves to, and were pulling him in the other direction," said Heisman. "I still wonder how some of the ball carriers escaped dismember-ment."[17]

Christy could relate to Heisman, missing several games at Bucknell due to injuries willingly afflicted by the opposition. "Against Penn," he said, "I thought my shoulders would be pried loose from my back-bone."[18]

During the 1905 season, there were 18 deaths and 159 serious inju-ries due to football, most in high school. Public opinion was stirred, a backlash arming to bury the entire sport. Many colleges, including Co-lumbia and MIT, banned the sport. Harvard president Charles Eliot sought to do the same.

That caused the president of the United States to burst into the discussion, Roosevelt accusing the leader of his alma mater of "doing the baby act.[19]

"As I emphatically disbelieve in seeing Harvard or any other college turn out molly coddles instead of vigorous men," said Roosevelt, "I may add that I do not in the least object to sport because it is rough."[20]

Insisting that football simply needed to clean up the "mucker play" with a few new rules, Roosevelt invited representatives from Harvard, Yale, and Princeton to the White House in the hopes of reaching a "gentleman's agreement." That instigated a larger gathering in New York City, represented by sixty-two of the eighty-two colleges that had football programs, planting the seed for the National Collegiate Athletic Association (NCAA). As for Harvard, the trustees agreed with President Roosevelt. Football had been saved.

New rules were added, the most anticipated being the introduction of the forward pass. Christy could have been a quarterback.

8

TINKER TO EVERS TO CHANCE, OH MY
(1906)

Christy would miss the first three weeks of the 1906 season, not throwing his first pitch until the fifth of May. He was fortunate, having survived a frightening bout of diphtheria, a highly contagious and killer disease.

Matty had become ill just after spring training in Memphis with what he initially thought was a bad cold. He was immediately quarantined, his upper respiratory system horribly damaged. It was tough on Jane, who was pregnant, and devastating to John McGraw, who had lost his mother, two brothers, and two sisters during an outbreak of diphtheria when he was but twelve years old.

New Yorkers were torn with worry, but the big story during Matty's illness was the disaster in California. An earthquake hit San Francisco on April 18, igniting a fire that would kill more than 3,000 people and essentially demolish the city.

When Christy did return home, he would tell Jane that he had never been so sick or prayed so much, but he knew that God was watching. He felt no fear.

McGraw was less cerebral than Christy, thankful his star pitcher would survive, but intent on getting back to the business of winning another championship. His first order of the 1906 season had been to replace the white "NY" lettering on the all-black uniforms with "WORLD CHAMPIONS" across the chest. New Yorkers loved the bold new look, which was largely viewed everywhere else as arrogant and disgusting. Of course, McGraw loved stirring the spirits of the enemy—the Giants packed the stadiums wherever they played.

The Giants were in first place when Christy joined the team in May. He was a bit shaky during his first outing, leaving after seven innings with a lead the Giants would eventually blow. Christy would not pitch for nine days and was not at full strength until July. Even so, he finished the season with a solid 22-12 record and a 2.97 earned run average. The Giants earned an impressive ninety-six victories, but were far short of the title. At least they had a good batch of excuses. Along with Matty's slow recovery, Roger Bresnahan was sidelined with continual dizzy spells after being beaned, and Turkey Mike Donlin broke his leg on a slide. Donlin, however, had better things to do than play baseball, marrying the beautiful actress Mabel Hite and joining her in vaudeville.

"He'll be an actor, all right," grumbled McGraw, "a bad actor."[1]

If anyone knew acting, it was McGraw, who would routinely escort Blanche to dinner and a theater performance. The McGraws could afford the best seats, but their many friends in the business usually left free tickets and backstage passes at the box office. For the bon vivant of Broadway, it was good to be in the company of John J. McGraw.

"The Giants and the entertainment world overlapped," said Blanche McGraw. "He was an important person because he knew more about the game than anyone else."[2]

And he was genuinely fun; a booming personality built for Gotham.

Before darkness, of course, he was the obsessed and cranky manager of the grandest team in sports . . . even if they were a distant second in the 1906 pennant race. It wasn't as if they hadn't been warned about the Chicago Cubs, the beginning of a dynasty that would win four of the next five National League titles.

Chicago's record of 116-36 is still a National League record; their road mark of 60-15 the greatest in Major League history. Mordecai "Three Finger" Brown would go 26-6, leading the league with nine shutouts and a 1.04 earned run average. A righty with a high-kicking delivery and crackling movement on the ball, Brown would become Matty's greatest pitching opponent, their twenty-four career face-offs underscoring a wonderful friendship. Along with Brownie, the Cubs had three other starters—Jack Pfiester, Ed Reulbach, and Orval Overall—all with sub-2.00 earned run averages.

Manager Frank Chance was also the best first baseman in the game, hitting .327, stealing 57 bases, and scoring 103 runs in his last injury-free season as a player. Don't think that playing slowed down his managerial skills. Like McGraw, Chance was delightful when he was away from the ballpark.

"But not even his best friend," wrote Ring Lardner, "could say that he is a pleasant party to have around when a close game is in progress."[3]

Chance also anchored the double-play duo of shortstop Joe Tinker and second sacker Johnny Evers, immortalized in the Tinker-to-Evers-to-Chance poem. Really, they may not have been the best combo, but Tinker and Evers were good, F. C. Lane calling them the "Siamese twins of baseball . . . they play the bag as if they were one man, not two."[4]

One other thing about Tinker and Evers—they refused to speak to one another; a legendary squabble with roots in a disputed cab fare, an on-field brawl in 1905, or Evers' claim that once, from close range, Tinker fired the ball so hard that it bent a finger, leading to a few choice words . . . and then nothing after that at all.

"That's the last word we had," Evers said years later. "Tinker and I hated each other, but we loved the Cubs. We wouldn't fight for each other, but we'd come close to killing people for our team. That was one of the answers to the Cubs' success."[5]

Another reason was the spark-plug speed of the fiery Evers and the uncanny clutch hitting of Tinker. He would definitely prove a thorn to Matty, owning a .350 career average against Big Six and nearly destroying him in 1908. Basically, the entire team was deep in talent and dangerous in every category.

But a strange thing happened in the 1906 World Series. Despite those 116 victories, the Cubs ran out of luck in the south side of Chicago, with the American League White Sox stunning them in six games.

Whatever was happening in baseball, nobody in the Mathewson home was paying attention. On October 19, Christy Junior, immediately nicknamed "Sonny," was born to a world of instant celebrity.

"He was a fat and chubby boy with light hair and blue eyes," said Blanche McGraw. "He was quite handsome."[6]

The McGraw-Mathewson apartment had been quite pleasant, but now that there was a baby, both families thought it best to find separate accommodations. Blanche and John moved into the Washington Inn.

Jane and Sonny. Courtesy of the National Baseball Hall of Fame

Cost was no concern for the McGraws, Brush having rewarded his manager after the 1905 series with a three-year contract at a whopping $24,000 per season—about five times the salary of the best ballplayers. Little Napoleon was the richest man in baseball, period.

Money was also not a problem for the Mathewsons, who had always stuck to a more frugal budget than the night-hound McGraws. With the new subway system, there would be plenty of connections to the Polo Grounds, but Christy and Jane instead settled in a large Washington Heights apartment, just above the home stadium.

As expected, they were wonderful parents. Sonny was healthy, energetic, curious, and coordinated. His first attempt at walking was an adventure of a dozen steps across the dining room floor. Like his father, he had no intention of slowing down.

Christy kept his politics quiet, but he greatly admired Theodore Roosevelt, the old Rough Rider—having been the nation's youngest president, only forty-two when he entered the White House—who won the election of 1904 while leading a progressive surge in America. Roosevelt's foreign policy emphasized America's rise as a world superpower—the Panama Canal, the Monroe Doctrine, the Great White Fleet. On the domestic front, Roosevelt fought political corruption and corporate greed, with his trust-busting Square Deal attempting to level the economic playing field for all Americans.

The president's effort to reform college football was commendable, but what really caught Christy's attention was Roosevelt's love of conservation, creating five national parks and 150 national forests on 230 million acres.

If either had ever found time in their nonstop schedules to meet, Matty and Roosevelt would have shared a host of interests. Like Matty, the president was obsessed with the outdoor life, vibrantly believing in a healthy body and moral mind. At an early age, he had wanted to be a naturalist, once writing a catalog on "The Summer Birds of the Adirondacks."

Because of size, coordination, and asthma; he did not have the talent to be a great athlete—but that was only a hurdle. Roosevelt exercised, boxed, rowed, hiked, hunted, rode horses, and played tennis. He was an intellectual with a retentive mind, believed in good sportsmanship, and did not like the night life.

His opponents dismissed him as an overgrown child; the president and his large family playing baseball on the White House lawn.

"People everywhere loved Roosevelt as a red-blooded, democratic American whose every action showed good sportsmanship and dynamic vitality," wrote historian Samuel Eliot Morison. "With the heart of a boy and the instincts of a man of action, Roosevelt had the brain of a states-man."[7]

Growing up, Matty and Teddy had certainly come from different backgrounds when it came to wealth, but both were deeply religious; Roosevelt was raised Presbyterian and Dutch Reform in a household that enjoyed daily Bible readings and prayer. Even during extensive travel, young Theodore and his family never missed church on Sunday. When Teddy left home to attend Harvard, his father advised him to "take care of your morals first." While attending Harvard, Teddy taught Sunday school. As a politician, Roosevelt kept his religious views quite conventional. Well, he occasionally made a point with the backing of scripture, once citing from the book of Micah (6:8), "To do justly, to show mercy, and to walk humbly before the Lord thy God."

Unlike Matty, Roosevelt was a fiery orator. There were problems in America, and the president had the ideas and energy to fix them. Better times were certainly ahead.

9

NICKEL PLATE ROAD (1907)

The life of a ballplayer was glamorous—fresh air, good pay, big crowds, a couple of hours work on a sunlit afternoon, riding the rails on the Nickel Plate Road (NPR) . . . oops, there goes the splendor.

A train ride on the NPR (New York, Chicago, & St. Louis Railway Company) was pictured—mostly by those not shrugging from one city to the next—to be filled with a beautiful journey across the fields of America, sun streaming through the window, casual dining in the Pullman.

In reality, trains were hot and stuffy, rides long and bumpy, and the hiss of steel and steam not quite as majestic as the poets might suggest. Reading inspired headaches, muscles began to crumble, and even the nonstop card games became drudgery. Weary passengers couldn't wait to escape, even if the prize was fifteen minutes in an Indiana depot.

There was a time that Christy would have instinctively lowered his shade as the train came to a halt, barely sensing the large crowds that always gathered on the depot platforms, gawking for a glimpse of the Great Mathewson. But that was the old days; when fame was new and he was hiding within his private war against immaturity.

One afternoon in Fort Wayne, Indiana, in August 1907, Christy straightened his collar and stepped off the train to the delight of a huge crowd, mostly kids. Once awkward and shy, the heroic ballplayer now understood his obligations; happily shaking hands, signing autographs, and thanking each for their kindness.

As the train departed, the Christian Gentleman stood in the doorway of his Pullman, waving to the fans who would love him forever.

Yet, he missed his family.

✿ ✿ ✿

The Giants had begun the 1907 campaign with expectations of a glorious spring training adventure in Los Angeles, where the team was hampered by three weeks of rain. Matty had his own problems, with the *Los Angeles Sun* telling readers on March 10 that he had "a lame arm because he pitched too hard."[1] Or perhaps it was just the damp weather. However, he was back in form within a couple of weeks and was pitching shutout ball by the time the team arrived in Nashville during the long haul back home for the new season.

Sore arm? New baby in the house? Matty seemed oblivious of distractions, opening with a 1-0 shutout against the Boston Braves at South End Grounds, Roger Bresnahan scoring the only run in the top of the ninth inning. Big Six did the same in the home opener at the sold-out Polo Grounds, beating Brooklyn 1-0 on a two-hitter.

New York looked strong early in the season, but then tumbled to fourth place. Matty looked solid throughout with a 24-12 record with a 2.00 earned run average while leading the league in wins, shutouts, and strikeouts. The Cubs captured their second straight National League pennant, then buried Ty Cobb and the Detroit Tigers in the 1907 World Series.

One sidebar from the season was the ongoing exploits of Matty's catcher, the irascible Roger Bresnahan. With seemingly the exact personality as John McGraw, Bresnahan was a wonderfully kind and considerate gentleman when not playing baseball. But don't mess with "The Duke of Tralee" on the ball diamond. With explosive speed and a superb bat, he was the only catcher in the game employed as a leadoff hitter. Bresnahan was tough, aggressive, and one tick from mayhem; one reporter described him as "highly strung and almost abnormally emotional."[2]

With the ability to play any position, he was once an outstanding pitcher, hooking up with McGraw and the Baltimore Orioles back in 1901, the first season of the American League. In New York, he was a fantastic centerfielder, hitting .350 in 1903. He would soon become the best catcher in baseball; definitely the smartest. In 1907, concerned with workplace safety, he became the first catcher to wear shin guards, bulky gear resembling the pads used for cricket. As with most new ideas, Bresnahan's self-designed protective gear was roundly ridiculed. Pittsburgh manager Fred Clarke complained that the pads might harm sliding runners. Others howled that Bresnahan was a coward . . . and then ran.

Bresnahan also was the first person to wear a batting helmet. After being badly beaned and hospitalized in 1905, he designed an offshoot of a leather football helmet, perfect protection for his tendency to crowd the plate.

In his autobiography, McGraw called Mathewson and Bresnahan the greatest pitching-catching combination of all time.

❖ ❖ ❖

Hard work, sportsmanship, honesty, moral values, and muscular Christianity . . . these were the qualities of Frank Merriwell, an enormously admired fictional character created by Gilbert Patten in 1896 for *Tip Top Weekly*. The Frank Merriwell series became so popular that it was soon a staple of the dime novel. The main character was the All-American Boy—athletic, intelligent, and forever getting ambushed at the edge of disaster—somehow finding a way to survive and to win . . . fair and square, of course. Faith in God also pulled Frank Merriwell through plenty of tough situations, fitting well with the "muscular Christianity" movement that was continuing to make an impact in schools and churches across the nation. The YMCA, Boy Scouts, Salvation Army, Teddy Roosevelt, Walter Rauschenbusch, Billy Sunday, and John Howard Harris all agreed—there was nothing weak about being a Christian. Nothing wrong with a clean-living follower of Jesus being healthy, dynamic, and athletic.

"For when the One Great Scorer comes to mark against your name," Grantland Rice would pen at the end of his famous poem "Football Alumnus," "He writes—not that you won or lost—but how you played the game."[3]

"He's a regular Frank Merriwell" was a common description for a person who practiced good sportsmanship.

Without a doubt, that would define Christopher Mathewson, portrayed by writers as a near-perfect athlete and gentleman.

"He gripped the imagination of a country that held a hundred million people," said Grantland Rice, "and held that grip with a firmer hold than any man of his day or time. There might be rumors and reports concerning others, but here was one man who was clean clear through."[4]

The legend of Matty would flourish in a world where communication mostly traveled by newspapers and word of mouth. Although stories were usually based on truth, they could also carry a good dose of folklore. Sportswriters reported the facts . . . and then some.

As fact and fiction harmoniously weaved through the palate of Americana, this man of faith took center stage. He was handsome, athletically gifted, virtuous, distinguished, impeccably dressed, unique . . . absolutely no one on earth carried such an indisputably perfect image.

These were the known ingredients: Christy Mathewson was an extremely smart and clean-living small-town farm boy from northeast Pennsylvania who went off to Bucknell, where he excelled in academics and three sports. He was an All-America football player and class president and a member of two literary societies. He was tall, stunningly handsome, and muscular—both competitor and sportsman. Polite, honest, and well spoken, he loved and respected his parents. With sound mind, body, and character, he was the definition of muscular Christianity. Didn't he make a promise to his mother that he would never play baseball on Sunday?

As with any legend, many of the details surrounding Matty's life were enhanced with a harmless measure of illusion: no liquor, no tobacco, no vulgarity; absolute purity of heart and mind; the emblem of all that is good and honest; a brilliant man who single-handedly brought dignity and sportsmanship to baseball, lifting the game from the dregs of vice to the summit of integrity.

First, Matty was not perfect. His teammates knew plenty about the man who was not quite as spotless as the public poster boy.

Laughing Larry Doyle, one of Matty's best friends, once said, "We were a rough, tough lot in those days. All except Matty. But he was no namby-pamby. He'd gamble, play cards, curse now and then and take a drink now and then. But he was always quiet and had a lot of dignity."[5]

The Christian Gentleman. Courtesy of Bucknell University

"The public thought Matty was faultless," wrote Frank Deford in *The Old Ball Game*, "while those who knew him thought he was wonderfully human."[6]

To the fans, The Christian Gentleman could do no wrong, and nothing could possibly demean his status . . . even when he occasionally did blunder.

Some narratives were absolutely true—he was an honor student at Bucknell. Some accounts were a stretch—he never questioned an umpire's decision. And some were downright fables—as a collegian, he dropkicked a football right through the middle of the goal posts from seventy-five yards away.

As the tales were passed around the cities, towns, and farmlands (the nation was then two-thirds rural), the rapidly escalating multitude of worshipers couldn't get enough. It didn't matter that most had never actually seen him, they knew all about the Christian Gentleman, all while living in a world with no radio, no television, and no instant replay.

The story goes that Matty was sliding into home plate with the winning run. The play was close, the hard (but clean) slide kicking so much dust into the air that the umpire lost view of the tag. Not knowing if Matty was safe or out, the umpire looked into the Great Mathewson's eyes.

"He got me," said Matty, the umpire then lifted his fist to signal "out" as the Polo Grounds crowd gasped in shock.

"Why would you do that?" the opposing catcher asked.

"Because," said Matty, "I'm a church elder."[7]

Matty possessed a "spiritual energy" and followed the Golden Rule without fault, quietly representing a wholesome ethical code that he learned from his parents and Pastor Harris at the old Factoryville First Baptist Church.

Except for the Sundays when he was on a train, Matty always attended church, at home with Jane and on the road by himself or with teammates. He kept his Bible close, checking and annotating what he might consider the most profound verses; reciting to himself, or when asked by Jane, some of his favorites.[8]

From Isaiah 40:31, "He who trusts in the Lord will find new strength. He will soar high on wings like eagles; he will not grow weary."

Another was Philippians 4:6–7, again word for word with perfect understanding: "Don't worry about anything; instead, pray about everything. Tell God what you need, and thank him for all he has done. Then you will experience God's peace, which exceeds anything we can understand. His peace will guard your hearts and minds as you live in Christ Jesus."

The Christian Gentleman even taught Sunday school.

"He held public faith in dark days when others were trying to destroy his faith," said Rice. "He was not walking along easy paths, yet his character was such that he held even the respect of those who had no ideals of any sort, but could still pay tribute to the rugged strength of one who was indifferent to any mockery or taunts."[9]

"Mathewson was steady as a rock," said Damon Runyon, "a man of high morality and restraint, a preacher by word and precept of decent living."[10]

How exactly it all unfolded was beyond him. Matty didn't court the spotlight as much as it fell on him. And if fame was thrown his way, why duck? The best explanation is that he walked into the perfect moment; the game desperately needed a wholesome poster boy and America took notice. Celebrity just happened and off it went.

Although he was often astonished at the scope of the adoration, he realized his good fortune. He knew the nation's perception and did not want to disappoint. Plus, it was basically true because even the myths defined his values. He was a good person who believed in a wholesome lifestyle and always tried to follow his moral compass. The conundrum was that Christy was a bit uneasy about expectations, always coveting his privacy. Remember, behind the artist on the baseball diamond, a quiet, discreet, and reserved kid at times still lingered.

But he loved the game, the tributes, and the glory. Best of all, he truly cherished being a role model.

"I feel strongly that it is my duty to show youth the good, clean, honest values that I was taught by my mother," he said. "That really is all I can do."[11]

"How we loved to play for him," said catcher Jack "Chief" Meyers. "We'd break our necks for the guy. If you made an error behind him or anything of that sort, he'd never get mad or sulk. He'd come over and pat you on the back. He had the sweetest, most gentle nature. Gentle in every way."[12]

Was Matty a regular Frank Merriwell or Merriwell a regular Christy Mathewson? Whichever, Matty was christened the role model for all boys, the matinee superhero, a beacon of virtue leading the nation down a righteous path.

10

THE SMARTEST BONEHEAD IN BASEBALL (1908)

Two outs, bottom of the ninth, and chaotic bliss was rocking the stadium as Freddie Merkle rounded first, his clutch single down the right-field line sending Moose McCormick to third with the potential game-winning run. Pardon Merkle's swagger, but the nineteen-year-old rookie's first heroic moment might pierce the heart of a blistering pennant race.

Freddie Merkle's life was about to forever be defined.

* * *

The 1908 season had been extraordinary.

On July 16 in Chicago, Giants rookie Otis "Doc" Crandall was sailing along with a 4-1 lead with one out in the ninth inning. Just to be safe, McGraw had Matty warming up in the outfield bullpen, but Big Six figured the game was in the bag, so he headed for the clubhouse to take an early shower. Unfortunately, Crandall lost his control, walked three straight Cubs, and McGraw signaled to the bullpen for Matty . . . who was gone. Furious, Little Napoleon ordered his bench players to find the missing ace while the Giants on the field began a series of stall tactics that included Iron Man McGinnity slowly ambling to the pitcher's box to relieve Crandall. McGinnity was not ready, with Jimmy Slagle beating out an infield single to make it 4-2 as word was relayed from the clubhouse that Matty had been found, calmly taking a nice hot shower. To stretch out a few more minutes, the Giants instigated an argument with umpire Hank O'Day, leading to Laughing Larry Doyle getting tossed from the game. By now, Matty had carelessly thrown on his uniform, but couldn't get into his spikes because his feet were too wet. Nevertheless, he charged into the game from centerfield, the greatest pitcher in baseball, half dressed, still wet, and shoeless. The Chicago crowd—and most of the players—had reached high hilarity when Matty finally got the ball from Iron Man. No hat, but at least he had his glove. The Great Mathewson managed to put on his shoes, conspicuously avoided eye contact with McGraw, and threw two warm-up pitches to catcher Roger Bresnahan.

There was still only one out, the Cubs had closed the gap to 4-2, and the bases were loaded. Matty quickly induced a groundout, then struck out Del Howard with a fastball and two fade-aways. Game over.

Little Napoleon would have the last word. "The next time," he told Matty, "don't take your shower in the middle of a pennant race."[1]

There was plenty of action in New York. Roger Bresnahan caught a record 139 games and the new hit song, "Take Me Out to the Ballgame," had been inspired by a billboard announcing an afternoon ballgame at the Polo Grounds. Annoyed by a fan, Turkey Mike Donlin slugged the man in the eye, Hooks Wiltse won a ten-inning Independence Day no-hitter, the Giants signed minor league prospect Richard "Rube" Marquard to an unprecedented contract. Branded by sportswriters as the "$11,000 lemon," Marquard would eventually reach greatness, but not in 1908.

In Chicago, the electric scoreboard was invented by George Baird and, on September 26, Ed Reulbach of the Cubs pitched both games of a double-header against Brooklyn, allowing no runs. The feat occurred in the midst of Reulbach's string of forty-four straight scoreless innings. Big deal, rookie Walter "Big Train" Johnson of the Washington Senators shut out the New York Highlanders three times in four days. How fast was the Big Train? Fearful of a cloudy day in Washington, Ty Cobb coined the famous expression, "you can't hit what you can't see."[2]

There was the usual: Cobb winning the American League batting title at .324 with Honus Wagner a major league best of .354. Wagner also led the National League in hits, steals, doubles, triples, and total bases.

For a hefty dose of drama, on the final day of the 1908 regular season, the American and National Leagues were each deadlocked in extraordinary three-way races—Detroit, Cleveland, and the Chicago White Sox in the American League; New York, Pittsburgh, and the Chicago Cubs in the National League. The nation may have been excited, but the Giants were downright angry—they figured they had already won the title.

Two weeks earlier, Christy and company were "robbed" of certain victory in what still remains the most controversial game ever played.

On September 23, as traces of dusk began to filter the Polo Grounds, the Cubs and Giants were engaged in a 1-1 pitcher's duel. Matty seemed to be stronger with every pitch, but Chicago's Jack Pfiester was obviously tired, his arm heavy from nine innings of stress and too many curveballs. With some rookie named Merkle having just singled Moose McCormick to third, the 30,000 Giants rooters were primed for victory.

As Giants' shortstop Al Bridwell approached the plate, he realized Merkle might be leading off first a bit too far. With the winning run at third, the Giants couldn't afford a stupid blunder at first, even though *Sporting Life* had recently mentioned that Merkle possessed great potential and used "good judgment on the bases."[3]

After motioning the rookie to shorten his lead, Bridwell turned his focus to Pfiester, surprised to see an eye-popping fastball right down the middle of the plate. Ever so smoothly, Bridwell smacked the ball so hard that it nearly nailed umpire Bob Emslie positioned in shallow center. Cubs' outfielder Circus Solly Hoffman had no chance as the ball found the gap and bounded under the makeshift ropes used to partition part of the overflow crowd.

Game over. Moose stomped on home plate and Bridwell triumphantly rounded first. Immediately, teammates and thousands of rooters stormed the field to celebrate.

It may have looked like bedlam, but drama had not yet arrived . . .

It seems that Merkle had stopped ten feet short of the second-base bag, gleefully observed the moment, and instinctively rushed toward the centerfield locker room.

Okay, he never touched second . . . it was tradition.

"Merkle, like all players before him, simply ran down toward second," said manager John McGraw. "Having shown that he could have

After games, rooters walked across the field to exit the Polo Grounds, a trigger to the most controversial moment in baseball history. Courtesy of the National Baseball Hall of Fame

reached the bag had he wanted to, he turned off and ran to the club house."[4]

Now, McGraw prided himself on having total understanding of the rule book. And according to a strict interpretation of the rules, a runner must proceed safely to the next base to avert a force out. Then again, even most umpires considered the rule only applied to infield grounders, not a clear single to the outfield. Plus, the obscure rule had never previously been enforced.

With the Giants' clubhouse located right next to the main exit in centerfield, it made sense to get off the field. There were literally thousands of people—and a few brave players—heading in the same direction.

"As soon as a game ended, the people would all pour out and rush at you," said rookie Fred Snodgrass. "Of course, all they wanted to do was touch you, or congratulate you, or maybe cuss you out a bit. But, because of that, we bench warmers all made it a practice to sprint from the bench to the clubhouse as fast as we could."[5]

Back to this game . . . and here's where it gets dicey. You see, there were no moving pictures, no instant replay, just a multitude of different versions as to what precisely happened. Not even the twenty New York and Chicago newspaper reports could agree.

All things considered, here's one more attempt.

With the field now swamped by jubilant fans, Chicago second baseman Johnny "The Crab" Evers—another student of the rule book—began shouting for Circus Solly to retrieve and throw the baseball. In Evers's mind, if Merkle is forced out at second, then the inning is over and McCormick's run doesn't count.

Iron Man McGinnity, who had been coaching first base for the Giants, noticed what Evers was doing as Hoffman worked his way through the outfield crowd to retrieve the ball. Matty, also seeing the sudden commotion, grabbed Merkle to get him safely to second. On the way, however, he asked the field umpire, Bob Emslie, if Merkle needed to touch the bag. "It's all right," said the ump. "You've got the game."[6]

The Cubs sure didn't think it was over, nor did McGinnity, now running full speed toward Evers at second. At 125 pounds, Evers was the smallest man on the field and Iron Man a 206-pound former muleskinner. As the ball finally arrived from Circus Solly, so did the Iron Man, plowing into Evers with the full force of a middle linebacker. Needless to say, McGinnity won the ball and threw it as far as he could into the stands.

By this time, home plate umpire Hank O'Day had made his way to second, the two officials observing the heightened confusion.

According to one of the more popular descriptions of the incident, a reserve pitcher on the Cubs, Floyd "Rube" Kroh, went into the stands to request the ball back from a tall, middle-aged man wearing a brown bowler hat. When the fan refused to hand over the baseball, Kroh simply smashed the bowler over his eyes.

Stealing the ball from the blinded rooter, Kroh heaved it to Joe Tinker for the relay to Evers, who now tagged second, prize to the sky so that Umpire O'Day could take note.

O'Day could have easily walked away, but the exact same thing had happened under his watch several weeks earlier with the Cubs. When one of the Pirates didn't touch second, Evers stomped on second, unsuccessfully demanding that the winning run be negated. When O'Day decided the Pirates had won the game, the always high-strung Evers blasted him for choosing tradition over a rule that was right there, somewhere, in the rule book.

Not that O'Day was afraid of getting chewed out by Evers, who paraded an ego and vocabulary that could rival McGraw, but the obscure rule was still fresh in the umpire's mind.

As both sides argued frantically with O'Day and Emslie, the hundreds of fans still milling on the now darkened field vigorously joined the home team's argument . . . leading to a near riot and an emergency umpire evacuation under police protection.

Later that evening, O'Day decided that Merkle had not touched second—even though neither umpire saw the entire play—and, therefore, the winning run had not scored. O'Day ruled the game a tie.

Was it the proper call? After all, Merkle was following a custom with deep roots.

"Any ballplayer on any ball club would have done the same thing Merkle did," Al Bridwell would recall many years later. "They did it all the time in those days."[7]

Umpire Bill Klem, who was working in a different city that day, surmised that the rule was not designed for clear, game-winning hits to the outfield. O'Day, according to Klem, had made "the rottenest decision in the history of baseball."[8]

When word reached the Giants that their victory had been negated, they initially thought someone was playing a joke.

"When the boys heard this in the clubhouse, they laughed," said Mathewson, "for it didn't seem like a situation to be taken seriously."[9]

Merkle, however, was distraught.

"It was a terrible thing to have happened," he said. "I wished that a large hole would open up and swallow me."[10]

Fueled over the years by a puzzling jumble of fact and fiction, truth has been lost to history. Some say Kroh grabbed a new and different baseball from the Cubs dugout. McGraw charged that Kroh—an illegal participant because he was not even in the game—was tackled by Iron Man, who threw the fake baseball into the stands. Others say it was Chicago's first baseman (and manager) Frank Chance who grabbed a different ball and personally took it to second where he stomped on the bag.

Not one New York newspaper carried a similar account. The *Evening Herald* had Tinker going into the crowd; the *Evening Journal*

Chicago's Johnny Evers (front) and Joe Tinker. Courtesy of the National Baseball Hall of Fame

claimed Merkle was standing on second when Cubs' catcher Johnny Kling corralled the baseball, and the *Sun* argued that Merkle would have easily reached second base except that "two or three Chicagoans were hanging on to him."[11]

"No play was made at second with the ball that had been hit," roared McGraw. "To get a picture of this confusion you must bear in mind that thousands of fans were running all over the diamond."[12]

Another twist was that Merkle actually came back and touched second while McGinnity was pummeling Evers or Kroh. Actually, umpire Hank O'Day said that McGinnity was fighting with Cubs pitcher Jack Pfiester.

Along with the accusations that neither Merkle or Evers or any baseball on the entire planet ever actually arrived at second base was the spicy conspiracy theory that the home plate umpire hated McGraw and his Giants. And even though Hank O'Day was universally considered to be 100 percent honest, he was in fact born in Chicago. The theory sinks because, back in the 1890s, O'Day had pitched for New York.

But the biggest backlash was hurled at rookie Freddie Merkle. Remember, this was his first major league start.

Sportswriter W. W. Aulick of the *New York Times* proclaimed that "Merkle's bonehead play was the dumbest mistake ever made by a player."[13]

Aulick's somewhat tongue-in-cheek account of the game has become a classic.

"The merry villagers flock on the field to worship the hollow where the Mathewson feet have pressed, and all of a sudden there is a doings around second base," he wrote. "And then begins the argument which will keep us in talk for the rest of the season, and then some."[14]

To their final moments on earth, players and other witnesses refused to budge on their various interpretations. Evers argued he did indeed complete the delayed out. New York catcher Roger Bresnahan, nearly four decades after the game, quipped that "Johnny Evers hasn't completed the force-out of Merkle yet."[15]

Al Bridwell, the man with what would have been the game-winning hit, also never saw Evers touch second base. Bridwell had other concerns, as well.

"I wish I'd never gotten that hit that set off the whole Merkle incident," he said. "I wish I'd struck out instead."[16]

❖ ❖ ❖

The entire matter might have tumbled into obscurity except for one circumstance. Sure enough, after a wild scramble with the Pirates exiting on the final day of the regular season, the Giants and Cubs were deadlocked in first. The tie game would need to be replayed. That would occur on October 8 at the Polo Grounds, the winner to face the Detroit Tigers in the World Series.

Christy would later call the one-game playoff to decide the National League pennant "the most dramatic and important contest in the history of baseball."[17]

The Giants and their fans were furious, some of the players wanting to boycott what they considered an unjust technicality. They still believed that they had been shafted in the "tie game" of September 23 and that the playoff "would be fighting for what they had already won."[18] To a majority of New Yorkers, the Chicago Cubs had advanced from bitter rival to hated monsters.

Despite all the animosity, it was the Giants who were hurting. Roger Bresnahan (sciatic rheumatism), Mike Donlin (muscle spasms), and Fred Tenney (two hamstrings) should not have been playing. Larry Doyle was badly spiked and had just gotten out of the hospital.

"How are the cripples?" McGraw bellowed as the players arrived to the ballpark. "Any more to add to the list of identified dead?"[19]

And then there was Freddie Merkle. He had lost weight, and his eyes were hollow with depression.

"He was drawn up in the corner of the bench, pulling away from us as if he had some contagious disease," said Christy. "We tried to cheer him up, but he was inconsolable."[20]

During the stretch run for the pennant, Christy had pitched nine times in two weeks and thrown nearly 400 innings for the season. His arm felt heavy and stiff. Before heading to the park on October 8, he told Jane, "I'm not fit to pitch today."[21]

She gave him a hug and kiss, encouraging him to do his best. She also wanted him to remember that she and Sonny would be at the park cheering. Perhaps they should have watched from their apartment.

Newspapers estimated that 250,000 people invaded the Polo Grounds for the big game. The *Washington Times* would carry three headlines the next day, including "Fans Storm Gates Hours before

Memorable Struggle" and "Millions Neglect Daily Duties to Await Returns."

The invasion was probably closer to 100,000 people, but because only 40,000 could possibly fit into the stadium, many resorted to illegal methods of entrance. The fifteen-foot walls of the outfield—despite a topping of barbed wire—proved no defense for groups of riotous fans as they skirted the fire department's high-powered hoses to bash through or over the wooden fences. It was estimated that 10,000 were able to break in without tickets, a few arriving through a sewer tunnel.

"Thousands piled upon thousands in a fearful tangle," observed a reporter. "The police were swept aside like corks before a torrent. And the horses of the mounted men were pushed and jammed against the walls surrounding the grounds."[22]

The Cubs couldn't even get into the stadium—policemen had revolvers drawn to escort them through the gates.

Those not willing to break the law charged up Coogan's Bluff to watch from the "elevated tracks, telegraph poles, tree tops, flag staffs and every precipice that afforded a fingernail grip."[23] Two spectators fell to their deaths from the elevated train track. That was after an initial stampede that injured hundreds of fans. In fact, on the way to the park with their tickets, Jane and two-year-old Sonny were momentarily caught in the middle of the onslaught, fortunately being pulled to safety by a policeman.

There was even a rumor that Fred Merkle had killed himself.

From beginning until end, the Cubs were showered with obscenities.

"I never heard as many foul names as the Giants fans called us that day," said Chicago pitcher Three-Finger Brown.[24]

On the field, Frank Chance punched Iron Man McGinnity in the jaw, instigating a bench-clearing, pregame fistfight. Again, that's one story. Matty claimed McGinnity stepped on Chance's foot and shoved him backward. Another version was that Iron Man punched Chance in the chin, but there was no retaliation because the Cubs' manager and first sacker knew it was a ploy to get him tossed from the game. The only certainty was that the two combatants, away from the ballpark, were great friends.

Later, Chance suffered a ruptured cartilage in his neck, after being hit by a flying pop bottle from the stands. Catcher Johnny Kling would snag a foul pop-up in "a shower of beer bottles."

"The Polo Grounds," said Three-Finger Brown, "was the closest to a lunatic asylum as any place I've ever seen."[25]

Long story short, the Giants lost 4-2, Brown earning the victory in relief.

"I never had less on the ball in my life," said Matty.[26]

The season in ashes, John Brush presented each of his players with a medal: "The Real Champions, 1908." He also gave them $10,000 to divide equally, awarding McGraw a new car.

Material rewards seemed of little consequence.

Now and forevermore known as "Bonehead" and "Wrong Way" and "Leather Skull," Merkle would be blasted by the newspapers and ruthlessly heckled by fans, haunted by the incident for the remainder of his life. "Hey Bonehead, don't forget to touch second," the cranks would holler from the stands.

"I suppose when I die," Merkle once said, "they'll put on my tombstone, 'Here Lies Bonehead Merkle.'"[27]

McGraw and the Giants always stood strong in Merkle's defense.

"The bonehead! What a misnomer! One of the smartest men in baseball, Fred Merkle," said Chief Meyers. "It's the truth. It shows what the newspapers can do to you."[28]

"It is criminal to say that Merkle is stupid and to blame the loss of the pennant on him," said McGraw. "In the first place, he is one of the smartest and best players on this ball club. In the second place, he didn't cost us the pennant. We lost a dozen games we should have won."[29]

Matty would call Merkle "one of the gamest players who ever stood on a diamond."[30]

Mathewson had quite a season in 1908, leading the National League in victories (37), earned run average (1.43), shutouts (11), complete games (34), saves (5), and strikeouts (259). In 390 innings, he allowed only forty-two walks and threw but two wild pitches. His won-lost mark was an amazing 37-11 (still a National League best). If not for that wicked twist on September 23, his record would have been 38-10.

"I have never weakened in my opinion that the awarding of that pennant to the Cubs on a technicality was unjust," said McGraw. "Bridwell's hit really won the championship."[31]

McGraw also knew that the Giants could have easily cruised to the pennant had they not crumbled in the final days of the season, even losing three times in less than a week to a rookie left-handed pitcher the Philadelphia Phillies had just purchased from the minors—Harry "The Giant Killer" Coveleski. As a side note, while Coveleski was darkening the Giants' chances, he was unknowingly bringing light into his younger brother Stanley's world back in the coal mines of Shamokin, Pennsylvania.

"Harry beating the Giants three times in 1908 probably changed my life more than it did his," said Stanley Coveleski. "See, I never played much baseball when I was a kid. How could I? When I was twelve years old I went to work in the coal mines."[32]

By 1908, Harry Coveleski's younger brother had already spent six years under ground, working six days a week all day long.

"I never knew the sun came up any day but Sunday," said Stanley Coveleski.[33]

At night, for entertainment, the youngster would throw stones against a tin can.

"There was nothing strange in those days about a twelve-year-old Polish kid in the mines for 72 hours a week at a nickel an hour. What was strange was that I ever got out of there."[34]

But Stanley Coveleski did leave the coal mines, carving a Hall of Fame career with a 215-142 pitching mark over fourteen major-league seasons. Older brother Harry was not quite as successful, although he did manage what has to be considered a miraculous comeback. Considered fried and done after 1910, he left the game with only 12 career victories. But wait . . . Harry "The Giant Killer" resurfaced in 1914 with the Detroit Tigers to notch three straight twenty-win seasons, eventually retiring with an 81-55 record.

To throw one more twist into the 1908 season, the Pittsburgh Pirates were actually the team that got robbed. Trailing the Cubs 5-2 in the top of the ninth inning at Chicago, Ed Abbaticchio launched high into the sky what appeared to be a ninth-inning grand slam homer down the line into the left-field stands. It looked fair to the Pirates, foul to the Cubs; the umpire hesitated, then agreed with Chicago—foul ball. A few minutes later, the Cubs had the victory and were headed to New York for the infamous playoff game. The poor Pirates, had they won that final game, would have eliminated the Cubs and mathematically bested the Giants.

The Pirates grumbled, but accepted the defeat . . . until a few weeks later when a fan brought suit for an injury suffered after being hit by Abbaticchio's drive while sitting in the outfield. As proof, she had a list of witnesses and her ticket stub. Funny, it turns out her seat was located in fair territory. The Pirates could have been champs if not for the errant call by the home plate umpire, none other than Hank O'Day.

11

A DEEPLY PRIVATE GRIEF (1909)

Matty wasn't the only baseball player in the family. Taller, thinner, and four years younger than his older brother, Henry Mathewson had graduated from Bucknell in 1906. Signed by the Giants as a pitcher, Henry managed a save in his first appearance, which unfortunately proved the greatest moment of his major league career. Earning a start against the Boston Doves—no longer the Beaneaters—Henry was not only shelled, but was mercilessly stranded on the mound while yielding a record fourteen walks. Sent down to Wilmington, Henry would never get another shot in the big time, his career record etched at 0-1.

However, the youngest brother, Nicholas, had the potential of being the best pitcher in Gilbert and Minerva Mathewson's family. But in January 1909, that would forever change.

During the Christmas holidays, Matty, Jane, and two-year-old Sonny had visited their hometowns. While in Factoryville, Hughie Jennings, manager of the Detroit Tigers, stopped by for a visit. Christy had the highest respect for Jennings, one of John McGraw's closest friends, once teammates on the old Baltimore Orioles.

Jennings was not there to visit Matty but to offer Nick Mathewson a $3,000 contract to sign with the Tigers. Only nineteen, Nick had just started college, he would pitch for Lafayette in the spring and was already set to play next summer for Nashville in the Southern League. Ask any baseballer in Central Pennsylvania and they would likely agree that Nick was destined to be the greatest Mathewson pitcher of all time.

It was there in the résumé—four years pitching for Keystone Academy without ever losing a game, his senior season not even allowing a run. Added to that, he had great success against the powerful town teams of Moosic and Pittston in the Pennsylvania summer leagues. Plus, like Christy, he was an exceptional student.

Nick wanted to sign, with the chance to play in Detroit with Ty Cobb and Sam "Wahoo" Crawford, on the same pitching staff with Wild Bill Donovan . . . $3,000 . . .

But Gilbert balked, and Christy supported the decision.

"I would advise a boy who has exceptional ability as a ballplayer to sign no contracts and to take no money for playing until he has finished college," Christy had written, ever angry at himself from not returning to Bucknell for that final year.

Nick wasn't listening. He was hurt, angry, and, for some odd reason, felt extremely tired. He went back to Easton, but unexpectedly returned home, complaining about sickness and stressed that he was missing school and falling behind.

On a cold afternoon in mid-January 1909, the youngster walked out to the barn, climbed the loft to the dry hay, wrote an illegible note, and put a pistol to his brain. He died the next morning; the family, including Matty, who had rushed to the Scranton hospital from New York, was at his bedside.

Four years later, Gilbert would blame himself.

"We didn't realize around the house how much he was worried, or that his mind was becoming at all unsettled," he quietly said. "He was just turned nineteen. It was a great blow to us."[1]

Their grief was slow to heal.

* * *

If bad luck had haunted the Giants in 1908, welcome back to the new season. Before a full house at the Polo Grounds, opening day pitcher Red Ames had a no-hitter through nine innings against Brooklyn, with the ball never leaving the infield. The problem was that the Giants were being shut out by Kaiser Wilhelm, who had tossed a no-hitter through eight innings.

Ames would lose his no-hitter in the tenth and the ballgame in the thirteenth, hard to swallow for the superstitious McGraw.

The Giants would tumble to a distant third in the 1909 standings, the Pirates easily besting the Cubs as Honus Wagner led the National League in hitting (.339) and runs batted in (100). Meanwhile, Ty Cobb won the Triple Crown, batting .377 with nine homers and 107 runs batted in. In what would be the final World Series for both Wagner and Cobb, Pittsburgh toppled Detroit in seven games.

While Three-Finger Brown would lead the National League with twenty-seven victories, Christy was marvelous, compiling a 25-6 record with a league-leading and career-best 1.14 earned run average. All that despite missing the first month of the season due to an injury suffered at spring training in Marlin, Texas. Harry "Moose" McCormick was the accidental culprit, lashing a liner that struck Christy in the hand.

Moose McCormick had been a good friend since college, definitely following in Matty's footsteps. Two years younger, Moose was a fraternity brother in Phi Gamma Delta and a teammate on the Bison football and basketball squads. In fact, the year Matty left school, Moose took his old position at fullback. Having graduated from Bucknell in 1904, McCormick was a good left fielder, and McGraw also used him as one of the game's first pinch hitters.

Few college athletes played professional baseball before 1900. Most notable was John Montgomery Ward, a graduate of Penn State and Columbia Law School, who threw a perfect game the summer of Christy's birth. But college graduates could forge much stronger careers in just about any field. Harold "Hal" McClure, the first Bucknell graduate to play pro baseball, hit .333 in two games for the Boston Red Caps in 1882 and then retired. Described as a man "with pure life and correct ideals," McClure dropped baseball to study law, eventually becoming one of the youngest judges in Pennsylvania. Before studying law at Cornell, Hughie Jennings took classes with John McGraw at St. Bonaventure. McGraw probably would have graduated if they had offered degrees in baseball.

Ward, Jennings, and McClure were exceptions. Most professional baseball players prior to the twentieth century were only slightly educated, some even illiterate. There was no job security and the pay was lacking; players were generally viewed with disdain.

The rise of the American League, cleaner standards, better pay, and the national love affair with Christy Mathewson opened a new door for the scholar athlete. Suddenly, a career playing baseball was socially

Ty Cobb notched a career .366 batting average. Courtesy of the National Baseball Hall of Fame

acceptable and encouraged. By the 1920s, roughly one-third of all pro players would have college backgrounds.

Along with Matty and Moose, Bucknell was a baseball factory in the early 1900s with fourteen players in the majors. When it came to college experience, the 1909 Giants had Art Devlin (Georgetown), Fred Snodgrass (Loyola Marymount), Jack "Chief" Meyers (Dartmouth), Fred Tenney (Brown), Red Murray (Lock Haven), and Buck Herzog (Maryland). The scattering of college boys across the majors in 1909 included Eddie Grant (Harvard), Branch Rickey (Ohio Wesleyan), Albert "Chief" Bender (Carlisle), Eddie Collins (Columbia), Harry Hooper (St. Mary's), Mickey Doolan (Villanova), and Jack Coombs (Colby).

Because writing for a newspaper could be highly attractive, many sportswriters had earned college degrees. There was W. O. McGeehan (Stanford), Sam Crane (MIT), and John Wheeler (Columbia). Bozeman Bulger (Alabama) and Grantland Rice (Vanderbilt) both met Matty in 1905, the three becoming great friends and competitors at cards, chess, checkers, and golf. Matty also enjoyed challenges from Heywood Broun, who arrived from Harvard with a reputation as a "checkers shark."

Social relationships between writers and players were quite common as they traveled together and stayed at the same hotels. To ensure full coverage in the various newspapers, teams would pay travel expenses for writers, including meals.

Plenty of writers became friends and fans, even believing they were an integral part of the team. Sam Crane not only played for the Giants in 1890, but was also credited for nicknaming Matty after New York's famous "Big Six" fire wagon. William Phelon told his readers that the usually reserved Mathewson was as "jolly, as sociable, as keenly alive to fun and laughter, as any man that ever lived."[2]

John Foster of the *New York Evening Telegraph* was a big fan who liked to insert fruit metaphors into his stories, such as Matty earned a "bowl of cherries," the Giants victory was "peachy," or the Cubs got "raspberries" because Foster hated them.

In Foster's defense, it was an age when writing style often embellished the mundane, with baseball games taking on the look of heroic epics complete with rainbows and candy canes.

"Sports writing was the most picturesque form of writing in America," said Connie Mack, "when imagination was permitted to run riot. Games in those early days were made to appear fantastic."[3]

Here's a piece from the *New York Herald* about how Big Six "toyed with the sphere as a cat would with a ball of yarn" as he dominated the Phillies: "Mighty Mathewson appeared in the box for the home talent, bright-eyed and rosy as a flower in June, and his performance was of the high-grade kind which glistens with quality and comes only in five-pound boxes."[4]

When Albert "Chief" Bender struck out Dan McGann, the *New York Times* reported that the Giants' first baseman "cut off three slices of air and walked away a heart-broken man."[5]

Fred Lieb of the *New York Press* said there were two schools of sportswriters—"Gee Whiz and Aw Nuts." Lieb was neither, bent on treating his writing and baseball "seriously as a profession."[6]

Even Damon Runyon succumbed to baseball as literary fantasy, saying that Matty was "a maker of magic when he fondled that baseball in the hollow of his old glove."[7]

Where Lieb and Grantland Rice would be lifetime sportswriters, Runyon and Ring Lardner were looking for different pastures. Runyon preferred to write about gamblers, hustlers, actors, and gangsters, the seedy side of New York and beyond. Years down the road, two of his short stories would become the basis for the famous Broadway musical *Guys and Dolls*. Lardner, one of the most famous short story writers of his time, loved baseball satire until his respect for the game dramatically soured after the Black Sox Scandal of 1919.

After retirement, Matty figured he would have a wealth of options.

In November 1909, on their way to California, the Mathewson family spent three weeks in Texas, with Matty signing a barnstorming contract. He would go undefeated for the El Paso White Sox, every game a sellout. That was only a taste of his western saga. At the YMCA, he opposed the top twelve Texas checkers players in a four-ring match. "Mathewson Trims Checker Sharps" was the headline story of the *El Paso Herald*, reporting that he went undefeated while playing "three men at one time and taking them into camp as fast as they could move their men."[8]

Turns out that the Christian Gentleman was a ringer. The second vice president of the American Checkers Association, he even enjoyed playing blindfolded against eight "seeing" opponents at the same time. He also spent evenings on the circuit playing at local chess clubs.

Baseball, horticulture, reading, puzzles, bridge, whist, poker, chess, and checkers—his calendar was always packed. Ring Lardner called Matty "the most brilliant master of games he ever encountered."[9] Would anyone like to play a round of golf?

Back in 1906, a month after his return from fighting diphtheria, Matty was back playing at the Westchester golf club, his presence causing such a disruption that "all the caddies deserted their posts to form a most admiring gallery."[10] With games starting in late afternoon, Matty would head to the links, often joined by sportswriters like Grantland Rice and Ring Lardner. Rice was exceptional, but Matty could hit the low eighties. Once, when the Giants were stuck in a losing streak, McGraw banned all golfing on game day. Matty was not pleased.

"I see no reason why a player's batting average should suffer from playing golf," he said. "The golf ball is much smaller. If anything, I should suppose that practice at hitting so small a sphere in exactly the way desired ought to be excellent experience for the batter."[11]

Mister McGraw, as he was addressed by all his players except Matty (who called him John), never shied away from imposing unpopular restrictions. Remember, after Big Six lost three games in a row in 1908, McGraw had ordered him to stop playing checkers.

Of course, Little Napoleon realized that Matty would probably ignore the order. Certainly, McGraw had no plans of busting up an underground round of checkers at the local YMCA.

✿ ✿ ✿

Kate Carew of the *New York Journal-American* had absolutely no interest in baseball. Noted for drawing celebrity caricatures to go along with her stories, she was nevertheless thrilled to interview and sketch Christy in April 1910.

"His shoulders were ever so broad, and his eyes ever so blue, and his hair ever so yellow, and his cheeks ever so red, and I thought of Phoebus, the sun-god, and a young Viking with a sword," Carew wrote of the then twenty-nine-year-old legend. "And, oh dear, the strength and gladness of youth were about him like a garment."[12]

Christy shows off his golf swing at the Giants' spring training facility in Marlin, Texas. Courtesy of Bucknell University

Carew wondered, since Christy was so handsome, did he receive "a great many letters from young ladies?"

"Mash notes? Oh yes," he said with a grin. "My wife answers those."

In a full-page article in the *Chicago Day Book* headlined "Christy Mathewson as Seen by a Woman," Idah McGlone Gibson seemed most impressed with his intelligence.

"He is perhaps the best talker of all the baseball men I have interviewed," she wrote. "His words are chosen with good taste; his intonation is cultured, and he points his speech with sincerity."[13]

Baseball was hot and Christy was everywhere. *Baseball* magazine suggested that he was better known than the president of the United States.[14] That would be William Howard Taft, a huge baseball fan and the first president to throw out the first pitch on Opening Day, but sadly lacking in the charisma of Teddy Roosevelt, who was then hunting rhino in Africa.

Actually, an "athletic craze" had been building in America for the past twenty years. The nation that had been two-thirds rural in 1890 was but ten years from having more people in urban areas; the old Victorian structure of families living together on the farm rapidly changed. The cities provided mobility to a middle and upper class now faced with an abundance of leisure time.

At home, they had parlor games, music, and reading. Within the cities were cultural choices of vaudeville, concerts, theaters, libraries, nickelodeons, and dance halls. Outdoors, the city parks were jammed, and lawn tennis was a favorite of the ladies with golf and cycling gaining stature. Crowds gathered for boxing, horse racing, football, basketball, and baseball.

For the first time in America, commercialized pleasure was becoming acceptable.

Big Six was an endorsement machine, promoting Coca-Cola, Blauvelt Sweaters, Arrow shirt collars, leg garters for socks, shaving razors, Tuxedo Chewing Tobacco, and other products. For the Christy Mathewson Parlor Baseball Game, he was given $1,000 in advance plus royalties of two cents per sale. As Christy's name equaled money, the board game was a huge success.

Which is why Big Six was approached by a group of wealthy businessmen with the idea of creating a drinking establishment called The Christy Mathewson. The only requirement would be to stop by the club for a few minutes each week, shake some hands, and earn thousands of dollars. Matty loved money, but not at the expense of his image. He was not interested.

"Money can cost too much," said Minerva Mathewson. "He told me, 'Mother, if I had to make money that way I wouldn't want any.' So you see Christy knows there is something in the world worth more than money."[15]

As did Jane: "All the money in the world would not pay to have my husband away from his home all the time."[16]

Besides, he was far too busy with other interests. He owned a successful insurance agency, played the stock market with Jane, was the big ticket for barnstorming, and loved to spend part of the winter with his family in California.

He starred in a silent movie, *The Umpire*, and collaborated on a Broadway play with famed playwright and songwriter Rida Johnson Young. Opening in October 1913, *The Girl and the Pennant* was billed as a "comedy of romance and baseball."[17]

Matty and his catcher, Chief Meyers, also played the Fifth Avenue Theater. Seventh on the program of a dozen vaudeville acts with two performances daily, *Curves* also featured May Tully, who cowrote the production with sportswriter Bozeman Bulger. Mathewson earned top billing as "the peerless pitcher" and Meyers "the Indian backstop."

Acting was definitely not Christy's passion, just a vehicle to somehow overcome an awkward shyness.

"He was conscious, and annoyed, that many people thought his timidity was arrogance or swell-headedness," said Bulger. "He hadn't that knack of making pleasant conversation upon meeting strangers and he struggled hard to overcome it. So he went on the stage for the sole purpose of training himself to feel at ease in making public talks and in addressing strangers. When he appeared ill at ease and non-communicative, it hurt him worse than the person he was addressing."[18]

Public speaking was not on the long-range agenda. Matty was intrigued with the life of a full-time writer. He talked with John Howard Harris about ideas for combining baseball with a Christian and moral message. To get started before retirement, he approached several friends to act as ghostwriters.

Several of his biggest sellers were *Won in the Ninth* (1910) and *Pitching in a Pinch* (1912); ghostwriter Jack Wheeler claimed he was simply an editor for a good writer and a voracious reader.

Christy also wrote a portion of *The Battle of Base-Ball* with journalist C. H. Claudy, whose usual genre was science fiction. He worked with Bozeman Bulger on magazine and newspaper articles. With sportswriter W. W. Aulick, Matty penned a string of popular children's books. Filled with action and wholesome values, he wrote in *Pitcher Pollock* that baseball is "just as respectable as medicine or law" and in *Catcher Sloan* that "you can be a professional ball player and be a gentleman, too."

Although Matty's appeal was universal, his most avid fan base was boys. He loved kids, often leaving free game tickets for groups of children along with autographed baseballs.

As a child, Arthur Daley—a future columnist for the *New York Times*—got to see his first baseball game, the Giants with Matty pitching. "To a kid growing up in New York," Daley recalled, "the now legendary Big Six was a god. He was a big, handsome man with a picture book delivery. So smooth was his pitching motion that he lulled batters into a false sense of security. He just seemed to lob the ball to the plate, yet it was past them before they could get their bats around."[19]

Specs Toporcer, who would one day become a star with the St. Louis Cardinals, was nine years old when the Giants fell to the Cubs in the one-game replay of 1908.

"I cried myself to sleep that night," said Specs, who often walked to the Polo Grounds with his good friend Jimmy Cagney, the boys watching from Coogan's Bluff when Matty pitched.[20]

It wasn't only the kids of New York who adored Matty. Raised in Cincinnati, famed Christian evangelist and writer Norman Vincent Peale was twelve years old when he got to shake Christy Mathewson's hand, one of the great memories of his childhood. Down in Baltimore, young George Herman Ruth loved Christy. "I was a rough kid," said Babe. "Maybe I didn't always know my lessons, but I always knew how many games Matty had won and lost. I read everything about him that I could get my hands on."[21]

"The youth of the land read every word they could find about him," said Damon Runyon, "and accepted him as their inspiration and guide."[22]

☼ ☼ ☼

In 1910, Matty would post a league-high 27-9 record with a 1.89 earned run average.

In early May, he nearly pitched a third career no-hitter, winning 6-0 in Brooklyn. The only hit by the Superbas was a routine grounder in the eighth inning that Giants' third baseman Art Devlin threw into the dirt at first. The Giants marked it as an error, but the official scorekeeper graciously awarded Pryor McElveen an infield hit. Forget that the *New York Times* blazed the banner headline that Matty had tossed a no-hitter, stating that an "untimely play by Arthur Devlin, which resulted in an error, was the only performance of the whole game that cast a blemish on the flinging of the big boxman."[23] The newspaper listed no hits in the box score and added that "the wiseacres who stayed on this side of the river yesterday and cackled up their sleeves at their friends for going way over to Brooklyn to see a ball game read the bulletin boards last night with their orbs popping out of their heads."[24]

Unfortunately for Big Six and the *New York Times*, the major league record book would side with the Brooklyn scorekeeper, giving credit to Matty for the fourth and final one-hitter of his career. His two no-hitters came against St. Louis (1901) and Chicago (1905).

He had plenty of impressive marks. Over the course of four seasons beginning in 1904, he beat the Cardinals twenty-four consecutive times. From 1908 to 1911, he took twenty-two straight from the Reds, causing Damon Runyon to write "Christy Mathewson pitched against Cincinnati yesterday. Another way of putting it is that Cincinnati lost a game of baseball. The first statement means the same as the second."[25]

By 1910, it had become customary for American and National League teams that had fallen short of a pennant to play a postseason rivalry series. It gave the players extra earnings and was fun for the fans, who never seemed to tire of the sport.

While the Athletics were besting the Cubs in the World Series, nobody seemed to care in the nation's largest city, now 4.7 million people. Seems that the Giants and Highlanders had both finished in second place, the two cross-town rivals agreeing to play a best-of-seven Manhattan Series.

The Manhattan Series would draw 103,033 fans, the Giants winning in six games over a team that sportswriters were beginning to call the "Yankees." In game one, Matty would defeat rookie Russell Ford and his "mysterious moist ball." Ford, who had won twenty-six games during the season, would scuff the ball with an emery board. For good measure, he would then spit on it.

Matty had a great series, winning three times as each player pocketed $1,100 for the extra week of work.

An interesting sidebar during the series happened at Hilltop Park when Giants' owner John T. Brush decided to leave his automobile inside the stadium by the right field wall. To the displeasure of the Highlanders and their fans, a liner by Charlie Hemphill that had the possibility of being a triple or inside-the-park homer was instead called a ground-rule double—the ball got stuck under the automobile.

Other than losing the series, the Highlanders were also on the short end when it came to fans. Even many of the kids who lived near Hilltop Park still cheered for Christy Mathewson and the Giants.

"Back in the days when a quarter was a fortune and we had to save for weeks to get the price of a bleacher seat, the Giants had been our favorites," recalled Lou Gehrig.[26]

Ten years later, Gehrig would get his big chance—a private tryout for John McGraw at the Polo Grounds. The star first baseman for Columbia University would crack seven straight into the right-field stands, but to McGraw's keen eye, Gehrig was too big, too slow, and too questionable on defense.

"He did not give me too much attention," said Gehrig, "nor did he seem to be impressed with my possibilities."[27]

Bruising muscle was not a good fit for the Giants, and McGraw was always seeking the quick and daring.

"The first thing I notice in youngsters when they report is their speed," McGraw would say in his autobiography. "If they have it, I pay more attention."[28]

Perhaps Gehrig could get a tryout with the Yankees . . .

12

HIGH SPIKES FOR THE CHIEF (1911)

Game one of the World Series, Matty was attempting to look tough as the Philadelphia Athletics walked past the Giants' dugout. Inside, Matty's teammates each held a shoe in one hand and a file in the other, busily sharpening their spikes.

The Athletics kept walking, some refusing to look. Chief Bender, however, stopped to peer into the long dugout and shook his head as he caught Matty's eye . . . both breaking into laughter.[1]

* * *

Naturally, the pregame spike-sharpening show had been McGraw's idea; a reminder to the visiting Athletics that the Giants were fast and dangerous. After all, they had stolen a record 347 bases for the season, literally "running away" with the pennant.

"The greatest base-running club I ever saw," said McGraw. "The players got the notion that they could steal on anybody."[2]

The 1911 World Series promised to be wild. Well, the season had been crazy, beginning for the Giants with spring training in Marlin, Texas. Located about 100 miles south of Dallas, Marlin had a population of around 4,000 and a mineral bath. Other than the big fish fry hosted by the townspeople to honor the Giants, there were no distractions. To McGraw, who had grown weary of five straight seasons without winning a pennant, the environment was perfect.

Matty would call it the "hardest five weeks' grind in the world."[3]

Every morning, already baking in the dry Texas heat, the players walked the railroad track one mile to the ballfield. Fortunately, groundskeeper John Murphy had arrived a few weeks early to prepare what "had been given up to steers, stray pigs, and horses."[4]

The dirt, said Matty, was so hard that it would tear and scar baseballs upon contact.

Late afternoon, worn weary from work, the team would walk the mile back to town for dinner and, as Matty pointed out, listen to the "same old stories that creep out of the bushes on crutches year after year."[5]

It was definitely too tame for Damon Runyon, the sports editor of the *New York American*, who was already thinking that he had more to write about than baseball and boxing.

"I can spend a lifetime writing about Matty," wrote Runyon, "and I shall know enough about Bucknell and other aspects of clean living to found a monastery."[6]

Although that seems to be a compliment, Runyon meant that he yearned for a more adventurous story. After a couple of days in Marlin, he headed west to the Mexican border town of Juarez to meet and write about Pancho Villa.

As the Giants slowly moved north, stopping in a host of southern cities to play exhibition games, the news from New York City was unsettling.

On March 25, a fire at the Triangle Shirtwaist Factory claimed the lives of 146 garment workers, mostly young women. They had been trapped; all of the doors and stairwells to the building locked from the outside. As hundreds of horrified New Yorkers watched and firefighters fought to somehow break through the locks, many of the employees broke out the windows on the ninth and tenth floors, jumping from the ledges to their deaths.

Locked inside while working? Public outrage and investigations would follow. To no one's surprise, working conditions at most garment factories were gutted by congestion, stale air, and safety hazards. A six-day, fifty-two-hour work week might bring in $7 to $12 (thirteen to twenty-three cents an hour). From that, workers were docked a number of fees, including sewing machine rental and the cost of thread.

At his trial, owner Max Blanck submitted the defense that the workers would have "robbed him blind" if he had not locked them inside. He was acquitted. Two years later, Blanck again sealed the doors at another of his factories. Using the same defense as he had for the Triangle disaster, he was fined the minimum $20 for the crime, with the judge apologizing that he was forced to uphold the law.[7]

A much different kind of fire occurred on the night of April 13. Long after the conclusion of the Opening Day double-header between the Giants and Philadelphia Phillies, the Polo Grounds was destroyed. Apparently a cigarette had smoldered; the immense fire quickly consumed the wooden structure, sparing only the left-field bleachers.

Except for the bad timing, the Polo Grounds was due for an upgrade, with the old wooden ballparks around the two leagues being replaced by modern stadiums of concrete and steel. Two years earlier, Shibe Park was erected in Philadelphia and Pittsburgh spent $1 million to build the spectacular Forbes Field. Chicago's Comiskey Park had been constructed in 1910 and Boston's Fenway Park would open in 1912.

Fortunately for the Giants, the cross-town Highlanders came to the rescue, renting Hilltop Park to them until the new Polo Grounds could be completed at the end of June. The new expansive horseshoe configuration was a whopping 483 feet to dead center, with power alleys down the foul lines, as if McGraw cared about home runs.

Although the beautiful new stadium could now seat 34,000 fans, there was one slight oversight—somebody forgot to include room for parking spaces.

True, at the turn of the century, America's 8,000 automobiles were considered playthings for the wealthy, a few without vision predicting a momentary phase. But, eleven years later, traffic was already getting "ugly" in New York City. Henry Ford would soon blast open the gate from novelty to necessity with the installation of the Detroit assembly line, considerably raising production and cutting costs. By 1917, there would be nearly five million cars on the road with an average price of $345 each.

❖ ❖ ❖

Under McGraw, the New York Giants were always entertaining. First, Muggsy liked to collect ballplayers in his own image—rough and gritty scrappers like Al Bridwell, Art Devlin, Art Fletcher, and Fred Snodgrass—small in stature and busting with fight. They were brutal, fearless, and easily agitated.

Naturally, Muggsy was usually at the heart of any insurgence.

"He was, distinctly, a robust temperament," said biographer Frank Graham. "He was generous and loyal to his friends, implacable to his foes. He irritated persons in the mass and charmed them as individuals."[8]

"I got along with McGraw fine," said Bridwell. "He only suspended me once, for two games. It was on account that I socked him."[9]

Neither held a grudge.

"He was a wonderful man," Bridwell added, "a real fighter."[10]

He was a master at the finer details of the game.

During a long midsummer road trip, McGraw had to telegraph home for replacement uniforms. "We arrived in Chicago with a club in rags and tatters," said McGraw. "Nearly every man on the club had slid the seat out of his uniform pants. We had patched and patched until the principal feature of our pants was safety pins."[11]

To the delight of the Chicago crowd, Josh Devore actually slid right out of his pants, having to be escorted from the field by a slew of surrounding teammates.

"It's great to be young and a Giant," said Laughing Larry Doyle.[12]

Aside from being fast, the Giants were also highly superstitious. Again, McGraw led the charge. If the team hit a batting slump, McGraw could break the slump by dumping a load of empty barrels on the ballfield. In the dugout, Art Devlin would attack any teammate who might be singing, humming, or sitting in his lucky spot.

Pitcher Red Ames broke a losing streak when he decided to wear a lucky multicolored necktie under his uniform.

"Ames used to sleep with it under his pillow alongside of his bank roll," said Matty, "and he didn't lose another game until the very end of the season."[13]

Matty may have been one of the most intelligent people in baseball, but he took jinxes quite seriously. For instance, it was bad luck to warm up with a third baseman. If you see a cross-eyed man, spit in your hat.

"Ballplayers are among the most superstitious persons in the world," wrote Matty. "A really true, on-the-level, honest-to-jiminy jinx can do all sorts of mean things."[14]

The Giants were known to crumble should one bat become crossed with another. Superstitions and jinxes do get complicated.

"I have seen a ball club," wrote Matty, "composed of educated men, carry a Kansas farmer, with two or three screws rattling loose in his dome, around the circuit because he came as a prophet and said that he was accompanied by Miss Fickle Fortune."

That ball club, of course, would be the Giants. In 1911, it was the presence of Charles "Victory" Faust, a rather strange character who had a vision that he would lead the Giants to a world championship. Whenever he talked his way into the dugout, the Giants won. Of course, the days he was missing—usually performing vaudeville—the Giants would lose. McGraw thought Charley was a quack, but the players loved his humor, and you don't mess with the supernatural.

✿ ✿ ✿

Back to baseball. The year 1911 saw the introduction of the cork-centered ball, which was thought might just have more pop. It certainly didn't when Matty was pitching, as he went 26-13 with a 1.99 earned run average. It would be the fifth and final time his earned run average finished below 2.00, although it was always close to that magical line that divides the great from the superhero.

Another line that every baseball player must acknowledge is the passage of his thirtieth birthday, the distinguished brand of a veteran. It didn't seem to bother the Christian Gentleman that he no longer possessed a stockpile of youthful energy.

At the beginning of the 1911 season, umpire Bill Klem noted that Matty had found a way to use age as a weapon.

"Matty knows how to pitch better than any other major leaguer and is still a wonder, but he hasn't the stuff he had four years ago," said Klem. "He is not as strong as he used to be and wins games through the use of his brain more than his brawn."[15]

The powerful Athletics had taken the pennant in 1910, thumping the Cubs for the world title. They were deep in pitching and had scored the most runs in baseball, their rugged third baseman Frank Baker having walloped a league-high eleven homers and 115 runs batted in. The Athletics were favored, just as they had been in the 1905 series when Matty notched three shutouts in six days.

McGraw came prepared, dressing his team in all-black uniforms as in 1905, having the boys sharpen their spikes, and adding a place on the bench for their secret weapon—Charles "Victory" Faust.

The plan seemed so perfect, especially when Matty won the opener, 2-1, in a classic pitching duel with Chief Bender. Matty then wrote about the victory for the *New York Herald*. Well, not really, Jack Wheeler ghostwrote the story under Matty's byline. With thirteen newspapers battling in New York City (seven morning and six evening), any edge could be worth a bundle in prestige and dollars.

But the Athletics took game two, with a homer by Frank Baker against Rube Marquard proving to be the difference. McGraw was upset because he had told Marquard exactly what not to throw to Baker. So, in Matty's newspaper column was the charge that Marquard made "a poor pitch" and there was "no excuse for it."[16] They may have been Wheeler's words, but the public only saw Matty's name.

Rube was not happy.

Matty was back in the box for the third game of the series and was only two outs from posting a 1-0 shutout when Baker hit another homer, with the Athletics eventually winning 2-1 in eleven innings.

Well, turns out that Marquard also had a newspaper column, giving the nod to his ghostwriter Frank Menke to get even. Menke obliged, writing that "Matty knew what he was talking about because he pitched the same thing."[17]

Matty versus Rube—and these were two close friends.

"It was amusing," said McGraw. "The players and the fans had a good laugh out of that."[18]

The rest of the series was not as humorous. After six days of rain, game four featured Mathewson against Bender, with Philadelphia winning 4-2. Perhaps most disappointing in Matty's two losses was that the Giants committed eight errors. The Athletics would go on to win their second straight World Series crown, McGraw praising their pitching but adding that his speedsters were "pretty well worn out and shot to pieces."[19]

Actually, he should have blamed Connie Mack, the Athletics' manager, for conjuring a magical antidote to McGraw's jinx machine.

For starters, the Athletics knew about the Giants' fear of crossed bats. So, whenever they needed a spark, the Athletics threw their bats wildly into the air in front of their dugout. Poor Giants, it just wasn't fair.

But that was just a taste of the double jinxing.

"They have a combination bat boy and mascot who is a hunchback," said Matty, "and he out-jinxed our champion jinx killer."[20]

No wonder the Athletics were so good . . .

* * *

Although baseball could be bizarre, it also mirrored society.

Nicknames, for example, often humorous or fanciful, could also demean. Luther "Dummy" Taylor was New York's third starting pitcher, winning 115 games in nine seasons. He played in the majors at the same time as Dummy Hoy, Dummy Dundon, Dummy Deegan, Dummy Leitner, Dummy Lynch, Dummy Murphy, and Dummy Stephenson—all deaf mutes.

Without doubt, verbal ammunition could be insensitive and vicious.

Although McGraw may have designed a roughhouse roster—and despite the regular measure of ethnic slurs, taunts, and insults that he and his players heaved at the opposition—the manager made certain that scorn and prejudice did not creep into his dugout. Under McGraw's iron watch, every player was embraced within the Giants' family.

"We could all read and speak sign language," said outfielder Fred Snodgrass, "because Dummy Taylor took it as an affront if you didn't learn to converse with him. If we went to the vaudeville show, he wanted to know what the joke was, and somebody had to tell him. So we all learned. We practiced all the time."[21]

Insensitivity went far beyond nicknames. In the modern world of the early 1900s, racism was a matter of fact, political and cultural correctness did not exist, and differences were open to scorn by all parties.

John Tortes "Chief" Meyers took over as Matty's catcher after Bresnahan was traded to the Cardinals in 1909. A Native American from the Cahuilla tribe of Southern California, Meyers had attended Dartmouth College. He was smart, humorous, calm, and cultured. He visited art galleries in every city the team played, had a keen understanding of politics and philosophy, devotedly studied the art of hitting, and loved the theater. He knew all about hatred and ridicule.

Big Six (left) and Jack "Chief" Meyers in Marlin, Texas. Courtesy of Bucknell University

"It was tough," said Meyers, "don't think it wasn't."[22]

Playing minor league baseball in Harrisburg, Pennsylvania, Meyers recalled that "nobody paid any more attention to me than they did to the bat bag."

In his first game, the Harrisburg spitball pitcher decided to switch signals on him, just to see how Meyers would react when he called for a slow curve and got a fastball instead. Meyers was charged with five passed balls in two innings.

At the plate, the first pitch was "right at the old head, you know," said Meyers. "Kind of tamed me down, but I'd figured it would be like that."[23]

For the record, Meyers hit the next pitch into the Susquehanna River for a game-winning three-run homer.

Although Meyers made a rapid climb to the Big Time, prejudice would not cool. For the talented group of Native Americans who played baseball, stereotypes were handed down through the same generic nickname—Chief Meyers, Chief Bender, Chief Chouneau, Chief Johnson, Chief Yellowhorse, Chief Youngblood . . . Jim Thorpe, Zack Wheat, and a few others somehow managed to escape the brand.

Besides being the same age, Matty and Meyers had much in common—from reading to bridge, from college football to the philosophy of life. Matty would scold himself for any slip of the tongue in calling Meyers "Chief," always preferring his first name, Jack. The two were great friends.

In fact, Matty also was close to Bender and Thorpe. Although Thorpe was an international hero, Bender heard plenty of "war hoots" from the stands. "Back to the teepee for yours" and "Giants grab heap much wampum" were caustically shouted at Bender by rooters, according to a straightforward account in the *New York Times* from the 1905 World Series.[24]

Bender never backed down, referring to the white baseball fans as "foreigners." One can only imagine what he thought of half the Giants. Again, from the *New York Times* story after Matty's 2-0 victory secured the 1905 series over Bender and the Athletics: "Let's get at the Indian and fix 'em," John McGraw yelled from the coaching line to his hitter, Mike Donlin. "I'm sorry, old Pitch-Em-Heap," Donlin jokingly remarked to Bender, "but here's where you go back to the reservation."[25]

Remember, Bender was a college graduate, hunter, golfer, gardener, and acclaimed painter. In sixteen seasons, he fashioned a 212-127 record on his way to induction into the Baseball Hall of Fame and never backed down from abuse, returning the chatter of bigoted hecklers while calling them "ignorant, ill-bred foreigners."[26]

Nevertheless, heritage was a major issue with many Americans. The Battle of Little Big Horn had occurred in 1876, the Wounded Knee Massacre in 1890. There still remained bitterness from both natives and whites.

"The wicked do not live out half their days," said John Howard Harris at the 1898 Bucknell commencement. "Non-moralized people do not live to a great age. The North American Indians die on an average in their twentieth year. The whites of Washington City, for instance, live for an average of fifty years. That is about the average of people as nearly Christianized as Americans."[27]

That was one of the few teachings from his old pastor that Matty never accepted, chalking it up to the blather of an older generation. President Harris quickly apologized for the statement that he soon realized had no merit; there was a quite different reason that Native Americans died young.

"In clearing away the forest, we have not always been wise," said Harris one year later. "The bear and the wolf have disappeared; but typhoid and diphtheria and a multitude of other germs sweep off yearly as many victims as the whole Indian population east of the Rocky Mountains."[28]

Harris often spoke of his disdain toward racism at any level.

"Despotisms depend on race hatred and religious bigotry," he said in 1915 before relating a true story that happened prior to the Civil War at a Southern rally for secession. One of the citizens actually suggested that perhaps they should reevaluate their treatment of the slaves.

"And that is the tree on which they hung him," said Harris. "Among them only one man was really sane and he was put to death."[29]

As badly as Native Americans were taunted by baseball fans, at least they could play. African Americans were not even allowed in the ballpark.

Racial lines were unbendable.

On a trip to Cuba in January 1912, Matty pitched against Jose Mendez, known locally as "The Black Mathewson." Although Big Six and the Giants earned a 4-0 shutout, Mendez was spectacular.

"If the unwritten law of baseball didn't ban Negroes from the Major Leagues," said McGraw, "I would give $50,000 for him and think I was getting a bargain."[30]

Of course, Little Napoleon knew the tall and gifted youngster would never pass the rigid major league color barrier.

"John bemoaned the failure of baseball, himself included, to cast aside custom or unwritten law, or whatever it was," said Blanche

The Giants relax during a barnstorming trip to Havana, Cuba. Courtesy of Bucknell University

McGraw, "and sign a player on ability alone, regardless of race or color."[31]

Christy would have welcomed the diversity. But, like most white Americans at the time, both he and Jane quietly accepted the status quo.

13

A FATEFUL DAY AT FENWAY (1912)

In 1912, at the age of thirteen, Specs Toporcer had the greatest job in the world. Every day after school, the youngster would rush to a nearby saloon where he would post inning-by-inning baseball scores. Using a large blackboard, Specs relayed the results of all the games as they arrived by Western Union ticker tape. He earned fifty cents a week, plus food, and never sipped a drink. Just like the city and team he loved, Specs was baseball hungry.

For a few splendid weeks that summer, Specs also had the distinction of announcing results of the daily events at the Olympic Games in Sweden, where the great Jim Thorpe claimed gold medals in the decathlon and pentathlon. Needing a positive distraction, New Yorkers turned to Matty, Thorpe, and the bunny hug. With close to 500 dance halls in the city, nightlife was hit with a craze that had once-normal folks now light on their feet to the turkey trot and grizzly bear. For the dancers who had not yet mastered the chicken scratch, there was the good old-fashioned cakewalk.

There also was the red-hot Giants, winning their second straight pennant while logging 103 victories. With a .330 batting average, Laughing Larry Doyle was named the National League's most valuable player, for which he was awarded a new Chalmers automobile prior to the first game of the World Series. Red Murray slashed twenty triples while Fred Merkle belted eleven home runs. Plus, the Giants were still fast, stealing a league-high 319 bases. At one point, Rube Marquard won nineteen straight ballgames and rookie spitball whiz Jeff Tesreau topped the league with a 1.96 earned run average. The Christian Gentleman finished 23-12, a twenty-game winner for the tenth consecutive year.

But the 1912 Boston Red Sox were loaded. Tris Speaker led the league with a .383 batting average and a league-record 53 doubles. Leading the pitching staff was Smoky Joe Wood, a phenomenal 34-5 for the season, at one point winning sixteen games in a row. When Walter Johnson of the Washington Senators was asked if he could throw harder than Wood, Big Train replied "there's no man alive can throw harder than Smoky Joe Wood."[1]

Best hitter, best pitcher . . . the Red Sox also had a brand new state-of-the-art stadium, Fenway Park.

Hugh Fullerton of the *New York Times* caused an uproar when he predicted the Red Sox were too strong for the Giants. To make matters worse, he suggested that Matty would probably get shelled.

"Against a team that can hit like Boston," Fullerton wrote, "one needs more than brains."[2]

It would be one of the most exciting World Series ever played.

McGraw had new uniforms for his team, this time off-gray with pinstripes and the big NY logo. He also tried to fool the Red Sox into thinking Matty would pitch the opener at the Polo Grounds, but instead started Jeff Tesreau. If that was McGraw's idea of trickery, it was lame compared to the innovative Red Sox voodoo. Leading the charge, as always, were the famous Royal Rooters, a group of rowdy Boston Irishmen whose exclusive club had roots back to the 1890s. The current leader was Michael "Nuf Ced" McGreevey, the lovable and chatty owner of the Third Base, the ultimate bar and all-year shrine to the Red Sox. One of the original Royal Rooters from two decades earlier, McGreevey earned his nickname from popping his hand on the bar when he had heard enough. "Nuf ced," he would command. As if Nuf Ced needed a partner at the top of the Rooters food chain, that would be the honorable John "Honey Fitz" Fitzgerald, the mayor of Boston. Men without a booming voice and undying fervor for their blessed Sox need not apply to a never-ending party that was always several hundred strong, swelling considerably for important encounters. Basically, the Royal Rooters were bent on causing wondrous havoc wherever they roamed. For every home game, they would parade around the field with their own band before the game and sit in their own private section out in the left-field bleachers. Although their enthusiasm sparked passion with the Fenway faithful, they also kept an extra bullet to annoy the opposition. That was easy for a group of fun fanatics who loved to drink, gamble, and sing the same song, "Tessie," over and over again. Had there been any rules of war, the exasperating tune would have been defined as torture.

> Tessie, you make me feel so badly
> Why don't you turn around?
> Tessie, you know I love you madly
> Babe, my heart weighs about a pound . . .

Sounds harmless enough, until you hear it for the 1,000th straight time.

The music and parade would continue after the game as well, the roaring Rooters singing and shouting allegiance to the beautiful Sox. It was fun; it was tradition.

For big games, such as the World Series, the Rooters took their show on the road. Three hundred reached Grand Central Station riding three special train cars in the early afternoon of the first game. Part of their finely dressed attire was straw boater hats with large red hatbands proclaiming "Oh! You Red Sox!" With trumpets blaring, they marched in parade formation to the Polo Grounds where they continued the pattern around the field to the not-so-neighborly jeers of 40,000 Giants' fans. The Rooters absorbed the mass cursing and smiled—McGraw had to be jealous.

The Royal Rooters were finally in their seats and already singing "Tessie," and the pregame conference was taking place at home plate, John "Don't call me Muggsy" McGraw chumming with his old adversary, umpire Bill "Never call me Catfish" Klem.

Ground rules covered, the umpire leaned past Boston manager Jake Stahl to speak directly to McGraw. "Let's not give anyone any reason to send you off to watch the rest of the game in the showers, okay John?" They both smiled. "Bill, you know how much I admire your work," said McGraw. "Just admire it quietly today," laughed Klem. "Do we have a deal?"[3]

Game one was phenomenal, Smoky Joe Wood desperately trying to hold a 4-3 lead in the bottom of the ninth with two runners in scoring position and only one out, the Polo Grounds in a frenzy. No problem, Smoky Joe struck out the final two Giants and the Sox were winners, the

New York hitting parade included (left to right): Josh Devore, Larry Doyle, Fred Snodgrass, Red Murray, Fred Merkle, Buck Herzog, Chief Meyers, and Art Fletcher. Courtesy of the National Baseball Hall of Fame

Rooters taking to the field for one last boisterous insult as the stadium quickly emptied.

Although it may sound foolish, the odd games (one, three, and five) were scheduled for New York and the even ones in Boston. If a game seven was needed, a flip of the coin determined the ultimate location. So, after the opener, both teams rushed to make the six o'clock train for a five-hour trip up the New Haven Railroad to Boston. Those who missed the Gilt Edge Express had to wait for the ten o'clock Owl, which after game one was three hours behind schedule, not arriving in Boston until seven o'clock the next morning. That was the train taken by the Royal Rooters (because they had been celebrating) and all of the newspaper reporters (because they had been writing). The series had only started and all of the sportswriters were cranky, each writing that baseball's back-and-forth scheduling was ridiculous and trying to catch a few hours of sleep while the sounds of "Tessie" echoed through the overnight Owl.

The next day at Fenway, the Giants committed five errors behind Matty and were probably lucky that the 6-6 game was called in the eleventh inning due to darkness. Back home, Specs Toporcer had moved his scoreboard outside and loudly announced the play-by-play results to a big crowd that paled in size to what was happening elsewhere in New York City. You could watch from special scoreboards in front of newspaper buildings, bars, businesses, or while sitting in Madison Square Garden. Overflow crowds were at every corner, causing Damon Runyon to observe that "there is no reason for any New Yorker at any time in their day today to be unaware of exactly what is transpiring in their sister city to the east."[4] An estimated crowd of 25,000 gathered in Times Square to gawk at the big electric scoreboard giving the lineups, the batter and pitching count—every detail a baseball fan would possibly need to know—a modern wonder. In fact, World Series scoreboard watching was becoming an event throughout the nation, with huge crowds gathering at newspapers and marketplaces from Pittsburgh to Chicago, Scranton to Seattle. In Southern California, Addie Snodgrass, mother of the great Giants' centerfielder, Fred, nervously watched the results unfold on a large, makeshift scoreboard in front of the Los Angeles Times building. With all this advancing technology, city folks could now enjoy the outdoors with a festive crowd, everyone pretending to be watching a baseball game while screaming at an ever-moving billboard. Hey, it was free.

Back in Beantown, when Matty got the call to pitch again, the Red Sox would hold a 2-1 series advantage. After three days of rest, the Christian Gentleman looked sharp at Fenway, retiring the last seventeen Sox in a row. The bad news was that Hugh Bedient (20-9 during the season) hurled a three hitter, and Larry Doyle's third-inning error was the difference in a 2-1 Boston triumph. Painfully, the Giants were on the brink of elimination.

To further the frustration, Big Six admitted that his arm felt dead.

"The muscles were so sore," he told reporters, "that it seemed as if a knife were shooting through me every time I threw a ball."[5]

Although the daily journeys between New York and Boston were grinding, the constant singing had become an irritant. But like their Sox, the Royal Rooters could not be silenced . . . or could they?

After Rube Marquard pitched the Giants to a 5-2 win at the Polo Grounds, as players boarded the train for the trip north, word came that Theodore Roosevelt had been shot in the chest, his condition unknown.

In Milwaukee, a man named John Schrank, shouting something about a "third term," had fired a gun from close range as the former president was leaving his hotel to give a campaign speech. Fortunately, the bullet was slowed by Roosevelt's jacket, his glasses case, and the thick folded papers of a prepared campaign speech—which he insisted to aides that he was going to present.

"I will make this speech or die," said Roosevelt, who was running under the progressive Bull Moose Party against Republican incumbent William Howard Taft and Democrat Woodrow Wilson; the November election was but a few weeks away.

A large Wisconsin audience sat stunned with anxious concern as a very pale Roosevelt, a trace of blood still on his coat, took the stage.

"It is true," he began in a subdued voice. "I am going to ask you to be very quiet and please excuse me from making a long speech. I'll do the best I can, but there is a bullet in my body."[6]

Roosevelt would finish the speech and be taken to the hospital, where it was determined the bullet had entered his right lung but the wound was not serious. The next morning, he asked about the series, finding the Giants had won.

"Outstanding," said Roosevelt, the former police commissioner and governor loving all things about New York City.

But the Giants were still in trouble, down 3-2 in the series, the Red Sox one win away from the crown. It was then that an already intense and somewhat wacky series would turn totally bizarre.

Game seven at Fenway, the Royal Rooters—now about 1,000 strong—paraded into the stadium as if they were the army of occupation, the newly freed Bostonians in the stands answering with deafening appreciation. As always, the band (mostly trumpets) led the march around the infield and headed out to the usual assigned seats in the left-field stands (Fenway's famous Green Monster did not yet exist). When the parade arrived at the bleacher entrance, it suddenly bottle-necked within a mass of confused shock—the seats reserved for the Royal Rooters were filled with spectators. Naturally, the not-entirely-polite Rooters ordered the intruders to move, but the people refused, producing tickets they had legally purchased. It got loud and ugly, the game unable to begin due to the uproar on the outfield grass—1,000 Rooters with nowhere to go. Making matters worse was the sudden appearance of six mounted policemen and their horses tromping across the playing field to restore order. It had all the makings for a full-scale riot . . . with a marching band to boot. A question arose for the mounted police: Do you actually arrest a crowd of ticketless "vagrants" whose leader just happens to be your own mayor? As time ticked away and worry began to emerge that the fidgety umpires gathered back at home plate just might forfeit this entire affair to the Giants, a deal between the Rooters and management was finally struck. The entire group of ticketless Rooters would be allowed to enter the bleachers and stand wherever they could find space . . . separated, unable and unwilling to sing, too angry to cheer, seething for blood.

Turns out the team secretary, Robert McRoy, sold the Rooters' tickets out from under them with the explanation that he wasn't sure if the team's number-one fans—who went to every game—were planning to attend this one, the seventh game of the World Series.

This, of course, provided the perfect backdrop for Mayor Fitzgerald to make a public statement.

"Secretary McRoy—who is from Chicago—should be retired from all connection with the Boston Baseball Club and a Boston man who understands conditions here given the place," bellowed Honey Fitz. "Boston money supports the club and there is certainly enough baseball brains in Boston to furnish a secretary."[7]

As politicians have an uncanny gift for knowing when other people are lying, it was quickly processed that McRoy knew that the game was sold out but long lines of Bostonians were still waiting in the street. Although he knew that the pile of bleacher tickets were reserved for the Royal Rooters, he figured by selling them the team would make a handsome profit and the Rooters would willingly stand somewhere else. It was a game-changing miscalculation.

Oh, there was also a baseball game. The Giants took full advantage of bedlam in the bleachers and scored six runs in the top of the first inning, producing an 11-4 thrashing and pushing the series to a deciding eighth game.

On October 16, with the teams remaining in Boston due to the Red Sox winning the dreaded coin flip, McGraw called upon Matty to bring home a championship. Where Fenway was packed beyond a fire marshal's warrant the previous day, it now seemed nearly empty. Still furious with their team's front office, the Royal Rooters had issued a call for all true Red Sox fans to boycott game eight and had set up a boisterous picket line outside the stadium. The attendance barely reached 17,000—half the crowd from the previous day. They would miss one of the truly great games in World Series history.

"I don't think Matty ever was much better than that autumn afternoon," said Boston's Tris Speaker.[8]

With New York leading 1-0 in the sixth, Doyle hit a deep drive toward the right center-field bleachers. Laughing Larry had already started his home run trot when outfielder Harry Hooper hit the short wall at full speed, falling backward into the crowd and popping back up with the baseball he had caught bare-handed. Umpire Cy Rigler, running from his position at first base, signaled an out.

"I was jinxed," bellowed Doyle as McGraw stormed from the dugout to confront the umpire.

"There's no way you can tell for sure that he caught that ball," screamed Muggsy. "For all you know, he picked it up off the ground after he fell into the stands. For all you know, a fan gave him the ball."[9]

Even Hooper could not believe that he had somehow made the unbelievable bare-handed snag. Afterward, he mentioned a prayer card he had found blowing over the outfield grass just before the game. He picked it up, read the thoughtful words, and put it in his pocket. Nuf Ced.

One other Giants' near-clincher was a long triple into the outfield corner by Buck Herzog. Because the earlier games of the series had people crowded into every edge of the stadium, it was decided that balls skipping into the corners would be automatically ruled as ground-rule doubles. That was fine for those games, but today's stadium was only half full. No matter, umpire Klem ordered Herzog to hold at second. Had he been on third, he would have scored on the next play. Instead, the inning ended with Herzog—who would have twelve hits for the series—still on base. New York would have several other great chances, but the Red Sox simply would not fold—or Hooper's prayer card proved to be a blessing for the entire team.

Finally, with the score knotted in the top of the tenth, Red Murray scored on Fred Merkle's single to give the Giants a 2-1 lead.

With Boston batting in the bottom of the tenth, Big Six was commanding, and Fenway Park was near quiet with the certainty that their
side was about to fall. And, when leadoff batter Clyde Engle hit a
routine fly ball to center, Fred "Snow" Snodgrass calmly waited as the
crowd moaned with a monotone disappointment. Stop . . . time to
backtrack to earlier innings and games at Fenway as Snodgrass became
the nonstop target of abusive chants and vulgar threats from the center-
field patrons. In the fifth game of the series, fans became so boisterous
that they accidentally pushed over the fencing, many tumbling onto the
field. The point is that there was a history as Snodgrass settled under
the high fly, happy to be one out closer to the title . . . except he
dropped the ball. It fell right out of his glove, with that universal moan
from the crowd changing to delirium before the ball could even hit the
ground.

"Well, I dropped the thing," said Snodgrass. [10]

No outs, the tying run on second.

What is lost in most history books is that Harry Hooper lined Matty's
next pitch to deep right center for what looked to be certain extra bases.
However, on a desperate sprint, Snodgrass made an extraordinary,
once-in-a-decade catch for the first out. After Steve Yerkes walked, it
seemed as if the Giants might be out of the woods as Tris Speaker hit a
high pop foul between home and first, directly in front of the Red Sox
dugout. Fred Merkle had the beat, but Matty called for his catcher to
make the grab. Merkle stopped, Chief Meyers dove, the ball skipped off
his glove.

Afterward, the Giants would blame the Red Sox bench, which was
hooting for everyone to take the ball.

"I think that confused Fred," said Meyers. "They just coached him
off it. Well, that's all right. It's all part of the game." [11]

As were Speaker's harsh words for Matty. "Well, you just called the
wrong man," he yelled. "It's gonna cost you this ball game." [12]

Speaker was absolutely correct, as he jumped on the next pitch for a
sharp single, sending Engle home with the tying run and Yerkes to
third. After an intentional walk, Larry Gardner followed with a long
sacrifice fly to right, and Engle easily scored for the 3-2 victory as
bedlam buried Fenway.

The Boston Red Sox were the world champs.

Matty stood stunned on the mound, then slowly walked to the dugout, his eyes staring at the ground. The euphoria of victory did not blind the Boston fans of their sympathy for the losing pitcher, with T. H. Murnane writing in the *Boston Globe*, "Mathewson, the baseball genius, was heartbroken and tears rolled down his sunburned cheeks as he was consoled by his fellow players. The greatest pitcher of all time had lost, after pitching a remarkable game. It was no fault of his."[13]

Out in California, at the foot of the Los Angeles Times scoreboard, Addie Snodgrass collapsed when she learned her son had made the critical error. Later, in an ambulance rushing to the hospital, after she regained consciousness, her first words would be, "My poor boy."[14]

In New York, Specs Toporcer was devastated.

"I broke down and found it almost impossible to announce the tragic events to the hushed crowd," he said. "After it was all over, I sat on the platform silently reading and re-reading the doleful news on the tape, as though repeated reading would erase the awful words."[15]

McGraw hugged Matty.

"I have never seen a gamer pitcher than you, son," said the manager. "You're the greatest boxman that the world's ever seen . . . it's a bad day for the Giants, but a wondrous one for you."[16]

When Big Six finally left the locker room, he was surrounded by well-wishing Red Sox fans, intent on letting him know once again how wonderfully he had pitched, how deeply he was admired.

Meanwhile, Jeff Tesreau and Josh Devore tried to comfort Snodgrass. "Boys, I lost the championship for you," said Snodgrass.[17]

"He was the most dejected looking person I ever saw," said Tesreau.[18]

All of the Giants walked lightly around their fallen outfielder. The *New York Times* would not be so kind.

"Write in the pages of world's series history the name of Snodgrass," the lead paragraph opened. "Write it large and black. Not as a hero; truly not. Put him rather with Merkle, who was in such a hurry that he gave away a National League championship. Snodgrass was in such a hurry that he gave away a world championship."[19]

Matty dismissed the *New York Times* article, reminding fans that all great players make errors.

"The team did not nurse bitterness about it," said Matty. "We were all pulling for him."[20]

But, like Merkle, Snodgrass would be forever branded by the public. Even the error was given a name, the "$30,000 muff," the difference between team shares awarded to the winning Red Sox and losing Giants.

"On the street, in my store, at my home . . . it's all the same," Snodgrass would say thirty years later. "They might choke up before they ask me and then hesitate, but they always ask."[21]

Fred Snodgrass died on April 5, 1974, more than six decades after that fateful error in Boston. On its obituary page, the *New York Times* took one more swipe with the headline, "Fred Snodgrass, 86, Dead, Ball Player Muffed 1912 Fly."[22]

Well, the whole team had suffered. Sportswriter Fred Lieb would recall that he had never witnessed "such dejection as that of the New York contingent."[23]

McGraw, described as strangely calm after the game, was still questioning Hooper's miracle catch back in the sixth. "But for that catch," Little Napoleon analyzed, "I am certain the Giants would have won."[24]

The Red Sox agreed. "It saved the game for us," beamed Wood, credited with three victories during the series. "It really took the heart out of the Giants."[25]

It was the first time that a World Series had been decided on the final pitch, after which the Royal Rooters headed for their favorite watering hole to celebrate—they were back in the fold and already had big plans for the next season.

The sting for the losing side would take at least that long to heal. Ring Lardner could not help but sympathize with The Christian Gentleman:

> Just as Steve Yerkes had crossed the plate with the run that gave the Boston's Red Sox the world's championship in the tenth inning of the deciding game of the greatest series ever played for the big title, while thousands, made temporarily crazy by a triumph entirely unexpected, yelled, screamed, stamped their feet, smashed hats and hugged one another, there was seen one of the saddest sights in the history of a sport that is a strange and wonderful mixture of joy and gloom. It was the spectacle of a man, old as baseball players are reckoned, walking from the middle of the field to the New York players' bench with bowed head and drooping shoulders, with tears streaming from his eyes, a man on whom his team's fortune had been

staked and lost, and a man who would have proved his clear title to the trust reposed in him if his mates had stood by him in the supreme test. The man was Christy Mathewson.[26]

Chief Meyers, the hard knock catcher with the sensitive soul, refused to blame any of his teammates, preferring that everyone go down together. Besides, his concern was deeper.

"I wouldn't have minded it half so much if it had been any pitcher but Matty," said Meyers. "I will regret to my dying day that this grand fellow was forced to suffer for our sins."[27]

* * *

Teddy Roosevelt would recover quickly, splashing back into the hearts of many Americans to earn one million more votes than the one-term William Taft, but two million less than the new president Woodrow Wilson.

It was probably fortunate for all three that Christy—who had the votes—was not a politician. Even as the years began to pile, the Christian Gentleman never lost control in anything. Speaking to 550 boys at the New York Juvenile Asylum, Big Six asked them to consider clean living and moral character.

"I might lecture you boys about control being the big thing in life," said Christy, "but just now I'll talk about pitching, and in that, also, control is everything."[28]

He'd been practicing his art since childhood, and it wasn't easy.

"Speed and curves meant little unless I could put them where I wanted them to go," said Christy, adding that he had to learn how to concentrate as well as throw.[29]

"But they ain't nobody in the world," wrote Ring Lardner, "can stick a ball as near as where they want to stick it as he can."[30]

As a student of the game, he took no shortcuts.

"He knew exactly what you couldn't hit, and that was all you had to hit at," said Johnny Evers of the Cubs, "for he could throw a ball into a tin cup at pitching range."[31]

Chief Meyers claimed that he could catch Big Six while sitting in a rocking chair.

"He had almost perfect control," said Meyers, who caught Matty for seven seasons. "Really, almost perfect."[32]

That would be tested when the Giants played an exhibition game against Army at West Point. Scheduled to pitch the next day in Boston against the Braves, Matty stood on the infield signing autographs and talking with a dozen cadets, one suggesting a bet that Big Six could not throw twenty straight strikes without Chief Meyers moving his glove. The cadets even offered 12-1 odds, Matty pulling a $20 bill from his wallet. Meyers never even twitched, the ball popping his glove twenty straight times. Matty collected $240 from the stunned cadets and divided the loot with his partner in crime.

Along with healthy living and careful training, there were secrets to Matty's success. "First control, second knowledge, and third ability," he said. "And through it all is the great factor of luck."[33] The cerebral pitcher played his game to precision.

"Here was a man with pinpoint control," wrote Arthur Daley, "a man who had all hitters' likes and dislikes so well catalogued that he was always pitching to weakness, never to strength."[34]

Max Carey, the Pirates great center fielder and former divinity student, was also a huge fan: "I've watched Mathewson closely and I've never seen him pitch a ballgame in which he didn't look as if he were having a lot of fun. It doesn't look to be work to him, but only pure sport, an afternoon romp."[35]

In an era when a good starting pitcher might throw 400 innings a season and seldom be relieved, Matty learned how to pace his strength. Perhaps never in the game before or since has there been a pitcher who could give up so many hits in the early and middle innings to eventual runners who would never score. If the Giants had a hefty lead, he purposely cruised. In the late innings, he took no prisoners.

He was not so much interested in strikeouts," observed Connie Mack, "as he was in placing the ball where it would be hit into his fielder's hands for an out. He did not waste his strength; he conserved it for the moments when the game was in danger, then he put on overwhelming speed."[36]

A rapid worker, Matty once threw a fourteen-hit shutout, allowing singles to the first two batters of each inning until the eighth inning. He retired the final six hitters in order.

"He seldom wasted energy early in a game," said McGraw. "In a pinch, when a hit meant a run or the game, he was as close to invincible as any pitcher could get."[37]

But, at times, McGraw could run out of patience. After an early six-run advantage, Matty's lead had been whittled to 6-5 by the ninth inning.

"Bear down, you big baboon," McGraw yelled from the dugout.

"Take it easy, Mac, it's more fun this way," replied Matty, who then struck out the final three batters.[38]

In a pinch, Matty often went to his against-the-grain fade-away, a pitch he had perfected through study and practice. Somewhat like the modern-day screwball, what Matty originally called his "freak pitch" broke inside to right-handed hitters and away from lefties, all the while taking a sudden drop as it reached the plate.

"After he got that ball perfected," said McGraw, "it was laughable to see the way some of the batters almost broke their necks going after it."[39]

※ ※ ※

Despite losing two straight World Series, the Giants were the hottest ticket in town. True, due to long work weeks for little pay, most New Yorkers were denied an afternoon at the Polo Grounds. But the hard knocks of life didn't keep them from loving their team, with Grantland Rice noting that "the swagger and grittiness of the Giants gave them their largest following amongst working-class New Yorkers."[40]

Rice had only been at the *New York Evening Mail* for two baseball seasons, but the Vanderbilt grad knew he was in the midst of something special, covering a team with an "attitude . . . brazen, boisterous, fun-loving, arrogant, cocksure and glamorous. They were winner, and they were stars."[41]

Putting a further stamp on that swagger was that the Giants were also idolized by the glamorous gathering in the box seats. Prior to the games, one of McGraw's favorite rituals was to hobnob with the slew of actors, comedians, and New York elite. There was Will Rogers, W. C. Fields, Lillian Russell, Mabel Hite, Eddie Foy, May Tully, George Dillingham, and DeWolf Hopper (who performed "Casey at the Bat"). Mayor William Jay Gaynor had season tickets, as did George M. Cohan and former heavyweight boxing champion Gentleman Jim Corbett. Even the world-famous Irish tenor John McCormack was a regular.

Although it would have been easy to be swallowed by fame, the Mathewsons had no interest in chumming with the celebrities of Broadway, leaving the nightlife to John and Blanche.

"In all of Manhattan," wrote a gossip columnist, "Matty is the hardest celebrity to find. That's because he's always home."[42]

Although Christy and Jane didn't entertain society's Upper Ten, they did welcome some interesting guests.

Christy cherished his teammates, and they him. Jack Meyers enjoyed many home-cooked meals at the Mathewson home, often playing bridge with Christy, Jane, and Freddie Merkle. Meyers once called "Bonehead" Merkle the smartest person on the team, no offense to Matty. That probably explains why Matty and Bonehead were bridge partners when the team was traveling.

Laughing Larry Doyle had been Matty's road roommate. At the same time, Jane and Larry's wife, Gertrude, became good friends. Jane hung out with many of the wives. But, like her best friend, Blanche McGraw, many of the women seemed to have Broadway in their blood. Turkey Mike Donlin and Rube Marquard (a later road roommate with Matty) were both married to actresses, Mabel Hite and Blossom Seeley, respectively. Art Fletcher's wife was a high-society heiress, Irene Dieu.

Meanwhile, Christy had not strayed far from his old friends at Bucknell. President John Howard Harris and his wife, Mary, always enjoyed a couple of summer visits to New York, as did football coach Doc Hoskins. Along with wives and children, fraternity brothers stopping for extended visits included Ernest Sterling and Reese Harris.

Lewis and Mary Theiss did not have far to travel. After graduating in 1902, Lewis Edwin Theiss joined the editorial staff of the *New York Sun*. At Bucknell, he had played on the varsity basketball team with Matty, but had made his athletic mark as captain of the Bison track and field squad, holding the school pole vault record for 12 years. While Matty was the class president in 1900–1901, Lewis was voted to that post the following year.

Mary Bartol Theiss and Jane had been friends since childhood, both eventually attending the Female Institute at Bucknell. Mary was now a freelance writer and women's suffragist, a movement Jane called "wonderfully good."

Other than a love for playing cards, there were plenty of interests and ties between the Theiss and Mathewson families. While the women chatted about the old days in Lewisburg and raising their young children, the men talked horticulture. Christy was fascinated with the subject, and Lewis was now the garden editor of two magazines, *Good Housekeeping* and *People's Home Journal*. He would eventually become head of the Bucknell journalism department, and by then he was one of the nation's leading authors of books for young men.

Lewis Theiss realized Matty's watershed contribution to baseball. "It was because of his genuine sportsmanship, his integrity, his cleanness of life, his high ideals, that baseball was made over and raised to a cleaner, higher, level," wrote Theiss. "In all history, there is perhaps no more striking case of the force of a good example."[43]

Another friend, Andy Wyant, put it more succinctly. "He believed in God," said Wyant. "He gave God the central place in his life."[44]

There was a comforting grace about the Mathewson home, most days tranquil and unassuming. Then the relatives arrived from Lewisburg and Factoryville, or old college chums, business associates, or ballplayers and their families. There was always plenty of room.

Yes, even Ty Cobb—whom Bozeman Bulger once said "was possessed by the furies"—visited Matty; hopefully on his best behavior. Matty and Ty were both vice presidents of the newly formed Baseball Players Fraternity, an early attempt to organize for better working conditions. Cobb never hid his admiration for the Christian Gentleman.

"You couldn't help but love Matty," said the Georgia Peach.[45]

14

PEBBLES ON A BARREN SHORE (1913)

John McGraw worshiped springtime in Marlin. Nothing like the scorching Texas sun to get the boys concentrating on baseball. Hard work with no distractions; the man could smell another pennant. Except in 1913, Little Napoleon was irked that his beloved spring training had turned into a circus, with newspaper and magazine writers flooding his ballfield to huddle around an untested rookie.

What did Muggsy expect? He had just signed the greatest athlete in the world . . . Jim Thorpe.

"I realize that he will be a big novelty," McGraw said.[1]

McGraw's self-inflicted wound must have stung; trying to balance the publicity he always cherished with his demand of total focus from his team was not going to be easy.

Born of the Sac and Fox nation, Thorpe had won two gold medals at the 1912 Summer Olympics. At Carlisle College, Thorpe had starred in track and field, baseball, football, basketball, and lacrosse. He had even won the intercollegiate ballroom dancing championship. His junior year in college, he had four field goals and scored a touchdown in the big upset of Harvard. Returning from Sweden for his senior season, Thorpe led Carlisle to a 12-1-1 record. In a highly hyped meeting against Army, led by future president Dwight D. Eisenhower, Carlisle pulled out a stunning 27-6 victory with Thorpe galloping for a ninety-seven-yard touchdown.

Thorpe, Matty, Moose McCormick, Chief Meyers, Freddie Merkle . . . the Giants could have put together a pretty rugged football team.

But McGraw had signed Thorpe for his athletic prowess and potential with a secondary awareness that he would be a ticket-selling jackpot.

"I expect to turn him into a good player," said the veteran manager.[2]

Plus, Jim Thorpe was lightning quick, immediately crowned the fastest man in baseball with the possible exception of the Phillies' Hans Lobert.

But Lobert could hit the curve and Thorpe had never seen major league pitching.

Matty predicted Thorpe would become a .300 hitter within a year, but that proved to be a stretch. Thorpe would only hit .143 his rookie season, playing in just nineteen games. Thorpe would describe the Giants as the "wildest, fighting, and blood thirsty bunch he'd ever known."[3]

Wait a second, this was from a man who also played professional football for the Canton Bulldogs.

* * *

Pick any game at the Polo Grounds and long before the first pitch, the crowd would have already reached peak hysteria, a thunderous welcome for their New York Giants, entering from the center-field clubhouse, spread out and walking slow as if they owned the entire diamond. In the heart of the entrance would be none other than the privately reserved Christopher Mathewson, now a mature and charismatic showman.

"I can still see Christy Mathewson making his lordly entrance," recalled Three Finger Brown many years later. "He'd always wait until about ten minutes before game time, then he'd come from the clubhouse across the field in a long linen duster that auto drivers wore in those days, and at every step the crowd would yell louder and louder."[4]

After the 1912 World Series loss to the Red Sox, Giants' fans had given Big Six a forty-horsepower Columbia Touring automobile that cost $5,000. His grand pregame entrances were simply a way to thank his devoted admirers.

Giants' 1912 pitching staff (left to right): Rube Marquard, Jeff Tesreau, Christy Mathewson, Red Ames, Hooks Wiltse, and Doc Crandall. Courtesy of the National Baseball Hall of Fame

Big Six was "king, emperor and ruler of all baseball," the press acknowledged.[5]

Matty, who had loved automobiles since their inception, definitely enjoyed driving that big, magnificent Columbia. Although he was usually quite conscious of the many kids gleefully running beside his car, he had a heart for the open road and was once fined $100 for driving thirty-one miles per hour in a ten miles per hour zone. McGraw would not ride with Matty—he believed it was too dangerous.

Jane—described by *Literary Digest* as "intelligent and quite beautiful"—was one of the first female motorists in New York City. Most of the women who could afford to own a car were wealthy enough to hire a chauffeur. And they didn't necessarily want to deal with the cumbersome hand cranks to start the engine, "starter's arm" becoming a major medical concern.

That didn't bother Jane, who drove as much for sport as convenience. Unfortunately she also would get stopped for speeding, driving eleven miles per hour.

Truthfully, the Mathewsons didn't need a car for navigating New York and beyond, their apartment overlooked the Polo Grounds. Except for the days the team was on the road, Christy worked in the afternoon and was home by evening. With their top floor apartment located at 155th Avenue and St. Nicholas Place, Jane could see the stadium scoreboard from the kitchen window, usually starting dinner in the seventh inning.

Jane was too busy with Sonny to attend all the games, but she did attend the games where her husband was the starter. She was not alone, fans calling the Mathewson home to ask when Christy would be pitching.

The center of the Mathewson household was their child; Christy amused that the first thing he would always see before entering their top floor apartment was Sonny's nose pressed against the windowpane, excitedly waiting for his dad.

Christy, himself, was still a big kid.

"He would come home grinning," Jane recalled of her husband, "like a boy who had committed some impish deed, and say, 'Well, I took those Reds again today.'"[6]

All things considered, they were simply a normal family.

As Sonny began to see the world beyond Washington Heights, he loved the many trips to see the relatives in Factoryville and Lewisburg, always a magnificent taste of his parents' small town, country upbringing. Still, Sonny and his puppy, Polo Grounds, had their own land of wonder, with a full run of Coogan's Bluff. Growing quickly, the boy was smart, curious, and did exceptionally well in school, where he had a ton of friends. On Sundays, he attended church with one or both parents, depending on the baseball schedule.

Always a welcome guest in the Giants' clubhouse, Sonny would be greeted by a parade of amazing ballplayers, instant playmates ever on their best behavior. Unfortunately, the first time that the youngster visited the dugout, he accidentally dropped a bat on his dad's toe.

Big for his age and quite athletic, Sonny played hours of catch with a father who never pushed, just encouraged. He also had his own set of miniature golf clubs, and the family often played at the Pelham and Van Courtlandt courses.

Even though "America's Proudest Boy" soon realized that his father was the most idolized man in the nation, Sonny was never consumed with fame; his upbringing was simply too grounded.

"Christy Junior is a fine, manly chap, and wholly unspoiled," said the *Scranton Republican* in 1913, adding that he would like to someday be a baseball pitcher.[7]

Actually, young Christy was already entranced with the skies, his secret ambition to someday be a pilot.

✿ ✿ ✿

Matty was consistent in 1913, going 25-11 while winning the earned run average title for the fifth time. At one point, he hurled 68 consecutive innings without allowing a base on balls, completing the season with

Christopher Jr. gets a few inside tips from his dad. Courtesy of the National Base-ball Hall of Fame

only 21 walks in 306 innings, an extraordinary 0.62 free passes per game.

Winning 101 games and a third straight pennant, New York had the best starting three in baseball—Matty, Rube Marquard (23-10), and Jeff Tesreau (22-13). Doyle, Meyers, Merkle, Snodgrass, and popular outfielder George Burns led the still-swift offensive attack. Burns popped thirty-seven doubles, but the real power in the National League came from Philadelphia's big slugger Gavvy Cravath, with an eye-popping 19 home runs and 128 runs batted in. Born and raised in the Southern California town of Escondido, Cactus Gavvy would win the National League home run crown six times, including twenty-four homers in 1915, a major league record that would last four seasons, until a kid named Babe Ruth became the new sheriff in town.

Over in the American circuit, Detroit's Cobb (.390) and Cleveland's Shoeless Joe Jackson (.373) were the best hitters in the game. However, the Athletics had regained the top spot, thanks in great part to their pitching trio of Chief Bender, Eddie Plank, and Bullet Joe Bush.

Philadelphia looked to win its third World Series in four years; the Giants hoped to win their first in three, provided they could weather untimely injuries to Meyers, Snodgrass, and Merkle. They couldn't. The Athletics won in five games, the lone New York victory a 3-0 shutout by Matty, who only allowed two runs in nineteen innings.

Mathewson was still the "king, emperor, and ruler of all baseball pitchers," according to the *New York Tribune*.[8]

Unknown at the time, this would be his last World Series, what started back in 1905 as the greatest pitching feat of all time would end with a string of powerful performances blanketed by defeat. Although Matty's overall record in those four fall classics was 5-5, he posted a remarkable 1.13 earned run average and allowed less than one walk per game.

After the finale, the *New York Herald*, as it now had for three postseasons, saluted the Christian Gentleman: "Once more the old master stood out like the Rock of Gibraltar, but his teammates were like a lot of pebbles on a barren shore."[9]

After the 1913 series, Matty caused a bit of a stir when he wrote "Why We Lost Three World's Championships" for *Everybody's* magazine.[10]

According to Christy, because John McGraw "absolutely directs the game," most of his players "cannot stand on their own feet because they have never had to."[11] Matty further charged that the "Giants are the greatest newspaper ballclub I know. Most of the men read everything that is printed about them."[12]

Put these facts together and the team developed, for three straight Octobers, a bad case of World Series nerves.

"The Giants did not obey orders," wrote Christy. "They either forgot or else convinced themselves that they knew more than the wonderful little manager who had guided them so long. Not only did they fail to execute McGraw's commands properly, but they became so upset that they made bullheaded plays that you would never have seen during the regular league campaign."[13]

Amazingly, Christy Mathewson was somehow able to be critical without causing waves.

"I sincerely hope no one will accuse me of poor sportsmanship," Matty concluded. "I have not squealed, only analyzed the situation from things that I know."[14]

15

THE WORLD'S LONGEST BASEBALL
ADVENTURE (1913–1914)

Barely six days after dropping the 1913 World Series to the Athletics, Matty and most of the Giants left New York City for the World Baseball Tour. Starting in Cincinnati, the Giants and White Sox began a thunderous 30,000-mile adventure through twenty-seven American cities and thirteen foreign countries, with the intent to bring the game of baseball to the rest of the world.

"We do not expect to make any money on the trip," John McGraw proclaimed to reporters gathered for the big sendoff at Grand Central Station. "Our trip is solely to exhibit the national game in foreign lands. It's a treat for the boys."[1]

Oh, there would be money. The ever humorous Ring Lardner suggested that the real purpose of the venture was "to prove to the foreign element that baseball is better than cricket, roulette, hopscotch . . . or any of the other sports in vogue abroad."[2]

The plan had been hatched the year before while McGraw was in Chicago entertaining a sixteen-week vaudeville contract. Basically, the Giants manager told baseball tales and answered questions for a lucrative $3,000 per week. For a time, McGraw was not only the highest paid baseball manager, but he also ranked number one in vaudeville as well.

In December 1912, Little Napoleon met with Charles A. Comiskey, a one-time first baseman turned owner of the White Sox. Talk about an odd couple—"The Old Roman" was six feet tall and three times wider than Little Napoleon. Although McGraw was rich, Comiskey had amassed a fortune. But that wasn't the biggest difference. Muggsy was fiery, but had a soft heart for his players, always sure they were properly paid. On the other hand, "Commy"—as he was called—was an intensely self-absorbed miser who looked upon his players as serfs and paid them accordingly. The White Sox were one of the strongest teams in the American League, but its players' salaries ranked dead last in both leagues. At a time when meal money for the most financially strapped teams was $4 per day, the White Sox paid its players $3. Commy also charged them for any broken bats or torn uniforms. He was the biggest tightwad in baseball, a trait that would help seed the infamous Black Sox scandal still six years in the future.

Comiskey may have been nasty to his employees, but when it came to his own wants, he was extravagant. A hound for self-publicity, he treated reporters like royalty. But, best of all, he was willing to provide a lot of the necessary capital for the World Tour—what he correctly viewed as a smart investment. Upfront, Comiskey and McGraw would tout the goodwill aspect of the global trek, but behind the curtain they were financially covered by contracts at every stop. But to the fans feasting on the newspaper coverage, predicted profit margins took a back seat to the excitement of this grand spectacle.

By any standard—particularly in the realities of 1913—the trip itinerary was mind-boggling. Around the world in three months, the adventure would first head west through the United States, then jump to Japan, China, the Philippines, Australia, India, Egypt, Austria, Belgium, France, Germany, Ireland, England, and Scotland.

Both teams had talent. After finishing in the middle of the American League pack, the White Sox played a postseason City Series against the crosstown Cubs, winning in seven games. The Sox were led by Buck Weaver, the twenty-three-year-old shortstop who had already earned superstar billing. Ray Schalk was not only one of the finest catchers in the game, but his straight-arrow character was worthy for the "Book of Matty." Hal Chase, the ultratalented first baseman, would never be lauded for character. Already suspected of throwing baseball games for unscrupulous gamblers, "the man with the corkscrew brain" would eventually be exposed to the ruin of what might have been a Hall of Fame career. For Chase, the worst was yet to come.

Comiskey also recruited some big-time stars for the tour, including Wahoo Sam Crawford (Detroit Tigers), Tris Speaker (Boston Red Sox), and Germany Schaefer (Washington Senators). All three were outstanding ballplayers, with Schaefer adding the element of humor.

"What stunts he could pull," said Davy Jones, who had teamed with Schaefer on the Cubs and Tigers. "I used to laugh at that guy till I cried. Far and away the funniest man I ever saw. He could beat Charlie Chaplin any day of the week."[3]

Back to the tour, the Giants brought Matty, Laughing Larry Doyle, Turkey Mike Donlin, Jack "Chief" Meyers, Jim Thorpe, Freddie Merkle, Hooks Wiltse, Fred Snodgrass, and Jeff Tesreau. Among McGraw's recruits were Mickey Doolan and Hans Lobert of the Phillies and Ivy Wingo and Lee Magee of the Cardinals. Magee, whose birth name was Leopold Hoernschemeyer, would take thousands of photographs during the journey.

The Giants and White Sox met in Cincinnati—the birthplace of professional baseball forty-four years earlier. Despite a gracious city ceremony to welcome the tourists, no one expected a particularly large crowd at Redland Field. Hadn't they already suffered enough with their seventh-place Reds bungling through a long and arduous season? Still, a crowd of 2,500 baseball addicts turned out, most looking to see some American Leaguers for the first time. They were hardly impressed with Speaker, Weaver, and company as Matty and the Giants prevailed 11-2 in what the *Chicago Inter-Ocean* headlined as a "punk" game; the *Cincinnati Enquirer* griped that it was "worse than terrible."[4]

At least the new outfits looked cool. The Giants were adorned in white uniforms with blue pinstripes and a blue cap, both carrying a patriotic U.S. Olympic emblem with thirteen stripes and thirteen stars. Should the weather on the trip turn cold—and it would—they had beautifully knitted navy blue warm-up sweaters. The White Sox were just as sharp in their dark blue uniforms with white socks that carried a blue stripe. They had an American flag embroidered on each sleeve and blue caps with white stripes. Their double-breasted warm-up jackets also included the flag on each sleeve.

After being hosted by local dignitaries for a lavish dinner party, the two teams and their entourage boarded the midnight train, the Cincinnati depot packed with baseball fans looking for a hero-worshiping party, a pattern that would be repeated in city upon town during the great journey west and beyond.

Little Napoleon and Big Six. Courtesy of the National Baseball Hall of Fame

By the way, this was not just any train the Giants and White Sox were boarding. It was chartered, specially designed for comfort and lavishly decorated for the correctly predicted ballyhoo. The tour was a big deal, particularly to a baseball-hungry nation that was reading the coverage of the trip in just about every newspaper and magazine. Boxing, football, and horse racing were major sports in 1913, but none could match the "National Pastime." And now there were rumblings that a third major league was about to hatch. Backed by big money, the proposed Federal League was expected to finalize its plans in early November. This, as most players realized, could mean a nice bump in pay.

But for now, the world was waiting.

Bound for Chicago, the special train had separate sleeping cars for the Giants and White Sox. There were dining cars and, naturally, Comiskey had his own lavish coach. There were accommodations for umpires, reporters, and fans. The train even had a Pullman that was exclusively designed for a group of players and their new wives. Thorpe, Crawford, Doyle, Chase, Lorbert, Tesreau, and Reb Russell were among the newlyweds. Turns out that Iva Thorpe received about as much publicity as her husband. She was beautiful, charming, and a wonderful dancer. Remember, Jim Thorpe won the national collegiate ballroom dancing championship two years earlier at Carlisle. Across the world, the Thorpes were big news and a solid hit.

This unique gathering of baseball players and their new wives made for great journalism, and the train was soon being dubbed "The Honeymoon Express."

There was baseball to be played. Chicago, the second and final city on the travel agenda that actually had major league baseball, was buzzing about the matchup—two great teams from opposing leagues. But mostly, this was Chicago versus New York, the two largest cities in the nation at that time. A huge crowd of brave fans battling bitter cold would witness a thrilling game won by the Giants with a ninth-inning rally.

Following the game would be another big dinner, another gathering of crazy fans at the depot (including some who tried to stowaway on the train), and a departure just before midnight, down the Rock Island Line to Springfield, Illinois. Players were already worn out but were still basking in a fresh excitement that would soon dissolve.

Hey, it was glorious, it was fun . . . it was just beginning.

On October 20, 1913, still in Illinois for the third stop of their baseball extravaganza, the players awoke to snow in Springfield. The citizens grimaced when the parade was canceled, heard rumors that the game was canceled, and prayed the sun would miraculously melt the snow. That didn't happen, but when 500 fans showed up anyway, McGraw and White Sox manager Jimmy Callahan decided to begin the game despite the falling snow. Most of the players wore their heavy sweaters. Thorpe and Doolan homered, the Giants won again, and everyone scrambled to the St. Nicholas Hotel for warmth, followed by another banquet to honor the heroes, especially Larry Doyle and his new bride, Gertrude. Back in 1907, Laughing Larry had played sixty-six games for Springfield's minor league club before his contract was purchased by the Giants for what would be a short-standing record of $4,500 (the following year, New York paid $11,000 for Rube Marquard). A native of Illinois, Doyle had been born and raised in Caseyville, and even worked five years as a coal miner before jumping to baseball in 1906. Now, the Giants' captain and the 1912 National League's most valuable player was considered one of the finest hitters in the game.

The fourth day was even worse, with the cold and wind in Peoria becoming a full-scale blizzard by the second inning. With the driving snow blocking their vision of the game, some of the rooters broke up the wooden stands and started small fires for warmth. They could have used a bonfire in the pitcher's box, with Hooks Wiltse and Walter Leverenz battling hitters and frostbite. Somehow, both pitched the entire game, with two triples by Wahoo Sam Crawford giving the White Sox their first victory.

But in the midst of bleakness there appeared Ottumwa, Iowa. It was still a bit brisk, but no snow and even a return of sunshine. Best of all, the town was crazy with enthusiastic fans, having traveled long distances to see the greats that they, prior to that day, had only been able to read about. There were chants for the Christian Gentleman, but few had seen him and, really, Matty was seldom thrilled to be at the center of a mob, no matter how friendly. In his stead, Germany Schaefer, ever the comic showman, would stand next to the train and entertain the gigantic crowds, even doing a special routine in which he impersonated the Great Mathewson. Schaefer could pull it off on personality alone, giving the fans a thrill and the players watching from inside the Pullman a good laugh.

Twenty-five towns in Iowa had made bids to host a game, with McGraw and Comiskey settling on Ottumwa and Sioux City. Both proved to be worthy selections. More than 3,500 fans packed the Ottumwa stadium, with an even bigger crowd the next day in Sioux City as autumn finally sparkled. It was so pleasantly warm that Matty and Turkey Mike Donlin unloaded their golf clubs, taking in a well-deserved eighteen holes.

Next stop, Blue Rapids, Kansas—the smallest town on the trip with the biggest breakout of baseball fever. Schools, stores, government offices . . . well, everything within traveling distance, took the day off for the event.

"It was the biggest day the town of Blue Rapids ever had," noted Gus Axelson of the *Chicago Daily Tribune*. "The country folk swarmed into the town early in the morning. They came in automobiles, top buggies, milk wagons, and lumber wagons. It is estimated that 500 automobiles were in town."[5]

Twenty-five of those automobiles carried the touring ballplayers around town in the splendor of an Independence Day parade. It was warm, it was wonderful . . . it was insane. Even Christy joined the funfest, agreeing to a challenge of firing a fastball from the pitcher's box to home plate with the intent of hitting a six-foot-high, quarter-inch-thick length of lumber. With his calling card of near perfect control, Big Six not only nailed the wood with his fastball, he broke it cleanly into two equal pieces.

Blue Rapids had 1,800 residents in 1913; the attendance that day hit 4,000.

"They crowded the little ballpark," reported Axelson, "hung on the fences like fringe, and peeked through all the knotholes."[6]

The players beamed about their stop in Kansas, and "The Honeymoon Express" headed for three games in Missouri—St. Joseph, Kansas City, and Joplin. The third game was already circled by every rooter in the country. Walter Johnson had signed a one-game contract to pitch for the White Sox. His opponent, imagine the surprise, would be Christy Mathewson. It would be the pitching matchup of the century, two men of strong Christian character, who, by the way, were the greatest in each of their leagues. Let the analysis and hot stove arguments begin.

In late 1913, Matty had won 337 games in fourteen seasons, not counting those five victories in the World Series. He had won twenty or more games eleven straight times, and his control kept getting better.

During the 1913 season, he only issued one base on balls for every two games he pitched . . . and never hit a single batter.

Seven years younger than Christy, Walter Johnson had two nicknames—Big Train and Barney. He also had back-to-back seasons as the American League's premier hurler, winning the 1913 Chalmers Award (most valuable player) with a 36-7 record, 1.14 earned run average, twenty-nine complete games, and eleven shutouts while leading the Washington Senators to a second-place finish behind the Athletics. The year before, Big Train was 33-12.

"I am for this game," Johnson told the *Joplin Daily Globe*. "Nothing ever pleased me more. I'm a great admirer of Mathewson, for he is a wonder in the box."[7]

Unfortunately, Joplin got laced with snow. The game itself was played, but the challenge between pitching greats was postponed until the next day in Tulsa. It would be cold, but no snow. Big Train would

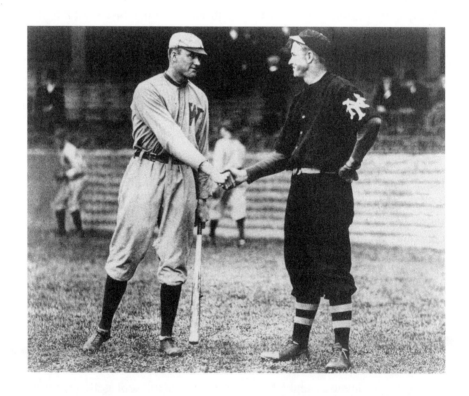

Alike in pitching greatness and Christian character, Walter Johnson and Matty would become close friends. Courtesy of the National Baseball Hall of Fame

face Big Six, and the packed stadium included the presence of numerous Native Americans excited to see Jim Thorpe and Jack "Chief" Meyers. But the main story unfolded half an hour before the game was
scheduled to start, when the wooden right-field bleachers, in need of
repair and under the weight of far too many people, suddenly collapsed.
Hundreds were injured, many rushed to the hospital. There was one
death, a soldier who had been walking in the back of the stands when
they collapsed. After a conference, the governor of Oklahoma asked for
the game to be played. Matty would allow but two runs, but would leave
after four innings due to fatigue. Johnson would be fresh and powerful,
pitching a complete game shutout. There was the usual evening feast
that had been meticulously planned by state and local dignitaries, but
no one could ignore the tension of the tragedy. After a stop in Musko-
gee, the teams would play seven games across Texas. By the time they
left Dallas, the series was tied 7-7, and everyone's early-trip adrenaline
had vanished.

Matty, for one, was tired. Yes, he was used to the rigors of barnstorming, but he was thirty-three years old and had pitched 325 innings
(including the World Series) before what was now a grueling journey.
He was looking forward to Sunday, November 2, in Houston. That
promise he made to his mother also applied to postseason contests.
Instead of attending the game, Matty went duck hunting. To him, it
may have seemed innocent. However, when the newspapers ran the
reason for his absence, the backlash was humbling. He may have been
America's favorite son, but he was a bad boy in Houston. The local
papers turned belligerent against the nation's idol. They wondered how
Mathewson, knowing his obligation to the fans, decided not to even
show up for an important event in which he could have at least signed
autographs for the now disheartened young boys who had saved their
allowances for weeks in anticipation of seeing him. No, Big Six would
rather hunt ducks.

The good news for Matty was that, by the time the Houston papers
hit the streets, the tour had already reached wonderful and quiet Marlin, where he was generally considered to be incapable of misguided
actions. It was as if they had returned home, the good guys winning 11-
1.

By the time the tour exited El Paso, the teams had each won ten
times and player excitement was revitalized. After two games in Arizo-

na, they would be playing baseball on the west coast. Matty was still tired from pitching, but happy that Jane and seven-year-old Sonny had now joined him for the tour. Plus, the family loved California.

On November 8, in the beautiful city of Los Angeles, Matty would once again take the ball; but his arm was gone, his performance weak. The huge crowd may have been disappointed, but many simply reassured themselves that their Pacific Coast League played the greatest baseball in America. The league was definitely powerful, many exceptional ballplayers turning down offers from the two major leagues, preferring the pleasant western environment to the perceived eastern grind. So, a crowd of 6,000 Angelinos were happy to witness a sloppy game at Washington Park. And if they wanted to hoot at mediocre baseball, they enjoyed the same treat the following day.

There was another huge crowd in San Diego, this time 4,400 strong, most of the Cahuilla Nation on hand to welcome home their favorite son, the great catcher John Tortes "Chief" Meyers. With a touch of magic, Meyers would clout a two-strike, game-winning homer in the bottom of the ninth. Although Meyers was the king of San Diego, Fred Snodgrass would be the returning hometown hero in Oxnard. What a day it would be, from an early morning ox roast to the seventh-inning "horse" race. Hans Lobert, who could run the diamond bases in less than fourteen seconds, was the only man in baseball faster than Thorpe. That morning, at the outdoor feast, the mayor of Oxnard challenged Lobert to a footrace against the area's best horse.

"I'm not here to run horses around the bases," Lobert told the mayor. "I'm here to play baseball."[8]

But the mayor, with McGraw at his side, persisted. Word that Lobert would run spread quickly, with more than 5,000 spectators cramming the field with several hundred cowboys on horses in the outfield. Man versus Horse . . . apparently there also was a lot of wagering involved.

"Nobody wanted to see the game," said Lobert, who was under contract to the Phillies. "They all wanted to see this race between the man and the horse."[9]

It would be high drama, filmed by a moving picture crew no less.

"From this mass of cowboys encircling the outfield, out steps the most beautiful black animal you ever saw," said Lobert, "with a Mexican cowboy on him all dressed up in chaps and spangles. Both he and horse were glittering like jewels in the sunlight."[10]

To add to the unfair advantage of having four legs, the cow pony was trained for sharp turns. The rules were simple—Lobert would touch the inside of each base, the horse would go outside the bag to avoid any unpleasant collisions. Umpire Bill Klem raised a starting pistol and they were off, Lobert leading by five feet at first base and stretching the advantage by the halfway mark.

"I was in perfect stride, hitting each bag with my right foot and going faster all the time," he said. "But instead of the horse keeping his distance, he crowded me between second and third and I had to dodge to avoid being knocked down."[11]

His stride interrupted, Lobert still had the lead rounding third, but was edged by a nose at home plate. By the way, despite his weary pitching tools, Matty hurled the Giants to a 3-2 victory, one of his best outings of the tour.

Ring Lardner, reporting for the *Chicago Daily Tribune*, explained that Matty's arm was only sore because on the trip he had "shaken hands about five million times."[12]

By the time the crew reached San Francisco, rumors were flying that some of the players, including Matty, would not be sailing overseas once the teams reached the end of the American leg in Seattle. McGraw claimed to have no idea what Matty would decide.

"He would like to make the trip," McGraw told the *San Francisco Chronicle*, "but he is a little bit afraid of the water. I am hoping at the last moment that he will decide to continue around the world with us."[13]

There would be three games in Frisco, one a masterpiece by the Christian Gentleman before an overflow crowd of 10,000 fans.

"Matty is all that he has been pictured," observed the *San Francisco Examiner*. "He is an artist. Deliberate, cool under fire, the guiding genius of the machine behind him, Matty pitched as he always does. It was a distinctive Mathewson victory."[14]

Tired, susceptible to seasickness, Christy decided it would be best for him and his family to spend the rest of the winter in Southern California. San Francisco would be his last stop. It would be a great disappointment to fans, but probably the best decision for his future. He needed the rest and yearned to play golf. Los Angeles had more than quadrupled in size since the turn of the century, now bursting with more than 400,000 residents. From the San Gabriel Mountains to the Pacific Ocean, the beautiful valley included endless miles of orange groves, mild winter weather, and pure air. It was a paradise where Matty could play golf and, hopefully, not be recognized. They rented a comfortable home at 1337 West 47th Street, Sonny enrolling in elementary school.

On January 8, 1914, a man from Chicago sent a postcard to New York. He addressed it to "6" . . . nothing more, just a large, four-inch-long numerical six, cut from a newspaper headline and pasted on the card. On the back he had written, "Matty, if you get this please let me know. G. Irwin." With a two-cent stamp, it headed to Gotham, where the postal clerk immediately realized the recipient was Big Six. With a blue pencil, he wrote in the corner of the card next to the stamp and below the giant "6" to "Try Los Angeles, Cal." The postcard was forwarded across the country, the clerk in Los Angeles handing it to a mail carrier who delivered it directly to Matty.

Meanwhile, the World Tour never slowed. By the time the Giants and White Sox boarded the R.M.S. *Empress of Japan* out of Victoria, British Columbia, they had played thirty-one games in thirty-three days before more than 100,000 fans. If they thought the weather had been bad in the United States, they were sadly heading into multiple storms, beginning with a typhoon in the Far East carrying sixty-foot waves. Oh, the seasickness. It also was a disaster in Italy and France, seven days of rain canceling every contest. On the final day of February, they would depart Liverpool, England, aboard on the S.S. *Lusitania* for New York City.

For the record, the White Sox would win the overall series 24-21 with one tie due to darkness. But who's keeping score? All told, the entire trip had been a wild and glorious adventure. No matter the elements and the seemingly never-ending pace, the playing had been generally good, sometimes brilliant, occasionally ugly, and always entertaining. Although nothing could top the Hans Lobert horse race in Oxnard, Lee Magee gave it a shot with a spectacular outfield catch in Medford, Oregon. It would not have been that big of a deal except that Magee made the play in a driving rainstorm, glove in one hand and an open umbrella in the other.

There were parades and keys to the city; celebrity banquets and morning ox roasts; snowstorms in Illinois and bone-wilting heat baths in Australia.

Once they landed on foreign soil, the athletes had realized that they were goodwill ambassadors for both baseball and the United States. They would meet the pope in Rome, play before the king of England, and tour Europe less than a year before the outbreak of the Great War. And by the time they sailed past the Statue of Liberty on March 7, it was time to get ready for spring training.

* * *

Entering 1914, Matty felt his first twinge of age discrimination, a few suddenly noisy skeptics wondering if the tank still had any gas. He was thirty-three years old, his arm had weathered more than 4,200 innings in fourteen major league seasons, and nobody pitches forever. Ring Lardner blazed to his good friend's defense: "Leave him get warmed up, then give him a good look. This spring was hard on old soupers. You can't expect a bird that's been hurlin' the pill in the big show all these years to set the league afire. Don't talk like he was gone and ask me what kind of a pitcher he *was*."[15]

"The strong arm which Mathewson possessed at the outset of his career lost much of its iron endurance long ago," said William Phelon in *Baseball* magazine. "And yet this man has surmounted every handicap with impressive ease and approaches middle age with his skill supreme."[16]

Matty would go 24-13 in 1914, completing twenty-nine of thirty-five starts, and walking only twenty-three batters in 312 innings. However, the Giants finished second to Boston; the "miracle Braves" having jumped from fifth place in 1913 after spending the previous four years in the National League cellar. The entire matter was a great disappointment for those New Yorkers seeking to right the ship after three straight postseason stumbles.

At least Matty was strong, public opinion blissfully thinking the gifted veteran could sail along for another twenty seasons. Well, he had won twenty or more for twelve straight years, including four with more than thirty victories. In fact, his lowest total over that span had been twenty-two wins in 1906, the year he had diphtheria.

Prior to spring training in Marlin, Christy received a cablegram from the president of the new Federal League asking if he would consider playing for their Brooklyn franchise. Christy had never made more than $10,000 a season playing for the Giants, but the Feds were offering a three-year $65,000 contract with $15,000 in advance.

"No player is worth that sum," surmised Christy. "Baseball cannot afford to pay so much money."[17]

Plenty of other baseball greats—including Chief Bender—may have disagreed as they shifted to the well-financed third major league. McGraw did not even need a heart-to-heart talk with his old friend; Christy quickly announcing that he would not leave the Giants.

There were then more than 100 million people in the United States, but three major leagues could not prosper. Attendance fell across the board, the Federal League surviving but two seasons.

Entering the 1915 season, Matty's control was flawless, his mind in total control . . . but his shoulder and back would suffer major problems. Almost overnight, it seemed, his body withered. His 3.58 earned run average was the worst since his three-game rookie struggle in 1900. His won-lost mark plunged to 8-14, the first time in a dozen years he had not been a twenty-game winner.

Big Six was "no real value to his club," wrote Frank Menke. "His arm seemed gone."[18]

Matty's "value" was reflected in the standings, with the Giants crashing to last place. Okay, it was an extremely balanced league, with New York but fourteen games behind the second-place Boston Braves, the Phillies taking the pennant.

Just in case Matty was thinking about retirement, Harvard asked if he would coach its college baseball team. Although he graciously declined, the door was left open. Matty figured that offseason rest would be the best therapy. Then again, relaxation was not always his best subject. Early in his career, he actually attempted to spend a lengthy vacation on an empty agenda.

"I loafed for one whole winter," he wrote in a 1914 article for *Baseball* magazine, "and it was the most unsatisfactory season I ever spent. I am determined never to spend another winter in that way so long as my health is good."[19]

So he joined an eighteen-city trap shooting tour with three other baseball players—Chief Bender, Otis Crandall, and Harry Davis. With each participant shooting 100 targets, the four players opposed a team of the area's top amateurs and "awakened a great enthusiasm for the sport."[20]

Naturally, the promoters decided to keep standings. Christy, a superb hunter but still injured, would finish third overall; his best performance was eighty-nine at Chicago. Four years younger than Matty, Bender would be crowned "King of the Traps" for the entire series, his best showing nailed 99 of 100 targets in Syracuse. The tour proved a good chance for Mathewson and Bender—always on the other side of the diamond from each other—to solidify a long friendship. Both were excellent golfers with an outdoor love for hunting, fishing, and hiking—not to mention intellectual discussions stretching from horticulture to philosophy—and, yes, the secrets of pitching.

Too bad umpire Bob Emslie wasn't included in the tour. Born in 1859 in Ontario, Canada, the even-tempered Emslie was an international superstar in the field of trap shooting. Once, having wearied of John McGraw calling him "Blind Bob," the ump proposed to "Muggsy" a $500 shooting wager that, from behind home plate, he could nail two apples atop second base. McGraw balked.

"Maybe you can see apples," said Little Napoleon, "but you can't see baseballs."[21]

For the record, Emslie would heave John McGraw from thirteen ballgames. Big deal, McGraw would hold the Major League record of 131 career ejections (including fourteen as a player) until it was finally broken in 2007 by Bobby Cox of the Atlanta Braves. Putting that into perspective, the volatile Leo "The Lip" Durocher and Earl Weaver are tied for third all time, each logging ninety-four expulsions. The closest to McGraw from the Deadball Era was Clark Griffith of the Washington Senators, whose career mark of sixty-one early showers was not even close to Little Napoleon's.

Emslie, who umpired from 1891 to 1924, had been an outstanding pitcher with the old Baltimore Orioles, his best season being 1884 when he finished 32-17 with a 2.75 earned run average. Unfortunately, he strained his arm from too many curves, having to retire in 1887. Although Matty considered Emslie "such a good fellow," players who made fun of his toupee or called him "Wig" would automatically be booted from the game.

Klem, who was six years younger than Christy, umpired in the majors from 1905 to 1941. His button could be pushed by any reference to his oversized lips. Naturally, disgruntled players who might dare to call him "Catfish" were always awarded with an early dismissal. There was no kidding that Klem was tough; he was the only umpire back in 1903 to survive the entire season in the Class B New York State League.

Little Napoleon, during a typical tirade against Klem, threatened to have the ump fired. "Mister Manager," Klem replied, "if it's possible for you to take my job away from me, I don't want it."[22]

Umpires. McGraw didn't like any of them; especially Hank O'Day, whom he never forgave for disallowing the winning run in the 1908 "Merkle" game.

A stern face on a rugged frame, O'Day was the only man in history to serve as a player, umpire, and manager. Born in Chicago, he was harsh and unsociable, a bad mood his calling card, particularly to those who addressed him as "Henry." The word around baseball was that his only friend was Emslie, the two sitting for hours in hotel lobbies without speaking.

Christy once witnessed O'Day trying to laugh. "His face acted as if it wasn't accustomed to the exercise and broke all in funny new wrinkles."[23]

Also a pitcher in his playing days, O'Day had a 73-110 career record, but got the taste for officiating when he started being used as a substitute umpire to avoid postponement should the assigned umpire be unable to work. He was a full-time umpire from 1895 to 1927, twice on sabbaticals to manage the Reds (1912) and Cubs (1914).

The encounters between O'Day and McGraw—both stubborn, bull-headed, and never wrong—were monumental. "O'Day had to be handled with shock absorbers," said Matty. "McGraw tries to do it, but shock absorbers do not fit him well, and the first thing that happens is usually a row."[24]

McGraw could explode over any detail that didn't fall his way. "O'Day cannot be reasoned with," said Big Six. "It is as dangerous to argue with him as it is to try to ascertain how much gasoline is in the tank of an automobile by sticking down the lighted end of a cigar."[25] It seemed that every club had a few players willing to light that match.

Just ask the high-strung Johnny Evers of the Cubs, who decided in 1915 to at least consider better behavior.

"I was fired out of so many games on my ear last summer by these human walruses in umpires's suits that I think my ears must have callouses on them," he said. "So far I have got along fine. I've been in two games already and haven't bawled anybody out yet."[26]

It would never last.

"Steam under pressure," said Evers, "exerts tremendous force and is liable to cause an explosion."[27]

Yet umpires are expected to remain calm during every storm.

"Look at O'Day," said American League umpire Silk O'Loughlin. "He's one of the best umpires, maybe the best today, but he's sour. Umpiring does something to you. The abuse you get from the players, the insults from the crowds, and the awful things they write about you in the newspapers take their toll."[28]

O'Loughlin, whom Christy defined as an "autocrat," was not about to break.

"There are no close plays," he once said. "A man is always out or safe, or it is a ball or a strike, and the umpire, if he is a good man and knows his business is always right. For instance, I am always right."[29]

Until the two-man crew was made mandatory in 1911, umpires often worked alone. The youngest—and largest—was Cy Rigler, standing six-feet tall with a claimed weight of 270 pounds. Umpiring from 1906 to 1935, Rigler seldom ejected anyone from a ballgame. Buck Herzog, however, stepped over the line one day in 1915 to shove, then purposely spike Rigler on the foot. Rather than toss the Cincinnati Reds manager, the umpire "decked Herzog with one punch."[30] Eventually, police would restore order.

16

SAY IT AIN'T SO, JOE (1916)

It was late August when the huge signs started popping up throughout Chicago, a picture of the two legendary rivals under the headline: "Brown versus Mathewson—Greatest Treat of the Year for Baseball Fans."

As part of a Labor Day double-header, the storied pitching matchup between Matty and Modecai "Three Finger" Brown would be revived for one final chapter.

The veteran rivals had met twenty-five times; Brown winning thirteen, Matty eleven, and one no-decision. Their most heralded encounter was the renowned 1908 playoff game, won by the Cubs over the Giants. Another classic was Matty's 1-0 no-hitter against Brown and the Cubs in 1905. Apparently motivated, Brown would roar to an eight-game, three-year winning streak over Big Six. But, entering their final encounter, Matty had won five of the past six meetings.

With 611 victories between them—plus another five apiece in the World Series—this would close two extraordinary careers. That both had lost their dominance hardly mattered to the sellout crowd at Chicago's spectacular Weeghman Park, which had been built in 1914 and would soon be renamed Wrigley Field.

There was one other striking difference to the final matchup—this would be the only time in his career that the Christian Gentleman would not be pitching for the New York Giants.

✦ ✦ ✦

Prior to the 1916 season, Matty had confided in McGraw that despite unceasing pain in the back of his left shoulder, his pitching arm felt strong. After missing the start of the season, Big Six tossed four complete games before shutting out the Braves on May 29. Yes, Matty had lost his zip, but he still had "the old gray matter of which he is possessed in such abundance."[1] Plus, the Giants had won seventeen straight games. Then the crash. The Giants streak would end the next day—they couldn't win forever. But the worst news was that Matty's back and shoulder were once again badly aching, his record sliding to 3-4 by mid-July, when he and McGraw sat down for a long chat.

Little Napoleon knew Big Six wanted to manage and understood his preference would be New York. But, at forty-three years old, McGraw was nowhere near retirement. With Matty's consent, he devised a deal with the Cincinnati Reds.

On July 20, the Giants and Reds pulled off a shocking trade. New York received Buck Herzog and Red Killefer; Cincy got Bill McKechnie, Edd Roush, and Christy Mathewson.

Big Six would be the player/manager of a terrible team with just a sprinkling of talent. Still, he was excited for the challenge. Owner August Hermann, known for his fairness, maintained Christy's $12,000 a year salary while also giving the rookie manager control of player acquisitions.

Looking back, the Reds clearly got the best of the deal with New York. Roush, a twenty-three-year-old centerfielder with great potential, had seen sporadic action with the Giants. In Cincinnati, he would become an instant superstar.

However, the monster story of that midsummer day was the unbelievable melancholy ripping through the heart of the baseball world. After seventeen seasons with the Giants, the greatest hurler in history was changing uniforms. To the fans, it seemed beyond belief, Damon Runyon observing that Matty on the Giants symbolized "the romance and the glamour and the glory of the game."[2]

To keep the club a contender, McGraw had parted with many fine players over the years. This time was different . . . and McGraw was hurting.

"It wasn't easy for me to part with Matty," said McGraw. "He not only was the greatest pitcher I ever saw, but he is my friend."[3]

"Of course, I realize I'm through as a pitcher," said Big Six. "But I appreciate McGraw making a place for me in baseball and getting me this managing job. He's doing me a favor, and I thanked him for it."[4]

In Matty's managerial debut against the Phillies at Cincinnati's Redland Field, young Roush sparked the Reds to a 6-4 victory, but the *Philadelphia Evening Ledger* led its game story by declaring Big Six had "written one of the cleanest and brightest annals of baseball."[5]

There was work to be done; one of the Christian Gentleman's first decisions was to hire a team trainer, his old Bucknell football coach George "Doc" Hoskins.

Matty would only hurl one game for the Reds, the Chicago Labor Day extravaganza in which both pitchers vowed to go the distance.

Four years younger than Christy, Mordecai Peter Centennial "Three Finger" Brown entered his final game with a 239-129 career mark, a phenomenal 2.06 earned run average, and a major league record of forty-nine career saves that would last until 1926.

"Brown is my idea of the almost perfect pitcher," Christy said during their prime. "He is always ready to work . . . a finished pitcher in all departments of the game. Besides being a great worker, he is a wonderful fielder and sure death on bunts."[6]

Born in Indiana, Mordecai was seven years old when he severed his right index finger in a corn shredder on his uncle's farm. Only his thumb was spared, as he lost parts of his two outside fingers with his middle finger mauled. In 1901, while working in the Indiana mines and playing semipro ball, he was signed by Terre Haute of the Three-I League. Over the next two seasons, "Miner" Brown would go 50-22, landing with the St. Louis Cardinals before being traded to the Cubs in 1904.

Noted for his great control, Brown conquered his hand deformity with a savage spin to his pitches—a fastball that would suddenly drop, a curve that resembled Matty's fade-away, equivalent to a modern-day screwball. Brown almost fell out of baseball due to a knee injury suffered in 1911, but landed with the Reds before jumping to the Federal League, leading Joe Tinker's Chicago Whales to a championship before the third circuit crashed after two seasons. Back with the Cubs in 1916 and nearing his fortieth birthday, Chicago's beloved Three Finger was ready to call it quits with the last showdown against Big Six.

The game was wild, Three Finger yielding nineteen hits and Matty fifteen. At least Big Six enhanced his batting average, getting three hits, including a double. What hurt the most, however, was that Laughing Larry Doyle now played second base for the Cubs, blistering his old roommate for a double and two singles. When it finally ended, Cincinnati was on top, 10-8, Christy registering his final career victory, number 373. Of course, 372 of those had occurred for the Giants.

The Christian Gentleman would make a graceful transition.

"How I love the game, the fighting, the glamour and the good will of the public," he said. "I don't know how I shall get along without them."[7]

The Reds were 25-43 under Matty's watch, finishing in a last-place tie with the Cardinals, the pennant won by the Brooklyn Robins, the franchise that had already been the Bridegrooms, Superbas, and Trolley Dodgers. Would they ever decide on a name?

Meanwhile, the unsteady Giants put together two long winning streaks and still finished fourth, McGraw vowing to rebuild.

But there was optimism in Cincinnati. Hal Chase had won the National League batting crown and Roush was easily the best young ballplayer in the game. Matty felt he could develop a young pitching staff to complement the talents of veteran Fred Toney. Manager Mathewson also welcomed Jim Thorpe on a loan from the Giants. Thorpe had an insignificant .195 batting average after three seasons in New York, but Matty still believed in his potential.

Under Matty's watch, Thorpe would be solid, Roush would hit .341, and the 1917 Reds would hurtle to fourth place while drawing a franchise-record 270,000 fans.

Christy was turning a club that had been "dying of dry rot" into a contender, establishing "harmony where chaos prevailed."[8]

The Christian Gentleman was now being acclaimed as a near perfect leader.

"Once in a while in the old days, Matty was panned by the pinheads because he refused to fraternize with the bums and preferred checkers and the YMCA to the red lights and the roysterers," declared *Sporting Life*. "There isn't a rookie or a vet on the whole Red outfit who wouldn't go to the limit and sprain a leg for him."[9]

But the 1917 season was far from perfect.

On July 1, despite many prayers, Christy would lose his brother Henry. Only thirty-one years old, Henry had been ravaged by the final

Manager Mathewson of the Cincinnati Reds. Courtesy of the National Baseball Hall of Fame

stages of tuberculosis, his wife and four children left behind. Christy, Jane, and Sonny took the first train to Factoryville. The national obituaries would remember Henry as the failed brother who pitched three games in the majors, going 0-1 with the record fourteen walks in one game. To Christy, of course, the statistics were meaningless . . . he had lost his last brother.

There also was the situation with Sunday baseball, of which the Christian Gentleman had mixed emotions. Although he never played on the Sabbath, it didn't matter in the five National League eastern cities ruled by blue laws. Only the three western cities—Chicago, Cincinnati, and St. Louis—could host games on Sunday, their clubs often scheduling double-headers against the Giants to keep Matty from pitching.

Not that baseball was totally clean in the east. In 1909, the New York Highlanders had played an "illegal" Sunday exhibition game against the minor league team in Jersey City. To keep the police from busting the party, the Jersey City ticket sellers distributed cards requesting the crowd not cheer or make any unnecessary noise. The Highlanders prevailed in what might have been the quietest game ever played.

Yes, Christy had made a promise to his mother, but over the years he realized that many New Yorkers had to work six days a week.

"New York has a much wider horizon than Factoryville," he said in 1914. "There is much to be said in favor of allowing the laboring man his only opportunity to see a baseball game on Sunday."[10]

Now that he was in Cincinnati, the Christian Gentleman had a big decision. Branch Rickey of the American League St. Louis Browns would not even manage his team on Sundays. Christy decided that he needed to be on duty for all games. In fact, on August 19, 1917, he and John McGraw violated New York City law by pitting their teams in the first Sunday baseball game played at the Polo Grounds. For that, they both were arrested, the judge quickly throwing out all charges, McGraw probably lucky that Matty was the other culprit.

Another major problem was Prince Hal Chase. When Matty became manager, the Reds ownership had passed on giving the position to Chase, who had long been suspected of shady dealings. It did not take Matty long to notice some odd play by his high-living first baseman. Matty watched, calculated, boiled.

Even more important was the backdrop of the Great War. On April 6, just five days before the start of the 1917 season, the United States declared war on Germany. Ever patriotic, Big Six immediately took a leading role in selling war bonds in Cincinnati and thinking deeply about the future. Actually, Matty had kept a close eye on developments for several years, particularly after the return of John Howard Harris from a frightening trip to Europe. In June 1914, the Bucknell president and his wife, Lucy, were sailing to Greece on an Austrian ship when Archduke Franz Ferdinand was assassinated. With a declaration of war, they were stuck for more than a month without transportation, eventually getting help from the American consul with a train to Holland, finally reaching London where they caught a ship to New York. Having visited the Mathewsons in New York before the departure, they had even more to talk about upon their return.

When the United States entered the war in 1917, Harris prepared for the Bucknell campus to follow many of the nation's colleges in being taken over by the War Department.

"I had served in the army in war time enough to know that everything must be subordinate to the military," said Harris, "and so whatever was asked was granted."[11]

With Americans focused on Europe and the home front, baseball would play a shortened, if not dramatic, season. Roush and Cincinnati were better in 1918, at times looking like a legitimate outside contender. Again, give credit to Big Six for the increasing predictions that the Reds had a superb future. The only complaint, occasionally raised, was that Matty was simply "too nice and easy-going" to be a great manager. For certain, he was no McGraw.

No matter how caring he was portrayed by the press, Matty had a line that nobody dare cross. Quite simply, cheating would not be tolerated. In early August, when pitcher Jimmy Ring entered a tight ballgame, Prince Hal Chase approached from his first-base position to whisper that he had money on the game and would share the spoils if the rookie made sure that the Reds lost.

Although Ring did his best to ignore the bribe and win the game, the Reds would fall. Afterward, a $50 bill appeared in Ring's locker. He reported the incident to his manager. It was not a surprise, just proof of what Matty had long suspected.

On August 9, Christy suspended Chase for "indifferent play" and forwarded his list of reasons to National League president John Heydler. It would take months for the league to hear all sides of the story and make a final decision.

Meanwhile, the surging Reds would finish in third place behind the Giants and the first-place Cubs, who would lose the Fall Classic to Babe

Ruth and the Red Sox. Cubs versus Red Sox . . . that had the makings of a once-in-a-lifetime encounter. The series would start in early September, with baseball closing its doors as players rushed to enlist.

Ruth would earn two victories for Boston, including a game one shutout. In all, only nineteen runs would be scored in the six-game series. The other two Boston victories would be earned by Carl Mays, a brilliant submarine pitcher with a headhunter for throwing high and tight, his moment of baseball history still two years down the road.

It was dark and overcast in New York City on August 16, 1920. They say that Cleveland's Ray Chapman never even saw the pitch, the ball striking him in the temple so hard that it rolled back to the pitcher— Carl Mays of the Yankees—who routinely tossed it to first-baseman Wally Pipp. It never touched the bat. Rushed to a New York hospital, Chapman died the next morning.

Seemingly unfazed and despite calls that he should be banned for life, Mays would go 26-11 in 1920 and a league best 27-9 the following year. There were boycotts every time he pitched, those who did attend showering him with hatred. It would last throughout a fifteen-year career in which Mays would win twenty or more games five times, chalk up a 207-126 record with twenty-nine shutouts . . . and have no chance for induction into the Hall of Fame.

Back to the World Series of 1918. Boston would claim its fifth crown in five appearances dating back to the first series in 1903. The franchise would not repeat for another eighty-six years.

It was even worse for Chicago. After taking their second World Series title in 1908—both at the expense of Detroit—the Cubs would lose their next seven trips to the Fall Classic, the last in 1945.

☼ ☼ ☼

Conducted in 1916, the nation's first accurate religious census identified 200 denominations with 41.9 million people attending 203,432 churches. There were 26.2 million Protestants, mostly Baptist and Methodist.[12] Catholicism, with its growth linked to immigration, was strongest in the big cities and northeast.

Continuing its swing toward the Social Gospel, Protestant churches were more and more involved with social issues. In order to save souls, religious institutions were realizing that they must first save society.

When twenty-seven Protestant churches created the Federal Council of the Churches of Christ in America in 1908, they included in its pact the abolition of child labor, the establishment of a living wage, safety rules in the workplace, and a day of rest once per week.

One thing the census did not include was the state of public opinion regarding the conflict in Europe. But prior to President Woodrow Wilson asking Congress for a declaration of war, most church-going Americans were isolationists. That would change in 1917 as patriotism scrambled to the spotlight. Liberal or conservative, Christians jumped to the cause without hesitation.

Even the fundamentalists who had vehemently argued against all involvement in culture and society were now raising the American flag. Nobody could accuse Billy Sunday—the eccentric, theatrical, king of evangelists—of not conducting a "God and country" revival. Claiming to be a fundamentalist who hated the Social Gospel, Sunday found detractors in every segment of Christianity. If the nation had thought Theodore Roosevelt spoke his mind, say hello to Billy Sunday.

"I don't know any more about theology than a jackrabbit knows about ping-pong," said Sunday, "but I'm on my way to glory."[13]

And he found plenty of followers, his revivals a huge hit in the nation's heartland.

Born in 1862, Sunday had once been a pretty fair baseball player in the 1880s, batting .248 during eight years in the majors with the Chicago White Stockings and Pittsburgh Alleghenys. Although extremely fast and coordinated, Sunday was an erratic fielder and hitter. After being drawn by gospel street singers and becoming a Christian, Sunday quit baseball to join a ministry where his job description called for him to visit the sick and dispossessed. An ordained Presbyterian, he soon established his own nondenominational ministry, first talking at churches and YMCAs, eventually barnstorming across the Midwest spreading revivalism with a good dose of vaudeville.

Yes, he was a conservative, but hardly a Calvinist. He was pro-business, but was strongly opposed to child labor. No one could say he didn't carry personal opinions regarding culture. He backed women's suffrage and hated all things alcohol. He was vehemently anti-immigration; warned against the evils of dancing, card playing, reading novels, or attending the theater. Baseball, on the other hand, was healthy and patriotic.

During his sermons, he would run across the stage waving the American flag, claiming that patriots would find heaven and traitors would end in hell.[14] Sunday was ready for war, leading a prayer at the U.S. House of Representatives by calling the Germans a "great pack of wolfish Huns whose fangs drip with blood and gore."[15]

When it came to fighting, the threads of Christianity weaved together in full agreement, with even the liberal Social Gospel modernists commending Billy Sunday.

"But the victory shall be ours," said former president Teddy Roosevelt, "and it shall be won as we have already won so many victories, by clean and honest fighting for the loftiest of causes. We fight in honorable fashion for the good of mankind. We stand at Armageddon, and we battle for the Lord."[16]

The churches, Boy Scouts, YMCA, and even the fictional Frank Merriwell believed that "Muscular Christianity" was the secret to victory as America mobilized with a passionate sendoff of 10,000 troops per day with a military now numbering four million.

Christy privately talked with Jane about joining the fight. She stressed his value on the home front. Although, at thirty-eight, he was too old to be drafted, Matty nevertheless felt a duty to enlist, particularly in light of the 254 other big league ballplayers going to war. Not all would return; Matty's former teammate "Harvard Eddie" Grant was the first ballplayer to be killed in action, the captain being hit by a shell in the Argonne Forest.

"Eddie Grant was a splendid fellow, a sportsman, and a first-class ballplayer," wrote W. A. Phelon for *Baseball* magazine. "May he rest in peace."[17]

In late August, Matty accepted a commission as captain in the Chemical Warfare Service of the U.S. Army.

"There is no worse crime than an aggressive war upon a peaceful country and no higher virtue than resistance," said President Harris from Bucknell, now home to 400 soldiers. "It is with reference to such defensive warfare that the Supreme Master gave His admonition, He that hath no sword, let him sell his coat and buy one."[18]

It would not be the war effort that Captain Mathewson intended to fight. In September, he became horribly seasick crossing the Atlantic. Barely recovered, he was hospitalized in Chaumont with influenza, an epidemic sweeping the world. When he finally joined the Gas and

Flame Division, he was reunited with his old baseball friends, Ty Cobb and Branch Rickey. Talk about a strange trio—two gentlemen and the Georgia Peach. The irascible Cobb, easily the most dangerous player in baseball, was a bully and a racist. Rickey, now president of the St. Louis Browns, would someday be known as the man who signed Jackie Robinson. If Matty read the Bible, Rickey quoted it.

Although Germany was close to surrender, Matty and Cobb were among eighty soldiers who marched into a chamber near Chaumont to practice the proper handling of their charcoal-filtered gas masks.

"Real mustard gas was to be released right after a signal was given warning us to snap masks into place and file out in an orderly way," said Cobb. "Then we were to dive into trenches as if under machine-gun fire. Well, the warning signal was poorly given and a lot of us missed it, including Christy and me."[19]

The two were lucky to get out of the chamber alive as twenty-four soldiers died and many others became sick, even crippled.

"Ty, I got a good dose of the stuff," Christy said. "I feel terrible."[20]

For the next few weeks, both would battle the same symptoms— weakness, cough, and a strange colorless discharge that drained from the chest. Cobb would recover.

"I saw Christy Mathewson doomed to die," Cobb would later say.

After the war ended in November 1918, Christy was assigned to Flanders, where he was exposed to another dose of mustard gas while examining ammunition dumps. His throat and upper lungs were wracked, the coughing spells immediately became unstoppable and severe.

Matty was in the hospital, battling the wicked cough and a second round of the flu, when August Hermann sent cablegrams asking him to again manage the Reds. Matty never received them and Hermann was forced to hire a new manager, Pat Moran.

Jane was deeply worried when Christy returned from Europe on the steamship *Rotterdam*. His skin was pale and pasty; his gait was slow, his body excessively fatigued . . . and he had a deep cough that would not subside. The doctors diagnosed it as chronic bronchitis, saying he just needed rest and warmth.

In the spring of 1919, John McGraw signed Christy to a $5,000 contract as the Giants' pitching coach.

Matty and Ty Cobb during the Great War. Courtesy of the National Baseball Hall of Fame

"It is my purpose to groom Matty for the job as manager," said McGraw, "and turn the team over to him in two or three years so that I can retire."

Matty had accumulated a managing mark of 164-176 with the Reds, but he had done a great job of building a contender. Joining the Giants at their Florida spring training site in Gainesville, Matty was reunited with Larry Doyle, Art Fletcher, Jim Thorpe, and Fred Toney. In New York, Jane could once again see Blanche on a daily basis and Christy Jr. was thrilled to be back at the Polo Grounds.

It all seemed a natural fit for Matty, except for two irritating problems. Playing first base for New York was none other than Prince Hal Chase. While Matty was overseas and unable to testify, Chase had been acquitted of trying to rig games despite rather substantial evidence. The matter was kept out of the newspapers, and baseball closed its eyes on scandal. Matty and Chase would not speak to each other for the entire season.

Frustrated that he had not recovered his strength, Big Six still constructed a solid pitching staff with great control, even coaching Jesse Barnes, previously a journeyman hurler, to a league-best 25-9 record. Nevertheless, the Giants finished second to the team Christy had rebuilt—the Cincinnati Reds.

※ ※ ※

That was the year of the infamous World Series between the Chicago White Sox and Cincinnati Reds. In a 140-game season, shortened for the second year due to the war, the Reds finished 96-44, nine games better than the second-place Giants. Led by Edd Roush and his National League–best .321 batting average, these were basically the same Reds that Matty had built into a contender. Still, they would be decided underdogs to the powerful White Sox.

Chicago (88-52) outdistanced Cleveland in the American League, but had the big guns in Shoeless Joe Jackson (.351), Eddie Collins, and Oscar "Happy" Felsch. They also had the pitching of Eddie Cicotte (29-7, 1.82 earned run average), leading the majors in victories and complete games.

The Reds would win the best-of-nine series in eight games, the effort by the White Sox boiling with suspicion. Working as a correspondent for the *New York Evening World*, Matty saw the fix unfold from the press box, comparing observations with sportswriter Hugh Fullerton of the *Chicago Herald*. They would send their notes to the National Baseball Commission. The following year, a small-time gambler named Billy Maharg spilled the beans of a grand plot involving eight veteran ballplayers and $100,000 in bribes (most never paid) to throw the World Series. The scandal rocked the nation. Leaving the courtroom, one of the eight—Shoeless Joe Jackson—walked past a young boy, tears in his eyes. "Say it ain't so, Joe," the boy sobbed. "Say it ain't so."

In 1920, Judge Kenesaw Mountain Landis was named the new commissioner of baseball. Although the undercurrent may have been that the White Sox players were angry for being so poorly paid by White Sox owner Charles Comiskey, Landis would not tolerate any reason for cheating. Eight Chicago players—Ed Cicotte, Shoeless Joe Jackson, Chick Gandil, Lefty Williams, Swede Risberg, Happy Felsch, Buck Weaver, and Fred McMullin—would be forever banned from the game.

"The game is bigger than the men who play it," said Matty, "and no small group can discredit it, even though they sell themselves out."[21]

Christy was back with the Giants in 1920, his nemesis Hal Chase having been released from the club after further evidence surfaced that he indeed was fixing games. No other Major League team would sign Prince Hal, even though he was still one of the finest fielders and hitters in the game.

As the season started, it became painfully obvious that Matty could not shake his health problems. He was frail and ashen, battled a constant low-grade fever, and his appetite had vanished. Returning to the doctor, he received a new and dreadful diagnosis. Matty had an advanced case of tuberculosis. He was given six months to live.

Matty left the Giants, traveling north with the family and dog to Saranac, New York, home of the Trudeau Sanitarium, one of the most notable tuberculosis treatment and research centers in the world.

17

THE SHADOW OF GREATER DAYS (1920)

Tuberculosis was horrid—the painful cough and uncontrollable chills, shallow breaths prodding raw cavities in the lungs, a body unable to work . . . so terribly tired.

Christy fought the disease with every fiber of his body and mind, with Jane at his side throughout. The worst, he told her, was the loss of control;[1] searching to remember the feeling of strength . . . to run the bases, to throw a fastball on the outside corner, to dropkick a football without pain . . . days that were now nothing more than a remote shadow.

* * *

In churches across the nation, preachers had long used Christy Mathewson as a talking point. Big Six exemplified character and sportsmanship; he believed in God and knew the Bible.

"Christy Mathewson is a modern masculine Christian," said the Rev. Christian F. Reisner of New York City's Grace Methodist Episcopal Church. "He belongs to the high type."[2]

It was trumpeted that Matty was steadfast in his faith, that "in his boyhood days he began to pattern his experiences upon the life of the Great Teacher of Galilee."[3]

The story of Christy's life was known in just about every household. What Americans soon learned was that he was extremely sick.

Christians prayed for his recovery.

❋ ❋ ❋

When Dr. Edward Livingston Trudeau founded his "wilderness cure" sanitarium at Saranac Lake in 1884, one in seven Americans were dying from tuberculosis. Starting with a cottage and several beds, Trudeau believed that the altitude of the Adirondack Mountains was restorative, that the "White Plague" could be fought with bed rest, healthy diet, and moderate exercise.

Even though tuberculosis was still killing more than 100,000 Americans each year, the number had steadily been declining to almost half the death rate of the early 1900s.

When the Mathewson family arrived in July 1920—five years after Dr. Trudeau's death—the center had expanded to 150 cottages with nearly 2,000 patients, a landscape of exquisitely manicured gardens fronting woods, lakes, streams, and mountains.

In a small and comfortable cottage at Saranac Lake, Jane dedicated her every moment to the rugged task of nursing her husband.

"There was so much to be done," she said, "that there was little time for brooding."[4]

Now fourteen years old, Christy Jr. assisted when not in school. It didn't help when he fell out of a tree and broke his arm, but that would pale beside his father's grave condition. After a dangerous and excruciating surgery, Matty remained bedridden, unable to even sit up. He quickly realized that his only weapon was a focused mind. Within the deepest despair, he would fight fear and pain with the Bible verses he had long known, reminding himself that this was but a temporary step to heaven. He would also think about baseball.

"When a fellow cannot read, or write, or talk, it requires some resourcefulness to keep his mind off his troubles," he said. "I started working out a baseball game, figuring every chance and studying how it should be played mechanically so as to offer the same chances as are offered on a ball field. It interested me and kept my mind engaged."[5]

Newspapers around the nation were reporting that he was near death—and this was true.

But in February 1921, he was starting to feel just a bit better, even able to sit up in bed for short segments. He had been bedridden for fifteen months, but now, with the help of Jane and their son, he began moving around the apartment in a wheelchair, then playing chess and checkers, looking out the window at Mount Pisgah, studying natural history.

Harry Hoffer, the one-time running champion who was also battling the disease, would bring Christy the daily newspapers from the railroad depot.

His reading appetite was stronger—Rudyard Kipling's *The Years Between*, William Roscoe Thayer's *Theodore Roosevelt*, and Irving Bacheller's *A Man for the Ages*. Christy Jr. even loaned his father *The Hidden Aerial* by Lewis Theiss.

When they couldn't visit, John and Blanche telephoned. Christy was still weak, but soon he was starting to take short walks and automobile rides, with Jane driving. He even conducted a few brief interviews with some of the reporters whom he considered more as friends.

"The doctors say he has a chance," wrote Bozeman Bulger. "That's why I know that he will win."[6]

For the public, Christy downplayed the affliction.

"Get out of your head that I am a real invalid or in any kind of bad shape," said Christy. "I don't know how the news of my illness got out. It sure spread. Somebody blabbed. I was surprised to find that some of the press reports have me at death's door."[7]

Christy blamed the tuberculosis on a bronchial cold that infected his throat and right lung.

"When McGraw found out about it he insisted upon my being shipped to the Adirondacks, so here I am. Take a peek at those hills; look at this beautiful lake."[8]

Of course, he knew how sick he had been, how he was far from cured. But he would fight, he would recover—just like *Pitching in a Pinch*, a regular Frank Merriwell—he'd somehow survive this scrape.

The stories caught the nation's passion, Christy hurling baseball analogies to define his battle for life: "You will never win if you quit . . . The game is never over until the last inning . . . Old T.B. won't get any decision over yours truly . . . You can't argue a call."[9]

Praising Matty's self-control as the "fight of a clean sportsman," *Outlook* magazine noted that "he appears to be winning a grim fight."[10]

In 1921, the Giants sponsored an old timer's "tribute game" for Big Six. The headliners included former teammates Larry Doyle, Moose

McCormick, Fred Merkle, Frank Bowerman, Iron Man McGinnity, Art Devlin, Hooks Wiltse, and Roger Bresnahan.

"We hold one dream of vanished years," wrote Grantland Rice, "when Matty's arm was young."[11]

Harry Stevens, the veteran Giants' peanut and scorecard vendor, co-chaired the event with Fred Lieb.

"Nothing we can do is too great for Matty," said Stevens. "I really love that guy."[12]

Lieb, a sportswriter who would live long enough to become a celebrated baseball historian, had to fend off colleague Heywood Broun, who suggested a great idea to boost attendance would be to hold a rattlesnake race between innings.

On behalf of McGraw, Lieb immediately squelched the idea, not wanting "to make a circus out of a tribute to a great athlete."[13]

Even with no snakes, more than $45,000 was raised for Matty's medical expenses.

"With such support," Christy telegraphed, "I cannot fail to win my game."[14]

And he did . . . or so it seemed.

In late summer, having just turned forty-one, Matty began a regimen of hiking in the Adirondacks, accompanied by Jane, their son, and Polo Grounds, their dog. Matty was definitely recovering.

In the spring of 1922, Matty threw out the first ball of the Saranac Lake baseball season. With the Adirondacks as his front yard, he focused on studying flowers, often comparing his findings with classmate Lewis Theiss, who was now the editor of publications for the National War Garden Commission. In a note from Lewisburg, Matty found out that he had been elected the first president of the Bucknell "B" Club.

Once a poor farming community, the beautiful town of Saranac now thrived with an economic base of health care and tourism. Christy spent hours in the lobby of the St. Regis Hotel, playing checkers against visitors from across the nation. Yes, he would often play blindfolded. He even defeated Newell Banks, the reigning world checkers champion.

In the fall of 1922, Christy was able to visit his parents in Factoryville, then attend his first World Series in three years, Babe Ruth and the Yankees against John McGraw's Giants. In the press box, Christy visited with his old sportswriter friends, including Grantland Rice and W. O. McGeehan calling the action on the radio. It was the first year the World Series would be broadcast, the new marvel of mass communications vaulting from a single AM outlet in 1921 to 556 stations within two years.

It also would prove to be John McGraw's third and final World Series championship.

That December, Christy spoke at the Christmas Tuberculosis Seals Benefit in New York City's Wannamaker Auditorium, shaking the pre-speech jitters with a calm demeanor once he got to talking to the sellout crowd.

"Not a bad place, Saranac," he said. "I lead the life of a country gentleman. Sometimes I ride in the morning and walk in the afternoon. Sometimes I walk in the morning and ride in the afternoon."[15]

At the same time, he did not downplay his battle against the dreaded disease.

"It's the hardest job I ever tackled in my life," he told the audience. "If I could just get out on that old diamond again."[16]

That winter, he again relapsed with an infection in his pleural cavity.

The world seemed to be moving quicker than it had in the old days. Half the nation now lived in cities, with fast cars and automobile trails providing a new and expansive freedom, the Lincoln Highway stretching from New York City to San Francisco. Sinclair Lewis wrote that George Babbitt's "motor car was poetry and tragedy, love and heroism. The office was his pirate ship, but the car his perilous excursion ashore."[17]

With the approaching spring of 1923, Christy was feeling strong enough to have a long talk with Jane about something she did not want to hear. Offered a part ownership with the Boston Braves, he was to be named team president. Jane, the doctors, anyone who understood the horrendous power of tuberculosis warned against the idea. But Christy was driven, which, as Jane said, was precisely the problem. Matty may have been an outstanding businessman, but he was still weak. He walked with a cane, could not see without glasses, and became easily fatigued. Jane knew he would give every ounce to his work. She knew the nature of the game, she knew the stress, and she knew that he would give too much.

He listened to her arguments, but he needed to be active, to have purpose and work. He signed the contract.

Matty at home in the Adirondacks. Courtesy of the National Baseball Hall of Fame

It was exciting to be on the ground floor of rebuilding a baseball franchise, the dead-last Braves having suffered 100 losses in 1922. In fact, Babe Ruth's thirty-five home runs that season for the Yankees was still three more than the entire Braves team.

Christy would represent the Braves at National League meetings and be involved in trades, acquisitions, and salaries. He could continue to live in Saranac and only travel as his health permitted.

On opening day of the 1923 season, the Braves visited the New York Giants. Christy's good friend Grantland Rice covered the game for the *New York Herald*: "A king walked out of the shadows of the past into the brilliant spring sunshine of the Polo Grounds yesterday as 30,000 loyal subjects paid him the tribute of a roaring acclaim that no crowned monarch could ever know."[18]

Matty's physical appearance had suffered from the past several years, but his composure was solid. In an article for *Good Housekeeping* called "Mathewson's Biggest Victory," Lucian Cary called him a "human thoroughbred," his pitching but a symbol for the beautiful control he maintained over his "own temper and own will."[19]

The Braves seemed in worse condition, their 54-100 record good for seventh in the standings and last in attendance.

In 1924, the construction of their brick home at 21 Old Military Road in Saranac Lake was completed. Beautiful and spacious, it had five bedrooms, three baths, and a living room that spelled instant comfort. Christy enjoyed reading by the fireplace or sitting on the porch in his "cure chair." The view and fresh air again brought tranquility, as did the baseball memorabilia and photos on the wall—college days, family, the 1905 Giants, John and Blanche McGraw.

Regarding baseball in Boston, Matty was beginning to realize that he should have listened to Jane. Once again he was extremely fatigued, handing the daily operations of the presidency to Emil Fuchs as the Braves tumbled back into the cellar, the club's third straight season with exactly 100 losses.

In the fall, Christy Jr., the salutatorian at Saranac Lake High School, enrolled as a freshman at Bucknell. With no plans to pursue baseball, he prepared to study electrical engineering.

John Howard Harris also remained on campus, but was now a professor of philosophy. Although he had retired as president in 1919, he was asked to give the commencement speech in June 1924. "Let there

**In September 1924, Matty and Jane visited Bucknell to enroll their son in college.
Courtesy of the National Baseball Hall of Fame**

be faith," he told the graduating seniors, "but let it be a living faith that issues in works." As if speaking to Matty, Dr. Harris added "let there be submission to Providence, but also increasing warfare against tuberculosis."[20]

The Christian Gentleman felt a resurgence of energy and that he could now push a bit harder. He attended the 1924 World Series, disheartened as the Giants fell in seven games to the Washington Senators, even if it was to his good friend Walter "Big Train" Johnson.

The following spring, Christy caught a common cold on the train bound for the Braves' spring training camp in St. Petersburg, Florida. It would not get better. Returning to Saranac Lake, he began to suffer blistering pain with each cough.

"Any man of ordinary makeup would have been gone by the end of the first six months," said his old friend from Bucknell, Andrew Wyant. "But Christy was more than ordinary. It was alone his strength of character, his unflinching courage and confidence that kept him alive as he passed down into the valley of the shadows."[21]

On April 4, 1925, John Howard Harris died of complications from influenza just shy of his seventy-eighth birthday. Praise flowed from around the world.

"He was warm and tender," said Crozer Theological Seminary president Milton Evans at the gravesite. "He called no one teacher except Jesus."[22]

Bucknell president Emory Hunt called his predecessor "a builder of character with marvelous self-control."[23]

Although the funeral took place in Scranton, Christy was too sick to attend. He prayed with Jane.

Down the road, W. O. McGeehan would write that The Christian Gentleman "in his prime had sinews of steel in his right arm, he had speed, he had everything, they said, but his greatest asset was his calm courage."

Christy spoke with Jane about his own funeral arrangements. He wanted the burial to take place in Lewisburg with "no fuss."[24]

For Matty, every breath became a reminder that death was now, without doubt, closing fast. Finally, he was unable to lift himself from bed, barely able to move at all.

In early October, Ty Cobb stopped in Saranac for a short visit.

"Big Six was a cripple," he said, "unable to move anything but his fingers and forearms."[25]

On October 7, Cobb was in Pittsburgh for the first game of the 1925 World Series between the Pirates and Washington Senators.

Back in Saranac, Christy called Jane to his side. He told her what train she should take to Lewisburg, that she needed a private drawing room.

"It's nearly over," he said. "Go out and have a good cry. Don't make it a long one. This is something we can't help."[26]

Jane held his hand.

"Are you sure you are all right?" he whispered to her . . . his last words.[27]

He died of tuberculosis pneumonia.

Game one in Pittsburgh was over, darkness had arrived, and the news spread fast. John McGraw was devastated, he called Blanche in New York and made quick plans to meet in Saranac to be with Jane, to do what they could. Big Train Johnson had pitched the Senators to victory that afternoon. When he heard about Christy, he turned "pale and silent, then openly wept."[28]

The nation was stunned. The next day in Pittsburgh, the flags at Forbes Field were lowered to half-mast, the players wore black armbands, a lone bugle played taps, the crowd of 43,000 baseball fans then sang "Nearer My God to Thee."

Every newspaper in America carried banner headlines with stories of deepest remembrance. "He was loved as no other American athlete has ever been loved" (*Oklahoma City Oklahoman*); "An even finer hero in the field of life" (*Boston Traveler*); "The squarest fellow you ever met" (*Chicago Tribune*); "There is sorrow felt beyond the realm of baseball" (*Harrisburg Patriot*); "More than a great athlete, he was a great soul" (*Minneapolis Herald*).

The *New York Herald-Tribune* printed an entire front page of photos and career highlights.

"It was not his prowess as an athlete that made him the idol of American manhood, young and old," wrote W. O. McGeehan. "It was the character of the man, the contempt for the chicanery that creeps into professional baseball and his frank and simple honesty."[29]

"How we loved to play for him," said Jack "Chief" Meyers. "We'd break our necks for the guy. If you made an error behind him or anything of that sort, he'd never get mad or sulk. He'd come over and pat you on the back. He had the sweetest, most gentle nature. Gentle in every way."[30]

❄ ❄ ❄

Early in World War I, on the bloody plains of France, a soldier wrote a poem about sacrifice, remembrance, and rebirth. Where thousands of young men had died, red poppies abundantly grew "In Flanders Fields."

Its seeds may be dormant for years, but when the earth is churned, the red poppy will grow once again.

❄ ❄ ❄

As Christy had planned, his remains would be brought to Jane's home in his old college town next to the Susquehanna River.

When the train left the Saranac station, hundreds stood silently on the platform. Even more gathered at each depot along the route to Lewisburg, where the Bucknell student body gathered at the edge of town to escort the body to the Stoughton home, a silent parade of grief.

The funeral service was held at the Stoughton home, filled with flowers from across the nation. Pastor Frank Everitt of the Presbyterian Church remarked that Christy looked like "a sun crowned man at peace," adding that he "did more than any one man to stabilize the moral standards of sport."[31]

The old coach, John McGraw, was visibly shaken, tears streaming from his weathered eyes.

"From an awkward kid, I watched him grow into the most finished artist in the world," said McGraw. "He had strength, intellect, and an uncanny memory. He gave our profession a dignity that it badly needed. He fully realized his early faults and worked constantly to over-come them. He did not want to be regarded as a hero. His was a natural dignity."[32]

It was a Saturday in Lewisburg. Standing with the kings of baseball and sport, townspeople lined the streets, flags silently draped at half-mast. All of the stores in town were closed and the Bucknell football game against George Washington was delayed until late afternoon so students could pay their respects.

At the Lewisburg Cemetery, their son stood by his mother's side, Christy's casket covered with white orchids and red roses. It had been a wonderful life, a long and unbearable struggle.

Ernest Sterling, the best man at Christy's wedding, was a pallbearer, as was McGraw and four dignitaries from the Braves, including Emil Fuchs. There were players, umpires, managers, reporters, classmates, students, and professors. There were relatives from Factoryville, friends from throughout the nation. Ty Cobb, who never attended funerals, hid within the crowd of black.

"Matty was a hero of mine," said Ty. "He was truly magnificent in every way."[33]

After the funeral, the first half of the Bucknell football game would be played without cheering, without noise.

"He never preached the code," proclaimed *Youth's Companion*, "he lived it."[34]

"Let none of us insult the memory of Christy Mathewson by making of him one of those sanctimonious and insufferably perfect heroes," said W. O. McGeehan. "He was a man's man. In all of sport, there never was such an influence for good, such an inspiration for young men. When they are asking who did most for baseball, they will have to say that the man was Christy Mathewson. Sport never will find his like again."[35]

Afterward, they covered Christy's gravesite with red poppies.

In Cooperstown, the plaque under the bust of The Christian Gentleman at the National Baseball Hall of Fame Museum reads, "Matty was Master of them All." The display includes his glove, checkers set, and Bible, open with personal annotations to Isaiah:

"He who trusts in the Lord will find new strength . . ."

The Christian Gentleman. Courtesy of the National Baseball Hall of Fame

18

THE FAMILY NAME (1929)

A small aircraft circled the Bucknell campus before descending upon the baseball field.

Practice disrupted, Coach John Plant's ball club watched in amazement as the Waco 10 made a perfect landing at the edge of the diamond. Exiting the plane, a tall and athletic-looking pilot wearing a long leather coat and flying helmet waved to the players and wished them a successful season.[1]

Christy Mathewson Jr. was born to be an air ace.

Forever compared to the legendary Big Six, the son carried many of his father's traits. They both were dynamic, confident, and held a competitive spirit that modestly embraced glory and courageously defied defeat. The story of their lives was always front-page news.

At Bucknell, Christy Jr. studied electrical engineering and was involved with student government and his father's old fraternity, Phi Gamma Delta. An exceptional musician and varsity tennis player, "Cricket" was described in the *L'Agenda* yearbook as "one of the most popular students on campus."[2]

"Everybody liked Christy," said classmate Anna Outwater Day, the last living member of the class of 1927. "All of the memories I have of him are that he was a wonderful person. He was fun, friendly, and mixed in with everybody. He never seemed to think of himself as important just because of his father. Like the girls say these days, he was hot."[3]

"He was drop-dead handsome," said Betty Cook of Lewisburg, a close friend with Jane in the later years. "Women were thrilled when he'd ask them to dance."[4]

Just over six feet tall with blue eyes and brown hair, Christy was quite athletic, although he shied away from baseball in favor of tennis, golf, and swimming.

But he did play one ballgame for the Bison varsity. In May 1926, he started in center field after being talked into the venture by manager Walter Blair, the former New York Highlanders catcher and longtime friend of the family.

"Wouldn't it be awful to have fans always pointing me out as my great dad's son," said Christy Jr. "It wouldn't be me, you see. Anyway, you don't know how awful a baseball player I am."[5]

He would retire after one game.

❊ ❊ ❊

The biggest story of 1927 occurred in May when Charles A. Lindbergh Jr., just twenty-five years old, flew the *Spirit of St. Louis* nonstop across the Atlantic Ocean, New York to Paris, in thirty-three hours and thirty-nine minutes. About the same time, Christy Jr. took his first flight, with good friend Eugene Keet piloting from Curtiss Field in Long Island. He was hooked.

Also in May, Christy Jr. graduated cum laude from Bucknell. Jane arrived from Saranac Lake, accompanied by John and Blanche McGraw. Although many of their relatives attended, Julia Stoughton was the only grandparent, Frank Stoughton having passed away several years earlier. When Christy died in 1925, his mother had not been able to shake her grief. Four months later, Minerva Mathewson died in Factoryville at the age of seventy. Gilbert Mathewson, nearing eighty and in the final year of his life, was too frail to travel.

Christy Jr. had a huge crowd of family and friends, including Lewis Theiss. One of his father's closest friends for all those years and the prolific writer of aviation books, Professor Theiss was now head of the Bucknell journalism department. Theiss presented young Christy with a copy of his latest book, *Piloting the US Air Mail; Flying for Uncle Sam.*

After graduation, Christy Jr. accepted a position as a researcher for General Electric in Schenectady, New York, and immediately took his first flying lesson.

While visiting the Philadelphia home of his best friend Arthur Phillips, he met Art's sister Margaret. She was a beautiful, nineteen-year-old student at Beaver College in Jenkintown. Peggy and Christy fell in love.

* * *

On June 5, 1928, the Christy Mathewson Memorial Gateway was dedicated at Bucknell. A gift from professional baseball to honor Big Six, the inscription across the top of the gateway reads, "Athlete—Soldier—Gentleman."

Dignitaries at the ceremony included a large group of players, owners, the presidents of both leagues, and the commissioner of baseball, Judge Kenesaw Mountain Landis. Jane and Christy Jr. also sat on stage as the commissioner made the presentation to the university.

"Matty had more than playing ability to carry him to the heights," said Landis. "It was his character, his integrity, and his heart which endeared him to every man and woman, boy and girl between the two oceans. He was the man who made baseball the truly national game it is today."[6]

There also had been talk of a rotunda to be built on campus, including the possibility of creating a future Baseball Hall of Fame.

After the ceremony had ended, Christy Jr. announced his plan to leave General Electric and forge a new career . . . flying airplanes. His first choice would be to join the Army Air Corps, but he also mentioned that mail pilots could earn nearly $1,000 a month.

It should not have been any surprise that his mother, her sisters, and seemingly everyone else on both sides of the family opposed the notion. The boy was undoubtedly caught up in the Charles Lindbergh craze, the barnstorming exploits of Eddie Rickenbacker, or perhaps he had just read too many books by Lewis Theiss.

But Christy's love of flying went much deeper, having grown up with a thirst for adventure, mechanics, and the skies. He also—unlike his father—was a very smooth talker, ever alert to unleash that sweet and wonderful smile into the conversation. Eventually he would win their understanding.

"His mother worshiped him," recalled Betty Cook many years later. "After his father died, all her love and interest went to her son. I think he was probably pretty spoiled."[7]

Nevertheless, he did not tell his mother about an early rush to the skies with Eugene Keets, the beginner pilots flying from Schenectady to Elmira.

"We had to fly through three snowstorms," Christy recalled, "following a railroad track, sometimes through ravines. And once the tracks went into a tunnel, and we had to pull a pretty stiff zoom to get over the hill."[8]

On their return trip to Schenectady, they ran into a fourth snowstorm.

"To add to that, our motor began missing. So we landed in the roughest air I've ever been in, and an automobile mechanic in a little town fixed up our engine."[9]

In July 1930, Christy completed advanced training at Kelly Field in San Antonio, Texas, graduating with honors to become a U.S. Army attack pilot.

"Here is for many tail spins and safe landings," Lieutenant Mathewson wrote to his cousin Al Stoughton, the Bucknell alumni secretary.[10]

"These were still the early years of aviation," said Cook, "so he was viewed by everyone as a real adventurer."[11]

Stationed at Mitchell Field in Long Island, Christy Jr. again had to shake the baseball questions.

"They have a baseball team here at the post and I suppose next spring they'll ask me to help out, but I'm afraid I won't be of much use to them," he said before pointing to an airplane. "There, I am able to do something on my own."[12]

He would definitely put a personal stamp on his next assignment. In light of the Japanese invasion of Manchuria and growing concern of war, the lieutenant was given a three-year tour to help build the Chinese air force. Assigned to Shanghai and later Hangchow, Christy and fifteen other American pilots taught young Chinese nationalists how to fly.

For Christy, life was good, particularly when his fiancée of four years agreed to travel to China for their marriage.

As a U.S. Army attack pilot in the early 1930s, Christy Jr. was stationed in China. Courtesy of Bucknell University

Margaret Phillips, accompanied by her future mother-in-law Jane Mathewson, left Philadelphia on Thanksgiving Day 1932 for a 9,000-mile journey by train and ship, the *Philadelphia Inquirer* reporting that she was "going to China, land of mystery, glamour, and adventure to the man she loved."[13] They arrived in Hangchow the day before an elegant Christmas Eve wedding. The story headlined society pages throughout the United States.

On January 8, 1933, after a two-week honeymoon in Shanghai, the couple prepared to return to Hangchow, Christy piloting a large Sikorsky amphibian plane.

Friends assembled on the shore of the Whangpoo River, saying that Peggy, twenty-three years old, was "thrilled with pride and excitement" as she sat next to Christy for her first plane ride.[14]

But thirty seconds into the flight, the huge plane suddenly dove nose downward into the water and crashed on a mudflat. Chinese river men, having witnessed the horrible crash from their small boats, rushed to the murky island. They tried to pull the Mathewsons from the wreckage. He was critical—awake, but unable to move—his body crushed.

"Never mind me," he pleaded. "Look after my wife."[15]

It was too late. Peggy would be pronounced dead within a few hours and newspapers across the world reported that he was near death . . . broken arms, shattered legs, internal injuries, head badly cut and bruised. He fought.

Deep in a coma, Christy continually called out "Margaret, Margaret." Doctors gave him less than a 5 percent chance to survive. When he did awaken, he was so fragile that doctors would not tell him that his wife had died.

Confined for six months in a Shanghai hospital, his left leg would be amputated two inches above the knee and doctors predicted he would never regain full use of his arms. Certainly, he would never again fly.

In late May 1933, Jimmy Doolittle visited Christy in the hospital to wish him well and talk about aviation. A major in the army reserves, Doolittle had been intensely involved in air racing, holding several world records.

"I have yet to hear anyone engaged in this work dying of old age," he said before retiring from air racing to a more secure vocation of testing aircraft. [16]

Christy was thrilled by the unexpected visit.

"The doctors promise me I will be out in another month," he said, "and then I want to get back to work." [17]

Doolittle asked the nurses to move Christy to the hospital veranda.

"I'll get my bearings outside," he said, "and I'll put on a show." [18]

Piloting a new U.S. army Curtiss Hawk pursuit plane, Doolittle performed a private stunting exhibition as Christy watched from a wheelchair.

A decade later, during World War II, Doolittle would be awarded the Medal of Honor by President Franklin D. Roosevelt. He would retire from the army as a general.

But, in 1933, who could predict what would soon unfold.

With his mother still at his side, Christy Jr. returned to Saranac Lake, learning to walk with an artificial leg. He hunted, fished, and climbed hills until he had regained his strength. His goal was to reenlist with the Army Air Corps.

"Looking at young Matty," wrote Grantland Rice, a family friend for nearly three decades, "I turned back to the older Matty I had seen face so many tight games in the past without a quiver. And his kid was in a worse spot." [19]

✻ ✻ ✻

On June 3, 1932, John McGraw stepped down from the Giants, ending a managerial career that had spanned three decades. There had been ten pennants and three world titles, but McGraw wanted more. He was only fifty-nine years old, but his health was rapidly failing. His final moment in the limelight would occur at the inaugural All-Star game the following July as part of the Chicago World's Fair. Little Napoleon managed the National League, with Connie Mack being his counterpart on the American League side. For the record, Babe Ruth would hit the first home run in All-Star history, a third-inning blast that would ultimately be the winning run in a 4-2 American League triumph. On February 25, 1934, McGraw died of cancer at his home in New Rochelle, New York. Having lived sixty years packed with wonder and turmoil, McGraw would be buried at the New Cathedral Cemetery in Baltimore.

On January 29, 1936, Christy Mathewson was one of five legendary ballplayers elected to the charter class of the new Baseball Hall of Fame. The others were Ty Cobb, Babe Ruth, Honus Wagner, and Walter "Big Train" Johnson. Three years later, the four living members of that first class would all attend the official induction ceremony with the opening of the Cooperstown museum. By then, twenty-one other greats had been added to the Cooperstown ledger, including John McGraw, Connie Mack, Cy Young, Tris Speaker, and Eddie Collins.

Jane had purposely stayed away from baseball.

"Since his death, I just can't bring myself to attend a game at the Polo Grounds," Jane said privately. "If I looked out on the field, at the pitching box where Christy stood so often, the memories would be too poignant."[20]

But, along with her son, Jane did attend the 1939 dedication, unveiling a bust of her late husband. The Mathewson plaque at the Cooperstown museum reads, "Matty was master of them all."

After the induction ceremonies, the inaugural Hall of Fame baseball game was held, the only one that would feature college teams. Johnny Evers, the old Cubs second sacker, threw out the first pitch, Bucknell falling to St. Lawrence 9-5.

✿ ✿ ✿

When Germany invaded Poland on the first day of September 1939, Christy Jr. was already writing letters requesting that he be reinstated into the army. Yes, he was disabled, but he could fly. He just wanted a chance. His requests were rejected, which only fueled his determination.

Although his father's fame certainly opened many doors, the young Mathewson always entered on his own terms. Organizing a flying taxi service in the Adirondacks, he continued his quest for reenlistment, at last able to impress the top military brass with a flawless solo flight. Still, once again, he was rejected. Again, he persisted.

Finally, as America entered World War II, the Air Corps relented. It was a desk job, but Captain Mathewson was ecstatic.

"I expect to be back flying again," he said. "They probably won't let me fly combat ships, but there's no reason I can't fly other types."[21]

The army also had high expectations, selecting Mathewson in early 1942 to command the Thunderbird Chinese Training Program at Arizona's Luke Field, fifteen miles from Phoenix. The headline of the *New York Sun* on May 25, 1942, read, "Like Father, Like Son—Courage."[22] Promoted to major, Christy helped prepare more than a thousand Chinese combat pilots and crews during the course of the war.

"These young men are eager, attentive, and serious students," he wrote Bucknell president Arnaud Marts, "a virtue, sir, that I am sure you will appreciate."[23]

*   *   *

On Saturday night, January 30, 1943, Christy was a headliner on a national radio broadcast commemorating President Franklin D. Roosevelt's sixty-first birthday and the March of Dimes campaign against infantile paralysis.

The program started in Washington, D.C., and ended in Hollywood. From the Great Lakes Naval Training Center in Illinois, Sammy Kaye and his orchestra teamed with 200 sailors for a special rendition of "Happy Birthday Mr. President." From Honolulu, Chief Petty Officer Artie Shaw and his Navy Band played "Begin the Beguine."

The heart of the broadcast took place in the Arizona desert as Major Mathewson's cadets sang "Happy Birthday" in Chinese. Christy Jr. spoke briefly about the training program he was commanding, predicting that his fighters would soon find "the exact center of Tokyo." Mathewson then introduced his good friend at the air base Sergeant Gene Autry, singing one of Roosevelt's favorite songs, "The Yellow Rose of

THE FAMILY NAME (1929)

Texas." Of course, Christy's favorite by the Singing Cowboy was "Back in the Saddle Again."

The Chinese Training Program was but a sector of Luke Field, the largest training base for fighter pilots of the U.S. Army Air Forces. Sergeant Autry did learn a bit of the Chinese language while there, eventually flying a C-47 air transport plane taking military supplies from India to China by way of the Himalayas, a dangerous run known as "The Hump." Christy would have done anything to earn that assignment.

☼ ☼ ☼

At the conclusion of the war, the Chinese government decorated Mathewson with the Special Badge Cloud Banner in the name of General Chiang Kai-Shek. Now a lieutenant colonel, Christy was transferred to London where he met and married actress Lola Finch.

After being discharged from military service in 1946, he and his new wife bought a ranch outside San Antonio, Texas, near the base where he had trained to be a combat pilot fifteen years earlier.

☼ ☼ ☼

The summer of 1950 marked the thirtieth anniversary of the Mathewson family moving to Saranac Lake. Now seventy years old, Jane had lived there for nearly a quarter of a century without her husband.

"Naturally, I cherish the all-too-few years I spent with Christy as the great experience of my life," she said.[24]

Jane's life in Saranac was quiet, content. She had made a small fortune in the stock market after her husband's death, but she was quite frugal. She never owned an air conditioner or television; she still made her own soap.

She loved to read and travel in the winter, particularly to Florida with Blanche and to Texas to see her son. She also enjoyed her trips to Lewisburg. But 1950 was a tough year as Jane lost two sisters—Margaret and Annie. Now, her only sibling was Bessie. Jane had hoped that Christy and his bride might settle in New York or Pennsylvania, but instead they bought the ranch near San Antonio.

Jane sometimes visited Laughing Larry Doyle in Saranac. A smoker and former coal miner, he was diagnosed with tuberculosis in 1942, five years after the death of his wife. Upon hearing that he was nearly destitute due to some bad investments, Jane and Blanche decided to establish a "free bed" in honor of Christy at the Trudeau Sanitarium. Larry Doyle had been the first recipient and was on his way to recovery.

Laughing Larry always referred to Jane as "my manager."

But, other than lasting friendships with former players and their wives, Jane stayed far away from the game itself. When John McGraw died, Blanche was given lifetime box seats at the Polo Grounds. Jane would visit Blanche, but would never see baseball. It was the same when Ford Frick, then the National League president, sent her a lifetime pass to every stadium, which she never used.

* * *

Jane had been her husband's full-time nurse for nearly a quarter of their twenty-two years of marriage. She had spent nearly two years nursing Christy Jr. back to health after his tragic plane crash. In the winter of 1941, when Christy Jr. was badly injured in a head-on automobile accident—the result of another car from the opposite direction skidding across the highway on an icy road—Jane rushed to his side . . . and again would help him back to health.

Despite physical and mental exhaustion, Jane was always strong, always selfless, always there.

* * *

On August 15, 1950, Christy Jr. was installing an electric dishwasher when a gas explosion swept his ranch house. Alone at the time, he dragged himself out of the basement and somehow drove himself to the nearest San Antonio hospital. He was conscious when he arrived, but 90 percent of his body had been badly burned. He died the next afternoon, at just forty-three years old.

Jane's world once again crashed.

Christy's remains would be brought back to the Lewisburg Cemetery to rest next to his father. After the funeral, Jane asked Bessie to live with her at Saranac Lake. But, not wanting to leave her friends, Bessie suggested that Jane return to Lewisburg.

"Alright," said Jane, "I don't care where I live anymore."[25]

That fall, she left the house she and her husband had built on Old Military Road and moved back to her childhood home.

* * *

At first glance, they might not appear as typical best friends. Jane Mathewson, now seventy-five years old, was half a century older than Betty Cook, a beautiful young woman she had long called the "grandchild we never had."

Betty and her parents had known Jane for many years. Living three doors down from the Stoughton home on Market Street, they had even driven Jane back to Saranac Lake on several occasions, a two-day trip covering 360 miles that had inevitably turned into a vacation . . . what with the huge house on Old Military Road filled with baseball memorabilia and a front yard to the Adirondack Mountains. On one visit in the late 1940s, Jane had even introduced a teenaged Betty to the great singer Kate Smith.

But now, Jane had been back in Lewisburg for close to five years. With a hint of disapproval, she opened a large white envelope, took a quick glance inside, and tossed it on the table.

"I don't know why they keep sending me these things," she said. "I never go."[26]

"What is it?" asked Betty.

"Oh, it's just another invitation from the Baseball Hall of Fame," said Jane. "I haven't been since that first year."

Curious, Betty picked up the invitation, her eyes immediately drawn to a cluster of magical words.

"Induction of Joseph Paul DiMaggio?" she blurted. "The Yankee Clipper . . ."

Jane looked up at her young friend, who was now reading aloud the invitation in what could only be described as an emotional frenzy. The Hall of Fame exhibition game would match Ted Williams and the Boston Red Sox against the Milwaukee Braves—Hank Aaron, Warren Spahn, Eddie Mathews.

Slowing down, Betty began from the beginning.

"The National Baseball Hall of Fame and Museum and the Village of Cooperstown, New York, cordially invite you and a guest to attend the dedication of plaques on Monday, July 25, 1955."[27]

Betty proudly announced the six inductees.

"Dazzy Vance, Ted Lyons, Gabby Hartnett, Ray Schalk, Home Run Baker, and Joltin' Joe DiMaggio."

Smiling, Jane interrupted.

"If you want to go," she said, "we will go."[28]

And so began an adventure that would take place every summer for the next dozen years—two hundred miles of back roads from Lewisburg to Cooperstown—Betty driving and Jane riding shotgun.

"Did you ever think about getting married again," Betty once asked her passenger. "I would guess you had many opportunities."

"Oh, my dear, Christy was my husband," said Jane. "No one could have possibly taken his place."[29]

⁂

At the 1955 Hall of Fame Induction Ceremony, Commissioner Ford Frick called forty-year-old Joe DiMaggio the "baby of the group." Gabby Hartnett and Ted Lyons were in their mid-fifties, Home Run Baker the oldest at sixty-nine.

The *New York Times* reported that DiMaggio "stole the spotlight," but Betty Cook would also meet Ty Cobb, Bill Terry, Frankie Frisch, Mel Ott, and Cy Young.

Approaching the final days of his life, Young was eighty-eight, Cobb a spry twenty years younger. Betty found both to be charming.

"According to Jane," said Betty, "Ty had mellowed by that time."

The *New York Times* also noted that four famous widows were in attendance at the induction ceremony—Mrs. Christy Mathewson, Mrs. John McGraw, Mrs. Roger Bresnahan, and Mrs. Eddie Collins.

"The men get all the attention," Jane joked. "The women are excess baggage."[30]

As for the fourteenth annual Hall of Fame exhibition game, Ted Williams slashed a two-run homer as the Red Sox downed the Braves 4-2.

⁂

Baseball movies were major box office hits in the 1940s and 1950s. In 1942, Gary Cooper played Lou Gehrig in the timeless classic *Pride of the Yankees.* William Bendix starred in the *Babe Ruth Story* in 1948, and James Stewart had a huge hit the following year with *The (Monty) Stratton Story*, about the White Sox pitcher who lost a leg but eventually returned to the mound. In 1952, *The Pride of St. Louis* featured Dan Dailey as Dizzy Dean. That was the same year Ronald Reagan played Grover Cleveland Alexander, starring with Doris Day in *The Winning Team.*

As can be imagined, *The Christy Mathewson Story* would have a phenomenal plot: the handsome Christian Gentleman, a college kid with a pure heart, overcoming the evils of professional baseball, personified by his coach and friend, Muggsy McGraw. It would be a certain box office blockbuster—or so the Hollywood producers thought who visited Jane, seeking her permission for the script to be written, a star to be signed, and filming to begin. Jane listened carefully to the proposals. Bottom line, she would not permit it.

In order to enhance their films, she reasoned, the studios took far too many liberties with the truth.

Blanche McGraw must have agreed with Jane's unwillingness to have Christy re-created for the big screen—imagine the revisions necessary for a movie about Little Napoleon.

❋ ❋ ❋

A sometimes needed respite from Manhattan, Lewisburg was one of Blanche's favorite destinations. Blanche had lost none of her youthful spirit. She was fun, educated, and well traveled. She loved to talk and was slow to judge. In fact, it was much easier to see Blanche and Jane as best friends than to understand the bond between their late husbands.

Over the years, Blanche had become quite close to all of Jane's sisters, particularly Bessie. Like Blanche, Bessie was both a firebrand and lady of fashion.

"Well, look at you, sitting at breakfast like Diamond Lil," Jane would kid her older sister.

"Papa always said that it's a poor house without at least one lady," Bessie would reply.[31]

Although Jane might often refuse Blanche's invitations to visit her home at 5th Avenue and 10th Street, Bessie loved the energy of Broadway and the Polo Grounds.

After John McGraw's death in 1934, the Giants honored Blanche with a lifetime box right behind the home dugout. Box 19 had eight seats and was always filled with Blanche and friends. Betty Cook and her mother sometimes visited Blanche, cheering for the likes of Johnny Antonelli, Monte Irvin, Red Schoendienst, Al Dark, Sal "The Barber" Maglie, and Willie Mays.

Blanche, a longtime stockholder with the Giants, had witnessed some remarkable moments over the years. In 1951, she saw Bobby Thomson's "Shot Heard Round the World" sink the Brooklyn Dodgers. Remarkably, the blast ended a mad dash in which the Giants somehow erased a thirteen-and-a-half-game deficit in the final weeks of the season, a feat forever known as the "Miracle of Coogan's Bluff." That set up a World Series showdown between the Giants and Yankees, the first postseason for Willie Mays and Mickey Mantle, both rookie sensations. When the teams moved to the Polo Grounds for game three, Blanche McGraw threw out the first pitch, the Giants winning 6-2. The Yankees, however, would capture the crown in six games.

The Giants would return to the Fall Classic in 1954, sweeping the favored Cleveland Indians, a series forever stamped by "The Catch" of Willie Mays.

The Giants had tumbled to third in 1955, followed by two straight seasons in sixth, but nothing was more heartbreaking for Blanche than the afternoon of September 29, 1957, the last Giants home game ever to be played in the Polo Grounds, the franchise moving to San Francisco. Before the game, manager Bill Rigney presented Blanche with a bouquet of red roses. Moose McCormick, Hooks Wiltse, and Rube Marquard were there from the old days, part of a bittersweet gathering of only 11,606 fans. In the bottom of the ninth, as the Pirates sealed a 9-1 romp, both teams rushed for the center-field locker rooms, trying to outmaneuver the fans rushing onto the field one last time. It was 1908 all over again . . . and then it was quiet.

Documented within the official history of baseball, Blanche McGraw—roses still in her hands—was the last person to leave the Polo Grounds.

Blanche never lost her love for the Giants. In April 1958, she attended the club's first game in San Francisco, played at Seals Stadium. Willie Mays was still the headliner, but a superb group of rookies—

Orlando Cepeda, Jim Davenport, Felipe Alou, and Willie Kirkland—helped propel the Giants once again into contenders.

There was no Hall of Fame induction ceremony in 1958, but they did play the annual exhibition game at Doubleday Field, the Washington Senators edging the Phillies, 5-4.

Following the game, at the Otesaga Hotel, Betty Cook was talking with a group of Phillies players when Jane arrived. Betty made the introduction.

"They about fell over," Betty said. "Everybody assumed that Mrs. Mathewson was dead. They didn't realize that she had been a widow for 33 years. They couldn't believe they were meeting her."[32]

Jack Sanford—a young pitching ace on the Phillies—politely reached for Jane's hand.

"Mrs. Mathewson," he said, "may I ask you a question? I always understood that your husband never drank, smoked, or swore. Just how straight and narrow was Christy?"

"Now Jack," she smiled, "you don't think I would marry such a prude, do you?"[33]

Of course, Jane had heard the question before, many times.

"There was nothing mamby-pamby or sissy about him," she said. "He was a real he-man. He did most of the things other players did, never tried to pose as a paragon of virtue, but no one could be around him long without recognizing the fine stuff in the man, his character, his ability, his inherent sense of decency."[34]

Educated, charming, fun; Jane became known as baseball's "most celebrated and gracious widow," a newspaper adding that "her young friend Betty was the belle of the ball."[35]

"We both were treated like royalty," said Betty.[36]

As was Blanche, with Cooperstown and San Francisco on her busy calendar. She would visit San Francisco again in April 1960 for the opening of Candlestick Park and even see the Giants in the 1962 World Series, attending all three games played at Yankee Stadium. The Giants had four world titles—1905, 1921, 1922, 1954—and Blanche had seen them all. But not a fifth . . . in game seven at Candlestick, the Yankees pulled out a 1-0 victory to secure a twentieth World Series championship. It would have driven John McGraw crazy.

Less than a month later, on November 5, 1962, Blanche Sindall McGraw passed away at the age of eighty.

* * *

Soon after Blanche's passing, Bessie Stoughton Cregar entered a nursing home. Now living alone, Jane had an open invitation for dinner at the home of Betty and her parents.

Edward and Anna Cook—both about the age of Jane's son—owned a huge three-story brick home that had been built in 1844, originally housing Lewisburg's first bank.

"We had air conditioning and a color TV," said Betty. "Jane never missed Mitch Miller or *Bonanza*. She had a great sense of humor. She was part of the family."[37]

Jane decided to will Christy's memorabilia to the Baseball Hall of Fame in Cooperstown and Keystone College in Factoryville. Meanwhile, she often donated significant gifts to the Presbyterian Church and Bucknell University, establishing the Jane and Christy Mathewson Memorial Scholarship. She also made donations to Phi Gamma Delta—in fact she still wore the fraternity pin that Christy had given to her in 1901 on all formal occasions.

Jane carried herself with great dignity, having a deep love for her husband and son that time could not weather. She had a strong faith and was dedicated to her church. There was reading, travel, a sewing bee, talking with Bucknell students and her many friends, riding around town in Betty's convertible, and their yearly trips to the Hall of Fame induction ceremony. Despite the burdens of old age, she created a life that was comfortable and good.

"People were always drawn to her," said Betty. "She was so charming."[38]

It was summer 1966 in Cooperstown, Jane sitting in a rocking chair on the front porch of the Ostesage Hotel talking with her good friend Claire Ruth. Casey Stengel, who would be inducted with Ted Williams, stopped by and recalled his early years with Brooklyn and his inability to hit against Big Six.

"Mrs. Mathewson was queen of the night, though she was unaware of it and the designation would horrify her," wrote Hall of Fame curator Ken Smith. "She was a woman of warmth and wisdom with a gentle spirit. We loved her."[39]

Jane Stoughton Mathewson. Courtesy of Betty Cook

Jane Stoughton Mathewson was eighty-seven years old when she threw out the first pitch to dedicate Lewisburg's new Wolfe Field in the spring of 1967. It would be her last public appearance. She passed away on May 29 . . . Memorial Day.

Once again, people arrived from across the nation, including a large contingent of friends from the Hall of Fame.

Christy, Jane, and their son are buried side by side on a beautiful hill in the Lewisburg Cemetery, within a stone's throw of Bucknell.

APPENDIX A

The Ups and Downs of Pitching Genius

Near perfect control, a wicked array of pitches, intellect, character, faith . . . Christy Mathewson had it all. In seventeen seasons of glory, he would win a mind-boggling 373 games. Then again, he also would get stung with 188 losses. Apparently, greatness is seldom easy.

Here's a glance at a few of his best and worst moments in the pitcher's box.

1900

July 17: Talk about first game jitters. In four innings of relief at Brooklyn's Washington Park, Matty stumbles to the wild side with two walks, four hit batsmen, and six runs. The Giants crumble 13-7; the college kid's not charged with the loss, only the blame.

September 26: In relief, Christy blows a three-run lead at Boston's South End Grounds. He is 0-3 after two rocky months in the majors, looking at a one-way trip back to the minors.

1901

April 26: Matty earns his first major league win by scattering four hits as the Giants thump Brooklyn 5-3 at the Polo Grounds. One month later, after a 1-0 victory over Cincinnati, Matty is 8-0 with four shutouts and the underachieving Giants are actually in first place. That would not last . . . nor will Matty's streak, ending on May 28 with a heartbreaking 1-0 loss to Jack Powell and the St. Louis Cardinals.

June 29: Matty's anticipated pitchers' duel against Rube Waddell explodes on impact, the Giants pounding the great lefty with nine runs in the first four innings. Matty tosses a four-hitter as New York pops Chicago 14-1.

July 15: In St. Louis, Christy earns his first career no-hitter, 5-0 over the Cardinals. The "Boy Wonder from Bucknell" has promise.

August 13: The classic pairing against Boston's veteran Kid Nichols is a double shutout for nine innings, a weary Matty folding in the tenth. Two days later, Nichols and Mathewson go eleven innings against each other before the game is called for darkness. On August 19, Matty and the Kid meet yet again. Boston pounds Christy for thirteen hits; the seventh-place Giants commit five errors and fall 11-6.

September 21: Yielding but three hits, Matty beats the Reds, 5-1, for his twentieth victory of the season.

1902

April 17: Before a huge crowd of 24,000 rooters at the Polo Grounds, Matty blanks Philadelphia 7-0. Two weeks later, he tosses a two-hit shutout against the Phillies.

July 24: Christy throws the first of two straight shutouts against Brooklyn, the second a two-hitter. New manager John McGraw is beaming.

August 9: Christy allows twelve hits and his hapless teammates play horribly in an embarrassing 8-2 home loss to the Chicago Orphans (soon to be Cubs).

August 26: At League Park in Cincinnati, Christy shuts outs the Reds 7-0. Poor Henry Thielman loses for the third time this year against Matty. The same age as Matty, the former Notre Dame fullback had started the season with the Giants. He would only pitch two years in the majors, notching a 9-19 overall record.

September 6: Nine runs, thirteen hits, five walks, four passed balls, one wild pitch, three errors, and one small grandstand fire directly behind the Giants bench . . . Pirates win 9-3.

October 4: In Boston, Christy loses his fourth straight, closing the year with a miserable 14-17 record despite throwing eight shutouts.

1903

June 13: Cincinnati's Joe Kelley triples in the first inning, but that's all the Reds can muster as Matty twirls a brilliant one-hit, 1-0 win against Noodles Hahn. By the way, New York is in first place.

July 31: Boston is bad news for Matty as he loses his fourth game in ten days, his record now 17-8.

August 21: Christy tops the Pirates and former college friend Bucky Veil. One year behind Matty at Bucknell, Veil would go 5-3 his rookie season. Christy's 1903 record against the eventual National League champs was 8-0.

September 21: Matty beats Chicago for his thirtieth victory of the season as the Giants secure second place over the Cubs. Pittsburgh claims the pennant.

1904

May 10: In St. Louis, Christy is yanked after giving up five runs in the first inning. Surprise, a frustrated McGraw blames umpire Bob Emslie for the disaster and gets tossed. Tag another loss on Matty two days later as he gives Cincinnati four runs in the first inning. In all, he yields thirteen hits and thirteen runs to the Reds, but at least he goes the distance.

June 16: Christy earns a 4-3 victory over St. Louis; the loss credited to Mike O'Neill, whose older brother Jack is the Cardinals' catcher. The O'Neill brothers had teamed with Christy in the Honesdale days of 1898–99. As a side note, this is the start of Matty's twenty-four straight victories over the Cardinals, a streak that would last more than four years.

October 3: Christy strikes out sixteen Cardinals in a 3-1 victory that takes only seventy-five minutes. With Matty compiling a 33-12 record, the Giants take the pennant but refuse to play the Boston Americans in the World Series.

1905

May 1: Christy registers his 100th career victory, baking Boston 8-2.

June 13: One of the all-time classics as Christy tosses a no-hitter at Chicago's West Side Park. He walks none and faces only twenty-eight batters, but on the other side of the ledger he is nearly matched by Mordecai "Three Finger" Brown, who has a one-hit shutout into the ninth inning, when the Giants get four straight hits and win 1-0.

October 14: Oh well, just the greatest World Series ever pitched, Matty stunning the Philadelphia Athletics and the baseball world with three shutouts in six days. As for the regular season, Mathewson goes 31-9 with a 1.27 earned run average; breaking the thirty-win barrier for the third straight year.

1906

May 18: In his third start of the season, still weakened by the effects of diphtheria, Matty allows fourteen hits in a 7-6 loss to Cincinnati. Two weeks later, Christy lasts but two-thirds of an inning as he walks six Phillies, questions the eyesight of umpire Bill Klem, and got thrown out of the game. That is definitely rare, but the worst occurs on June 7 as Mathewson once again cannot get out of the first inning. After giving the Cubs five quick runs, he is relieved by Iron Man McGinnity, who provides absolutely no help, allowing six more runs. By the time New York bats in the bottom of the first, the Cubs have scored eleven runs. Chicago wins 19-0.

June 15: After a much-needed eight days of rest, Matty regains the magic with a 2-1 win over St. Louis.

August 18: Every pitcher has his nemesis . . . hello Joe Tinker. The great Chicago shortstop pops Christy for three hits as the Cubs roll.

September 11: Despite his horrible bout with diphtheria to start the season, Matty hurls his sixth shutout of the year on his way to a 22-12 mark.

1907

May 8: Matty twirls his second straight shutout. After topping Brooklyn 1-0, he blanks Pittsburgh's tall and lanky Al "Lefty" Leifield.

June 14: Matty and Lefty Leifield battle again, this time the Pirates win in twelve innings. Matty goes the distance in spite of being hit in the stomach in the ninth inning by an errant Leifield fast ball.

July 20: At the Polo Grounds, Big Six beats the Cubs 1-0. He gives up only three hits with no walks.

August 17: Another gem against Three Finger Brown and the Cubs results in a twelve-inning, 3-2 loss.

September 24: Matty throws his eighth shutout of the year, downing the Pirates 2-0 in Pittsburgh. Lefty Leifield, who will notch a 20-17 record for the season, loses four of those games to Big Six. Meanwhile, Matty's final 1907 record is 24-12.

1908

April 22: Opening day at the Polo Grounds looks bad for Matty, trailing the Brooklyn Superbas 2-1 in the bottom of the ninth. No problem, Turkey Mike Donlin blasts a two-run, game-winning homer.

April 27: At Boston, Big Six tosses a 1-0 one-hitter against the Doves (formerly Beaneaters and not yet Rustlers or Braves).

May 18: The Reds maul Christy for nine runs on fifteen hits, his third loss in five days.

July 13: Christy fires a three-hit shutout in Pittsburgh. The loser, of course, is Lefty Leifield.

July 16: Matty is supposed to be warming up in the bullpen, but instead decides to sneak into the locker room for a quick shower in the ninth inning at Chicago. When things suddenly turn dicey in the game, he gets hauled back for relief duty. Give Big Six a soggy save.

July 17: Christy is dry and dangerous, matching zeroes against Three Finger Brown. The only difference is Joe Tinker with an inside-the-park home run. Cubs win 1-0.

July 25: A standing room crowd of 30,000 at the Polo Grounds comes to witness a certain New York victory. After all, it's Big Six against Lefty Leifield. Spoiler alert—Honus Wagner goes five for five and Lefty gets the win.

August 24: In a super tight pennant race between New York, Chicago, and Pittsburgh, the Giants squeeze into first as The Christian Gentleman whips the Pirates 5-1, his 200th career victory. All seems back to normal—Leifield gets the loss. Actually, Leifield is an excellent twirler, fashioning a 124-97 record (2.47 earned run average) in twelve seasons, most of them with the Bucs. But when it comes to facing Matty, he is not the only hard-luck pitcher in town. In 1908, Irv Young (Boston Doves) and Andy Coakley (Cincinnati Reds) each lose five times to Big Six.

September 8: Matty gets his thirtieth victory of the season and fourth of his career, downing Brooklyn 1-0 in eleven innings, Al Bridwell driving home the winner.

September 18: The largest crowd in major league history (35,000) crams into the Polo Grounds, many standing behind makeshift ropes in the outfield to watch Christy toss his eleventh shutout of the year, the Giants cruising past the Pirates 7-0 as Lefty Leifield watches from the bench.

September 23: The Merkle game . . . Freddie, all you had to do was run an extra few steps. When Hank O'Day rules the game a tie, most figure a replay will never happen. Well, it does, and the infamous make-up game is won by the Cubs on October 8.

1909

May 13: Due to a bruised hand, Matty misses nearly three weeks, his first game at home against none other than the hated Chicago Cubs. Neither Matty nor the home faithful had forgotten the vicious end to the 1908 season. For a touch of revenge, Matty four-hits the Cubs and the Giants roll 4-1.

June 8: One hit, two errors, two runs in the first inning and it has all the markings of another hard-luck outing against Three Finger Brown in Chicago. But Matty tosses one-hit ball the rest of the way and the Giants beat the Cubs 3-2.

May 24: How could this happen? After twenty-four straight wins over the Cardinals, Big Six loses. Well, the new St. Louis manager is Matty's old catcher and pitching consultant, Roger Bresnahan.

July 12: Christy has won thirteen games in a row, his record at 15-2 with half the season still to play. Jinxed, he's ambushed by the Pirates 3-1.

September 16: In Chicago, President William Howard Taft—a huge baseball fan—meets the players, then watches Matty outduel Three Finger Brown 2-1.

September 24: Christy beats Three Finger at the Polo Grounds. What is happening? After dropping eight straight to Brown over the course of four years, The Christian Gentleman takes three of four in 1909. It's quite a season for Matty. In 390 innings, he will go 25-6 (.806) with eleven shutouts and a league-leading 1.14 earned run average. Now twenty-nine years old, Christy records career personal bests in winning percentage, shutouts, earned run average, and innings pitched.

1910

May 2: At Brooklyn's Washington Park, Matty gets robbed of a no-hitter by the scorekeeper, who calls Art Devlin's error an infield hit.

May 28: A two-runs-batted-in double by Fred Snodgrass proves the difference as Matty and the Giants slip past Philadelphia 3-2.

June 15: Christy runs his 1910 record to 10-1 by thumping Lefty Leifield and the Pirates. Two weeks prior, he beat Cincinnati for the fourteenth straight time.

June 25: A three-run homer by Laughing Larry Doyle propels The Christian Gentleman over the Phillies. Four days later, Christy will be the hitting hero with a single in the bottom of the tenth to drive home Fred Merkle with the winning run against Philly.

August 15: Lefty Leifield figures out a way to beat Christy—he throws ten innings of shutout ball. They will meet again in a month, with Christy throwing the masterpiece.

August 19: Christy's seventeenth straight win over the Reds also gives him twenty victories for the year.

October 13: The Manhattan Series features the Giants and High-landers, and a crowd of 25,000 at the Polo Grounds sees Christy domi-nate. The Giants go on to win the series with Matty notching three victories and a save. Twenty-five-year-old shortstop Art Fletcher takes his $1,100 winner's share and marries Irene Dieu, his childhood sweet-heart.

1911

April 13: Late at night, after the Giants home opener, the wooden-structured Polo Grounds burns down. Thanks to the Highlanders, the Giants will use Hilltop Park until their new concrete-and-steel stadium can be constructed.

May 13: Fred Merkle accounts for six runs batted in during the first inning with a double and inside-the-park home run. Giants beat the Cardinals 19-5. In June, Merkle will again get two plate appearances in one inning. Trailing 1-0 at Chicago in the top of the ninth, Merkle doubles and triples during a seven-run uprising.

June 9: Different park (Forbes Field), but the same old story as Matty and the Giants beat Lefty Leifield and the Pirates.

June 28: In the first game at the rebuilt Polo Grounds, Matty hurls a nine-hit shutout and even steals home as the Giants down the Boston Rustlers 3-0. So now they're the Rustlers? Let's clear this up. One of the charter National League franchises, Boston was originally named the Red Stockings (1871–75), followed by the Red Caps (1876–82), Beaneaters (1883–1906), Doves (1907–10), and Rustlers (1911). They change their name to the Braves in 1912 and keep the name for twenty-three years until a big switch to the Boston Bees in 1936. In 1940, the name changes back to the Braves, which still stands . . . except for two new locations. The Braves moved to Milwaukee in 1953 and then Atlan-ta in 1966.

August 7: Matty and Three Finger both get roughed up during an 8-6 Cubs win. While the Giants outhit Chicago 13-10, Joe Tinker reaches Big Six for two singles, a double, and a triple.

August 19: After twenty-two straight losses to Big Six dating back to May 1908, the Reds finally break the streak.

September 12: In the only career matchup of Christy Mathewson and Cy Young, the Giants cruise.

September 28: As the Giants near the pennant, Joe Tinker doubles in two runs and the Cubs top Christy 2-1.

October 14: For the first time in six years, the Giants are back in the World Series. Christy enters with a 26-13 season record. Unlike 1905, the Philadelphia Athletics prevail, with Matty's great pitching efforts resulting in one win and two losses.

1912

May 18: Christy pitches at the dedication of Cincinnati's sparkling Redland Field. He loses 4-3. No problem, four days later he dominates the Reds, at one time retiring eighteen in a row.

July 4: Six days in July starts with Brooklyn ending the league-leading Giants sixteen-game winning streak, with Christy not escaping the third inning. But, since he's rested, Matty pitches again on July 5, taming the Superbas 5-1. On July 9, he beats the Cubs and Three Finger Brown.

August 3: Fred Merkle smacks two home runs and Christy beats the Reds 3-2.

August 6: Matty and Ty Cobb are named vice presidents of the new Player's Fraternity.

August 22: The Pirates sweep a doubleheader from the Giants before a sellout crowd of 27,000 at Forbes Field. Honus Wagner touches Big Six for three hits in the opener, then nails Rube Marquard for the cycle—single, double, triple, and homer. For the day, Wagner has seven hits, five runs, four runs batted in, and two stolen bases.

October 16: The Giants drop the final game of the World Series at Fenway Park, with Christy suffering a bewildering loss in ten innings. The Red Sox players each earn $4,024.68 and the Giants $2,566.47. For the season, Matty goes 23-12 with a 2.12 earned run average (the first time in five seasons he has been above 2.00). Strangely, for the first and only time in a complete season of work, he throws no shutouts.

1913

April 29: He's back with the zeroes . . . Matty baffles Brooklyn with a thirteen-inning shutout.

May 16: The Christian Gentleman beats Pittsburgh, but his record streak of forty-seven innings without issuing a walk is finally halted.

June 26: Laughing Larry Doyle hits a grand slam against the Braves, Matty saves the first game and wins the second.

June 30: At Philadelphia, Matty gets the save, the Giants capture first place, and John McGraw gets attacked by several unruly fans.

July 5: It's a great day for career win number 300, Christy thumping Brooklyn 6-1.

July 18: Matty's forty-seven-inning base on balls record certainly doesn't last long . . . he immediately breaks his own mark. During a 5-0 victory over the Cardinals at the Polo Grounds, the Christian Gentleman's new no walk record of sixty-eight innings comes to an end, not to be passed for nearly half a century.

August 14: New York manages to retire Honus Wagner one time . . . an inside pitch that accidentally hits the bat as he bails, then rolls fair for the easy out. Otherwise, Honus pounds the Giants with four hits and the Pirates roll past Christy 8-6.

August 30: When their storied careers end, Christy Mathewson and Grover Cleveland Alexander will share the National League record for most victories (373). Meeting in Philadelphia, the two aces are hardly the story in a wild game that has the Phillies leading 8-6 when McGraw protests that fans in the center-field bleachers are purposely distracting his hitters. Since umpire Bill Brennan has already evicted Philadelphia manager Red Dooin, he orders acting manager Mickey Doolan to stop the commotion in center field. Doolan refuses and Brennan forfeits the game to New York, causing such an uproar that police with drawn revolvers are needed at the train station to protect the umpires and Giants from a mob. The National League hierarchy eventually overturns the forfeit and orders the game to continue at the spot it was stopped, with the Phillies claiming the victory one month later on September 30. Christy will be hit with the loss, but he rebounds quickly to win the next regularly scheduled game. His final record for the season is 25-11 with a 2.06 earned run average and only twenty-one walks in 306 innings.

October 11: The Giants drop their third straight World Series despite a valiant effort by Big Six, who tosses a shutout against the Philadelphia Athletics for what will be his final postseason victory.

1914

July 4: The Christian Gentleman hurls a 3-0 shutout over the Phillies, good for his 350th career victory.

July 18: While Matty wins in Pittsburgh, the Boston Braves quietly exit the National League cellar. Really, nobody is paying attention . . . Boston has not logged a winning season since 1898.

August 15: Matty pitches nine scoreless innings against the Braves, but loses in the tenth.

September 7: With the surprising Braves making an impressive late-season pennant run, the Labor Day morning-afternoon doubleheader against the Giants is held at Fenway Park, three times the size of South End Grounds. Attendance for the two games is 74,163. Matty loses the morning game in the ninth, but the real fireworks occur in the late game. After Fred Snodgrass is hit by pitcher Lefty Tyler, he has a few words on his way to first. Striking back, Tyler pretends to reenact the routine fly ball that Snodgrass "muffed" in the 1912 World Series against the Red Sox. The benches clear, order is restored, but the already incensed crowd in center field is dangerously crazy when Snodgrass returns to his position, a shower of glass bottles thrown in his direction. At this point, the mayor of Boston, James Curley, actually runs on to the field and demands that Snodgrass be ejected from the game. Instead, McGraw replaces Snodgrass for his protection. The Giants win 10-1, with the Boston-New York rivalry alive in both circuits.

September 30: The "Miracle Braves" have won the pennant, but once again Mathewson is stellar; a 24-13 record and second straight season with more victories than walks rendered (only twenty-three passes in 312 innings).

1915

July 26: Christy loses to Pittsburgh, 2-1, both runs driven home by Honus Wagner.

August 27: Battling shoulder and back problems, Christy wins his final game of the season, 2-1 over the Pirates. His record for 1915 was 8-14 with a 3.58 earned run average, the worst full season of his career.

1916

May 29: In Boston, Christy beats the Braves 3-0, allowing only four hits for what will be his last shutout.

July 20: Matty's first game as manager of the Cincinnati Reds is spoiled by Grover Cleveland Alexander and the Phillies.

September 4: Matty outlasts Three Finger Brown in a Chicago Labor Day special at Weegham Park (Wrigley Field), his 373rd career victory and the only time he pitches for a team other than the Giants.

APPENDIX B

Old Giants

There are seasons in a ballplayer's life that touch perfection . . . rounding third at unrivaled speed, reflexes fueled by power and grace, the mind sharp within the moment.

"It's great to young and a Giant," Laughing Larry Doyle quipped to Damon Runyon in 1911.[1]

During the Deadball Era, most members of the mighty New York Giants were focused on hitting .300 or winning twenty games. Life beyond baseball? Now there's an abstract thought. Few seemed prepared when John McGraw took back their key to the Polo Grounds. But at least they knew how to battle, to struggle, to survive.

For eight seasons, **Luther "Dummy" Taylor** was a vital part of the Giants' family. Despite being deaf since childhood, Taylor refused to be hindered by any cultural stereotypes of the times, instead stepping to the heart of team chemistry, even teaching his teammates to use sign language. Although Taylor would routinely entertain the crowd before games with his juggling skills, he was a thorn to umpires in that he often mocked their decisions through humorous pantomime, such as wearing rubber boots onto the field when the umpire refused to call the game during a brisk rain. There was also the time Taylor used uncomplimentary sign language to describe Umpire Hank O'Day in an exchange with the Giants' dugout, the players howling with delight. Well, it seems that

O'Day had been raised by two deaf parents and knew exactly what Taylor was signing. The Giant got tossed.

A national role model for the deaf community, Luther Taylor was thirty-four years old when he was released from the Giants after the 1908 season, having compiled a 116-106 record in nine major league seasons. However, Taylor was not finished, pitching seven more years in the minors, at one point actually facing Joe "Iron Man" McGinnity. When he did leave baseball, Luther Taylor coached and taught for two decades at the Illinois School for the Deaf. In 1940, he began scouting for the Giants, passing away in 1958 at the age of eighty-two.

Barely educated, **Joe "Iron Man" McGinnity** was only eight years old when he began working in the coal mines of Illinois. Plenty of occupations would follow—iron worker, mule skinner, barkeeper, bouncer—and that was all before baseball. He was twenty-eight when he hit the majors, a decade older when the Giants released him in 1909, with a sparkling career mark of 246-142 with two thirty-win seasons, his best year being 1904 when he finished 35-8 with a 1.61 earned run average. The Giants would have probably been wise to keep Iron Man a bit longer. The new pitcher on the staff—young Rube Marquard—bombed his first few seasons, while McGinnity simply took his business to the Class-A Eastern League, purchased the Newark Indians for $50,000, and penciled himself into the lineup as player-manager, going 29-16 with eleven shutouts. All told, he would pitch another fourteen years in the minors, compile six twenty-win seasons and once break thirty. During that span, he was a part owner and player-manager for the Tacoma (Washington) Tigers and Butte (Montana) Miners. On July 28, 1925, at the age of fifty-four, he retired in true Iron Man fashion by pitching a doubleheader. Not ready to entirely leave the game, McGinnity became a coach for the Brooklyn Robins under Wilbert "Uncle Robbie" Robinson. Iron Man McGinnity was fifty-eight years old when he died in 1929; he was elected to the Hall of Fame in 1946.

Although **Turkey Mike Donlin** would carve out a blistering .333 career batting average, he would quit the game three times before actually retiring in 1914. The handsome husband of actress Mabel Hite was certain he could make more money on Broadway. "I can act," he boasted. "I'll break the hearts of all the gals in the country."[2] Unfortunately, Turkey Mike was a heavy drinker, and the heart most broken was usually his own.

After his playing days, Donlin managed the Memphis Chicks, promoted boxing in Cuba, and even taught baseball in France for the U.S. government during World War I—all while pursuing a stage and screen career. Moving to California, he became a supporting actor in a number of silent movies. Most notable was his role as a Union Army officer in Buster Keaton's *The General* (1926) and the role of Flask in *The Sea Beast*, starring his good friend John Barrymore. Mike Donlin died of a heart attack in 1933.

Laughing Larry Doyle was blessed with speed and unrelenting hustle, notching a .290 career batting average with 300 stolen bases that included seventeen swipes of home. Although his glove could be porous, Doyle was a wonderful team player with an exuberant personality. When the Giants captain and second baseman was awarded a new Chalmers automobile for being named the National League's most valuable player in 1912, he joked, "I didn't even know how to put gasoline in it."[3] In the final week of the 1913 season, he would accidentally crash the car into a tree, suffering shoulder and arm injuries, but he was back on the diamond for the World Series. As long as he could move without crutches, Doyle's therapy for his lengthy résumé of injuries was simply to play through the pain.

Retiring in 1920, Laughing Larry coached the Giants, many expecting him to be named manager upon McGraw's retirement in 1932. Instead, Bill Terry was awarded the helm, and Doyle continued in the Giants' organization by managing their high minor league teams in Toronto and Nashville. Diagnosed with tuberculosis in 1942, he not only survived the disease but was photographed in *Life* magazine as the last person to leave the Trudeau Sanitarium when it closed in 1954. Doyle was eighty-seven when he died in 1974.

Freddie Merkle always had a keen understanding of baseball; he just could never shake the disaster of 1908. If only he would have touched second base. Constantly abused by insensitive fans, Merkle often considered quitting the game. But even after being released by the Cubs in 1920, he played five more seasons for Rochester of the AAA International League, then signed with the Yankees for spot duty in the final weeks of 1925. He joined the Yankees' coaching staff in 1926 and managed in the minors. Then came the day when a young player called him "Bonehead" . . . Merkle walked off the field and never returned. Despite hard times in the Depression, he had saved enough money from his playing days to buy a fruit farm in Florida, where he was content playing bridge, golf, and chess.

Although he refused all interviews, he finally accepted an invitation to the 1950 Giants' Old-Timers' Day. It would prove to be a great moment for the embittered old first baseman. When the Polo Grounds crowd wildly cheered his introduction, Fred Merkle cried. "After all these years," he said. "I expected so much worse."[4] He died six years later, in his sleep, at the age of sixty-seven.

Unlike Merkle, **Fred "Snow" Snodgrass** did not dwell on the stain of embarrassing disaster, preferring to downplay the "muff" that cost the Giants the 1912 World Series. In nine seasons, the swift centerfielder would hit .275 with a career best .321 in 1910. After being released by the Boston Braves in the spring of 1917, he moved back home to California, played one year in the Pacific Coast League, and then became a successful businessman, banker, and politician in Oxnard, even serving as the mayor. In his later years, he bought a large ranch in Ventura, growing walnuts and lemons. Fred Snodgrass lived eighty-six years, passing in 1974.

It would have been hard to predict that, after retiring in 1925, **Richard "Rube" Marquard** would live quietly for the next fifty-five years. Yes, the tall and lanky lefty had been brilliant during the Giants' triple pennant run from 1911 to 1913, winning more than twenty games each season, including nineteen in a row in 1912. He was even busier off the field—multiple advertising endorsements, a lucrative vaudeville act with Blossom Seeley, and even starring in the silent movie, *Rube Marquard Wins*. With a 201-177 career record and one no-hitter, the tall lefty would manage in the minors for a few seasons, then work at the horse racing tracks of Baltimore.

He was eighty-four years old when inducted into the Baseball Hall of Fame in 1971 and would live for seven more years.

Although Rube Marquard got his nickname for his resemblance to Rube Waddell, **Charles "Jeff" Tesreau** (pronounced Tez-row) looked like heavyweight boxer Jim Jeffries. At six-feet-two-inches, 225 pounds, Tesreau also carried the nicknames of "Bullfrog" and "The Ozark Bear." Essentially, he threw hard, a sizzling spitball that, in his early days, had batters ducking for their lives. But under the tutelage of pitching coach Wilbert "Uncle Robbie" Robinson, Tesreau would find his control and advance to the Giants in 1912 to complete the powerful pitching trio with Matty and Marquard. Playing only for New York, Tesreau registered a 115-72 career record over five seasons, including a no-hitter against the Phillies in his rookie season.

After an argument with John McGraw, Tesreau walked off the team during the middle of the 1916 season. When McGraw refused to trade or release him, Tesreau instead went to work for Bethlehem Steel. At the end of World War I, he signed to coach the Dartmouth College baseball team, a position he held from 1919 until 1946. In twenty-seven seasons at Dartmouth, Tesreau compiled a 379-264 record with five championships. One of Dartmouth's Ivy League rivals, of course, was Yale University, which was managed for two decades by Smoky Joe Wood, Tesreau's rival during the 1912 World Series. While on a fishing trip in 1946, Jeff Tesreau suffered a stroke and died several days later at the age of fifty-seven.

John Tortes "Chief" Meyers—the gifted catcher and vaudeville performer—would retire from the majors in 1915 with a superb .291 career batting average. After serving in the U.S. Marines during World War I, he played a few more years in the minors, including a stint as player-manager for New Haven of the Eastern League, ultimately returning to his childhood home in California. In 1920, after being booed during a semipro game in San Diego, he quit baseball forever. Although a natural on the stage, Chief Meyers was not ready to be typecast for the "Indian" roles of the era. Instead, he became the police chief of the Mission Indian Agency near Riverside and would later work as a supervisor for the Department of the Interior.

Sensitive and intelligent, Meyers had a difficult time accepting the heightened pace of American life. "The world seems to be turned all upside down today," he said during an interview for *The Glory of Their Times* in the mid-1960s. "Progress, they call it . . . I guess I'm like the venerable old warrior . . . my eyes perceive the present, but my roots are imbedded deeply in the grandeur of the past."[5]

Meyers died in 1971 at the age of ninety.

With that special feisty, bulldog temperament that John McGraw so loved, **Art Fletcher** charted a solid career; hitting .277 in thirteen seasons with 238 doubles, 77 triples, and 32 homers. A cartoon published by Ripley in 1917 called Fletcher "the best hitting and fielding shortstop in baseball . . . and the most underrated."[6] A firestorm on the field, Fletch was just the opposite at home, a deeply religious and devoted family man who would be named manager of the Philadelphia Phillies in 1923, a promotion he would eventually regret. The Phillies had little talent, but their new manager was obsessed with his job. His wife, Irene, worried about the stress on her husband's health, asking him to step down. He listened. "Managing took too much out of me," said Fletch. "I couldn't take defeat and the Phillies had me almost as nutty as they were. The responsibilities of managing made me a nervous wreck."[7]

After four rugged years in Philadelphia, Fletcher switched leagues to coach third base for the Yankees, a position he would hold for the next nineteen years. What a change, from the last-place Phillies to one of the greatest teams of all time: the 1927 Yankees with Babe Ruth, Lou Gehrig, "Murderers Row," 110 victories before a World Series sweep of the Pirates, Ruth finishing the season with a record sixty home runs. When New York manager Miller Huggins died in 1929, Fletcher was named interim manager and offered the full-time job, but he turned it down, eventually spending fifteen years with Joe McCarthy. Fletcher soon became known as "the man who didn't want to manage the Yankees,"[8] although he did take over the helm whenever needed. Ever the showman, Fletch would whip off his cap whenever a Yankee player homered and spank the guy with a sweep of the arm as he rounded third. Regarded as the game's "master heckler," he was also called "the world's highest paid traffic cop," earning a coaching-record $15,000 for the 1944 season.[9]

Although never elected to the Baseball Hall of Fame, Art Fletcher was praised throughout baseball at his death in 1950 as one of the game's all-time greats.

Raised on the Sac and Fox nation in Oklahoma, Wa-Tho-Huk ("Bright Path"), known to millions as **Jim Thorpe**, would not be the "world's greatest athlete" when it came to baseball, logging a .252 career batting average over six seasons. Although he left the diamond in 1919, Thorpe continued to play football until 1928, one of the major players in the formation of what today is the National Football League. Thorpe would play in 52 NFL games, mostly for the Canton Bulldogs. But then came the slide. There were small parts in fifty movies, including a role in *White Heat*, the 1949 blockbuster starring James Cagney that had Thorpe in the unnamed role of the "Big Convict." But Thorpe was a heavy drinker, and he married three times while drifting through numerous jobs, including ditch digger, barroom bouncer, construction worker, security guard, and merchant marine. Although alcohol was a problem, he could not deal with the injustice of being stripped of his two gold medals from the 1912 Olympic Games. "It broke his heart," said Jack "Chief" Meyers, "and he never really recovered."[10] Jim Thorpe died in 1953. Thirty years later, the International Olympic Committee overturned the 1912 decision and reinstated his gold medals.

Roger Bresnahan could have played any position, the super-fast outfielder turned catcher beginning his baseball journey as a twirler, producing a 4-1 record in nine games. In a seventeen-year career, "The Duke of Tralee" would hit .279 with 212 stolen bases. The innovative designer of the early shin guard and batting helmet would eventually be a player-manager with the Cardinals and Cubs. When he was replaced by Joe Tinker as the Cubs manager, the Chicago franchise helped him purchase the Toledo Mud Hens, which he owned until 1924. With a career 328-432 record as a manager, he would coach on McGraw's Giants (1925–28), but he was buried by the stock market crash in 1929. After coaching two years with the Tigers, he suffered hard times during the Great Depression, finding jobs as a security guard, manual laborer, and beer salesman. Bresnahan died of a heart attack in December 1944 at the age of sixty-five. He was inducted into the Hall of Fame the following summer.

With a background in engineering, **Harry "Moose" McCormick** never had a problem with change. Matty's old college buddy from Bucknell only played five full seasons in the majors, but was one of the first and best pinch-hitting specialists, hitting .301 in ninety-three calls from the bench. Overall, he charted a .285 career mark, but was best remembered in baseball circles for scoring the run that didn't count to end the "Merkle Game" in 1908. Away from baseball, Moose worked in the steel industry, fought in France during the Great War, and was a civilian director with the army during World War II. In between, McCormick was a successful college baseball coach. At Bucknell from 1923 to 1925, his Bison were 27-15-1. He then succeeded Hans Lobert—the old Phillies outfielder—to run the baseball program at the U.S. Military Academy, going 83-59-1 from 1926 to 1936, including an 11-2 mark with the Cadets in 1932. There were also two seasons as Bucknell basketball coach, but a 2-10 overall record hardly tops his résumé. After World War II, Moose returned to Bucknell as director of alumni housing, with Betty Cook describing him as a "gruff old man with a heart of gold."[11] McCormick died in 1962 and is buried near the Mathewson gravesite in the Lewisburg Cemetery.

Most of the old Giants would manage to carve out a decent life after baseball. **Frank Bowerman** owned a 100-acre fruit farm in northern Michigan, **Hooks Wiltse** became a politician, **Art Devlin** a loan officer, **Red Ames** worked for a dairy company, and **George Burns** managed in the minors and ran a pool hall.

But not everyone found comfort. In 1910, **Dan McGann**—the first baseman who eight years earlier had jumped the Orioles to follow John McGraw—committed suicide. In 1953, **Buck Herzog** was found homeless and destitute in Baltimore, dying of tuberculosis. **Arthur "Bugs" Raymond**—the troubled alcoholic spitball pitcher—would run out of warnings from McGraw in June 1911. Bugs died the following summer of a fractured skull, the result of back-to-back Chicago bar fights that included being hit on the head with a baseball bat.

John McGraw, of course, always figured he would die going nose to nose with an umpire on the field of battle. But Little Napoleon's health threw a wicked curve, forcing his retirement on June 3, 1932. "Life without baseball," said Blanche McGraw, "had little meaning for him. It was his meat, his drink, his dream, his blood and breath, his reason for existence."[12]

John McGraw was sixty years old when cancer took his life on February 25, 1934.

APPENDIX C

Deadball Players in the Hall of Fame

The National Baseball Hall of Fame includes eighty-two inductees who were players, managers, umpires, or executives in the American or National Leagues during the Deadball Era. The list is arranged by the decade of induction, name (primary position and team).

Charter Class (1936): Ty Cobb (CF, Detroit Tigers); Walter "Big Train" Johnson (P, Washington Senators); Christy Mathewson (P, New York Giants); Babe Ruth (RF, New York Yankees); Honus Wagner (SS, Pittsburgh Pirates).

1930s: Ban Johnson (executive); Nap Lajoie (2B, Cleveland Indians); Connie Mack (MGR, Philadelphia Athletics); John McGraw (MGR, Giants); Tris Speaker (CF, Indians); Cy Young (P, Cleveland Spiders); Grover Cleveland Alexander (P, Philadelphia Phillies); Eddie Collins (2B, Athletics); Charles Comiskey (executive); Wee Willie Keeler (RF, New York Highlanders); George Sisler (1B, St. Louis Browns).

1940s: Rogers Hornsby (2B, St. Louis Cardinals); Roger Bresnahan (C, Giants); Fred Clarke (LF, Pirates); Jimmy Collins (3B, Pirates); Ed Delahanty (LF, Phillies); Hugh Duffy (CF, Boston Beaneaters); Hugh Jennings (SS, Baltimore Orioles–NL); Wilbert "Uncle Robbie" Robinson (MGR, Brooklyn Robins); Jesse Burkett (LF, Spiders); Frank Chance (1B, Chicago Cubs); Jack Chesbro (P, Highlanders); Johnny Evers (2B, Cubs); Clark Griffith (executive); Joe "Iron Man" McGinnity (P, Giants); Eddie Plank (P, Athletics); Joe Tinker (SS, Cubs); Rube

Waddell (P, Athletics); Ed Walsh (P, Chicago White Sox); Herb Pennock (P, Yankees); Mordecai "Three Finger" Brown (P, Cubs); Kid Nichols (P, Beaneaters).

1950s: Henry Heilmann (RF, Tigers); Charles Albert "Chief" Bender (P, Athletics); Tom Connolly (umpire); Bill Klem (umpire); Bobby Wallace (SS, Browns); Rabbit Maranville (SS, Boston Braves); Frank "Home Run" Baker (3B, Athletics); Ray Schalk (C, White Sox); Dazzy Vance (P, Dodgers); Sam "Wahoo" Crawford (RF, Tigers); Zack Wheat (LF, Dodgers).

1960s: Max Carey (CF, Pirates); Billy Hamilton (CF, Beaneaters); Bill McKechnie (MGR, Cincinnati Reds); Edd Roush (CF, Reds); Elmer Flick (RF, Indians); Sam Rice (RF, Senators); Eppa Rixey (P, Reds); Red Faber (P, White Sox); Burleigh Grimes (P, Dodgers); Miller Huggins (MGR, Yankees); Casey Stengel (MGR, Yankees); Branch Rickey (executive); Stan Coveleski (P, Indians); Waite Hoyte (P, Yankees).

1970s: Jesse Haines (P, Cardinals); Dave Bancroft (P, Phillies); Jake "Eagle Eye" Beckley (1B, Pirates); Harry Hooper (RF, Boston Red Sox); Joe Kelley (LF, Orioles–NL); Rube Marquard (P, Giants); Will Harridge (executive); Ross Youngs (RF, Giants); Billy Evans (umpire); George Kelly (1B, Giants); Sam Thompson (RF, Phillies); Amos Rusie (P, Giants); Addie Joss (P, Indians).

1990s: Vic Willis (P, Beaneaters); Ned Hanlon (MGR, Orioles–NL); George Davis (SS, Giants); Frank Selee (MGR, Beaneaters).

2000–2014: Barney Dreyfuss (executive); Hank O'Day (umpire); Jacob Rupert (executive).

There also are sixteen inductees from the early Negro Leagues who played in the first two decades of the twentieth century. A few, like Rube Foster and Jose Mendez, played in exhibition games against Christy Mathewson. Again, the list includes the decade of induction, name (position, primary team).

1970s: Judy Johnson (3B, Hilldale Daisies); Oscar Charleston (CF, Pittsburgh Crawfords); John Henry "Pop" Lloyd (SS, New York Lincoln Giants).

1980s: Charles "Bullet" Rogan (P, Kansas City Monarchs).

1990s: Rube Foster (MGR, Chicago American Giants), "Cyclone" Joe Williams (P, NY Lincoln Giants).

2000–2014: Frank Grant (2B, Philadelphia Giants); Pete Hill (CF, Cuban X-Giants); Jose Mendez (P, Cuban Stars); Alex Pompey (executive); Cum Posey (executive); Louis Santop (C, NY Lincoln Giants); Ben Taylor (1B, Indianapolis ABCs); Sol White (executive); Cristobal Torriente (CF, Cuban Stars); J. L. Wilkinson (executive).

NOTES

.

INTRODUCTION

1. Quoted from Tom Simon, ed., *Deadball Stars of the National League* (Cleveland: Society for American Baseball Research, 2004), 75.

I. THE BOY WONDER FROM BUCKNELL (1901)

1. Blanche Sindall McGraw, *The Real McGraw* (New York: McKay, 1953), 181.

2. Ibid., 183.

3. Arthur Daley quoting Fred Lieb, "The Early Years of Christy Mathewson," *New York Times*, December 13, 1942.

4. John Howard Harris, *Thirty Years as President of Bucknell* (Washington, D.C.: Roberts, 1926), 35.

5. Ibid., 139.

6. Ibid., 238

7. Grantland Rice, "Greater Than His Game," *New York Herald-Tribune*, October 9, 1925.

8. Connie Mack, *My 66 Years in the Big Leagues* (Philadelphia: John C. Winston, 1950), 99.

9. Arthur Daley, *Inside Baseball: A Half Century of the National Pastime* (New York: Grosset & Dunlap), 44.

10. Harris, 316.

11. Ibid., 332.

2. A NEAR PERFECT BOYHOOD (1889)

1. John Howard Harris, *Thirty Years as President of Bucknell* (Washington, D.C.: W.F. Roberts Company, 1926), 238.

2. Ibid., 139.

3. "Matty's Boyhood," *Literary Digest*, June 6, 1914.

4. Ibid.

5. "Mathewson's Folks," *Baseball* magazine, December 1914, 40.

6. C. H. Claudy and Christy Mathewson, *The Battle of Base-Ball* (New York: Century, 1912), 321.

7. Ibid., 317.

8. Christy Mathewson, "My Life So Far," *Baseball* magazine, December 1914, 53.

9. Harris, XX.

10. Ibid., XIII.

11. Ibid., XXVIII.

12. Ibid., XXVII.

13. Ibid., XVI.

14. Claudy and Mathewson, 319.

15. Ibid., 322.

16. Ibid.

17. Ibid., 323.

18. Ibid.

19. Mathewson, 54.

20. Claudy and Mathewson, 329.

21. Ibid., 330.

22. Ibid., 334

23. "Matty's Boyhood," 3.

24. Frank W. Stanton, "Those Were the Days," *Bucknell Alumnus*, January 1949, 1.

25. Ibid.

26. Harris, 255.

27. Ibid., 271.

28. Christy Mathewson, "Freshman Class History," *1900 Bucknell L'Agenda*.

29. Claudy and Mathewson, 336.

30. *Honesdale* (PA) *Citizen*, July 17, 1899.

31. Christy Mathewson letter to parents, National Baseball Hall of Fame, July 1899.

32. Mathewson, 55.

33. Ibid.

34. Ibid.

35. *New York Times*, October 5, 1899.

36. Ibid.

37. Ibid.

38. Ibid.

3. BREATHING IN THE SMOKER (1900)

1. C. H. Claudy and Christy Mathewson, *The Battle of Base-Ball* (New York: Century, 1912), 348.

2. Christy Mathewson, "My Life So Far," *Baseball* magazine, December 1914, 57.

3. Ibid., 56.

4. Ibid., 57.

5. Claudy and Mathewson, 340.

6. Bayard Still, *Mirror for Gotham: New York as Seen by Contemporaries* (New York: Fordham University Press, 1999), 279.

7. Ibid., 280.

8. Ibid., 276.

9. *New York Times*, December 31, 1899.

10. Still, 279.

11. Ibid., 277.

12. George B. Tindall and David E. Shi, *America: A Narrative History* (New York: Norton, 1984), 940.

13. J. G. Taylor Spink, "Down Memory Lane," *Sporting News*, April 20, 1959.

14. Mathewson, 58.

15. Fred Lieb, *Baseball as I Have Known It* (New York: Grosset & Dunlap, 1977), 42.

16. Mathewson, 59.

17. *St. Louis Daily-Globe Democrat*, July 16, 1901.

18. "Mathewson a Money-Maker," *New York Evening World*, October 9, 1901.

19. Mathewson, 60.

20. Blanche Sindall McGraw, *The Real McGraw* (New York: McKay, 1953), 181.

21. *New York Times*, April 18, 1902.

22. *New York Times*, May 22, 1902.

23. McGraw, 184.

24. *New York Times*, July 3, 1902.

25. Arthur Daley, "Sports of the Times," *New York Times*, December 13, 1948.

4. DUMPING ON THE YANNIGAN (1901)

1. Lawrence S. Ritter, *The Glory of Their Times: The Story of the Early Days of Baseball Told by the Men who Played It* (New York: Macmillan, 1966), 62.

2. Al Stump, *Cobb: A Biography* (Chapel Hill, N.C.: Algonquin, 1996), 119.

3. Ritter, 34.

4. Connie Mack, *My 66 Years in the Big Leagues* (Philadelphia: John C. Winston, 1950), 20.

5. Connie Mack, "The Bad Old Days," in *The American Story: The Drama and Adventure of Our Country since 1728 as told by The Saturday Evening Post* (Indianapolis: Curtis, 1975), 217.

6. Charles Fountain, *Sportswriter: The Life and Times of Grantland Rice* (New York: Oxford University Press, 1993), 122.

7. Frank Deford, *The Old Ball Game: How John McGraw, Christy Mathewson, and the New York Giants Created Modern Baseball* (New York: Atlantic Monthly Press, 2005), 27.

8. Tom Simon, ed., *Deadball Stars of the National League* (Washington, D.C.: Brasseys, 2004), 39.

9. John J. McGraw, *My Thirty Years in Baseball* (New York: Boni and Liveright, 1923), 175.

10. Simon, 5.

11. Anthony J. Connor, *Baseball for the Love of It: Hall of Famers Tell It Like It Was* (New York: Macmillan, 1982), 105.

12. Ritter, 99.

13. O. K. Armstrong and Marjorie Armstrong, *The Baptists in America* (New York: Doubleday, 1979), 225.

14. Justo L. Gonzalez, *The Story of Christianity, Volume II: The Reformation to the Present Day* (New York: HarperCollins, 2010), 342.

15. U.S. Department of Commerce, Bureau of the Census. *Historical Statistics of the United States: Colonial Times to 1970, Part 1* (Washington, D.C.: Author, 1975), 391.

5. HIT THE ROAD, SLACKER (1902)

1. Lawrence S. Ritter, *The Glory of Their Times* (New York: Macmillan, 1966), 91.

2. Frank Graham, *McGraw of the Giants: An Informal Biography* (New York: Putnam, 1944), 29.

3. John J. McGraw, *My Thirty Years in Baseball* (New York: Boni and Liveright, 1923), 139.

4. Ibid.

5. Blanche Sindall McGraw, *The Real McGraw* (New York: McKay, 1953), 220.

6. Anthony J. Connor, *Baseball for the Love of It*. (New York: Macmillan, 1982), 102.

7. Ibid., 103

8. John McGraw, 179.

9. *St. Louis Star-Times*, April 25, 1932.

10. *St. Louis Star*, July 6, 1902.

11. *Sporting Life*, December 6, 1902.

12. Ibid.

13. *St. Louis Post-Dispatch*, December 15, 1902.

14. *St. Louis Star*, July 6, 1902.

15. *St. Louis Star-Times*, April 25, 1932.

16. *Lewisburg Journal*, March 7, 1903.\

17. Ibid.

18. Blanche McGraw, 190.

19. Jane Mathewson memories (from interview with Betty Cook).

20. Blanche McGraw, 190.

21. Jane Mathewson memories.

22. Blanche McGraw, 190.

23. Ibid.

24. Ibid., 215.

25. Frank Deford, *The Old Ball Game* (New York: Atlantic Monthly Press, 2005), 172.

26. Ibid., 173.

27. John McGraw, 175.

28. Christy Mathewson, *Pitching in a Pinch* (New York: Grosset & Dunlap, 1912), 98.

29. John McGraw, 140.

30. Ibid., 141.

31. Blanche McGraw, 191.

32. Ibid.

33. Ibid., 194.

6. MATTY AND THE IRON MAN (1903)

1. Frank Graham, *McGraw of the Giants* (New York: Putnam, 1944), 35.
2. Blanche Sindall McGraw, *The Real McGraw* (New York: McKay, 1953), 203.
3. *New York Times*, September 1, 1903.
4. Connie Mack, *My 66 Years in the Big Leagues* (Philadelphia: John C. Winston, 1950), 65.
5. John J. McGraw, *My Thirty Years in Baseball* (New York: Boni and Liveright, 1923), 121.
6. Blanche Sindall McGraw, 191.
7. Frank Deford, *The Old Ball Game* (New York: Atlantic Monthly Press, 2005), 69 (emphasis in original).
8. Geoffrey C. Ward and Ken Burns, *Baseball: An Illustrated History* (New York: Knopf, 1994), 69.
9. Blanche Sindall McGraw, 202.
10. *New York Evening World*, October 1, 1904.
11. Ward and Burns, 68.

7. A BUSY MIND (1905)

1. John J. McGraw, *My Thirty Years in Baseball* (New York: Boni and Liveright, 1923), 142.
2. Ibid., 226.
3. Daniel Okrent and Harris Lewine, *The Ultimate Baseball Book* (Boston: Houghton Mifflin, 1979), 72.
4. Lawrence S. Ritter, *The Glory of Their Times* (New York: Macmillan, 1966), 96.
5. Damon Runyon, *Bucknell Alumni Monthly*, November 1925.
6. Bozeman Bulger, *New York Sun*, February 18, 1921.
7. Ray Robinson, *Matty: An American Hero* (New York: Oxford University Press, 1993), 123.
8. *Philadelphia Inquirer*, April 30, 1905.
9. McGraw, 159.
10. *Chicago Daily Tribune*, June 14, 1905.

11. Connie Mack, *My 66 Years in the Big Leagues* (Philadelphia: John C. Winston, 1950), 92.

12. Jane Mathewson letter, courtesy of Betty Cook.

13. Mack, 100.

14. *New York Times*, October 15, 1905.

15. Allison Danzig, *Oh, How They Played the Game: The Early Days of Football and the Heroes Who Made It Great* (New York: Macmillan, 1971), 202.

16. Robert J. Higgs, *God in the Stadium: Sports & Religion in America* (Lexington: University Press of Kentucky, 1995), 264.

17. Richard Whittingham, *Rites of Autumn: The Story of College Football* (New York: Free Press, 2001), 38.

18. Christy Mathewson, "My Life So Far," *Baseball* magazine, December 1914, 56.

19. H. W. Brands, *TR: The Last Romantic* (New York: Basic Books, 1998), 553.

20. Danzig, 152.

8. TINKER TO EVERS TO CHANCE, OH MY (1906)

1. Blanche Sindall McGraw, *The Real McGraw* (New York: McKay, 1953), 213.

2. Ibid.

3. Tom Simon, ed., *Deadball Stars of the National League* (Washington, D.C.: Brasseys, 2004), 91.

4. Ibid., 97.

5. Ibid., 100.

6. McGraw, 213.

7. Samuel Eliot Morison, *Oxford History of the American People* (New York: Oxford University Press, 1965), 816.

9. NICKEL PLATE ROAD (1907)

1. *Los Angeles Sun*, March 10, 1907.

2. Tom Simon, ed., *Deadball Stars of the National League* (Washington, D.C.: Brasseys, 2004), 348.

3. Grantland Rice, "Football Alumnus," *Pittsburgh Press*, November 2, 1914.

4. Grantland Rice, "Greater Than His Game," *New York Herald-Tribune*, October 9, 1925.

5. Frank Deford, *The Old Ball Game* (New York: Atlantic Monthly Press, 2005), 125.

6. Ibid., 124.

7. Ibid., 37.

8. Interview with Betty Cook.

9. *New York Herald-Tribune*, October 9, 1925.

10. Damon Runyon, *Bucknell Alumni Monthly*, November 1925.

11. Deford, 131.

12. Lawrence S. Ritter, *The Glory of Their Times* (New York: Macmillan, 1956), 176.

10. THE SMARTEST BONEHEAD IN BASEBALL (1908)

1. Ray Robinson, *Matty: An American Hero* (New York: Oxford University Press, 1993), 92.

2. John M. Rosenburg, *The Story of Baseball: A Completely Illustrated and Exciting History of America's National Game* (New York: Random House, 1973), 60.

3. *Sporting Life*, August 22, 1908.

4. John J. McGraw, *My Thirty Years in Baseball* (New York: Boni and Liveright, 1923), 181.

5. Lawrence S. Ritter, *The Glory of Their Times* (New York: Macmillan, 1966), 106.

6. Harry J. Casey, "Famous Bone-Head Plays," *Baseball* magazine, January 1914, 51.

7. Ritter, 136.

8. William Klem and William Slocum, "Jousting with McGraw," *Collier's* magazine, April 7, 1951, 50.

9. Christy Mathewson, *Pitching in a Pinch* (New York: Grosset & Dunlap, 1912), 189.

10. Cait Murphy, *Crazy '08: How a Cast of Cranks, Rogues, Boneheads, and Magnates Created the Greatest Year in Baseball History* (New York: Smithsonian Books, 2007), 195.

11. *New York Sun*, September 24, 1908.

12. McGraw, 181.

13. W. W. Aulick, *New York Times*, September 24, 1908.

14. Ibid.

15. Arthur Daley, *Inside Baseball* (New York: Grosset & Dunlap 1950), 33.

16. Ritter, 132.

17. Mathewson, 184.

18. Ibid.

19. Ibid., 191.

20. Ibid., 201.

21. Frank Deford, *The Old Ball Game* (New York: Atlantic Monthly Press, 2005), 146.

22. Rosenburg, 57.

23. Ibid.

24. Murphy, 264.

25. Deford, 146.

26. Mathewson, 185.

27. Harry Grayson, *They Played the Game* (New York: Barnes, 1945), 89.

28. Ritter, 180.

29. Joseph Durso, *The Days of Mr. McGraw* (Upper Saddle River, N.J: Prentiss-Hall, 1969), 75.

30. Mathewson, 205.

31. McGraw, 180.

32. Ritter, 118.

33. Ibid.

34. Ibid.

11. A DEEPLY PRIVATE GRIEF (1909)

1. "Mathewson's Folks," *Baseball* magazine, December 1914, 40.

2. William A. Phelon, "Reminiscences of Christy Mathewson," *Baseball* magazine, December 1914, 46.

3. Connie Mack, *My 66 Years in the Big Leagues* (Philadelphia: John C. Winston, 1950), 149.

4. *New York Herald*, May 5, 1908.

5. *New York Times*, October 15, 1905.

6. Fred Lieb, *Baseball as I Have Known It* (New York: Grosset & Dunlap, 1977), 29.

7. Robert E. Streeter, ed., *Bucknell Now & Then: A Sesquicentennial Miscellany* (Dallas: Taylor Publishing, 1995), 115.

8. "Mathewson Trims Checker Sharps," *El Paso Herald*, November 12, 1909.

9. Roger Kahn, *The Head Game: Baseball Seen from the Pitcher's Mound* (San Diego: Harcourt, 2000).

10. *New York Daily Tribune*, "Christy at the Tee: The Idol of Fans Plays Golf at Westchester," June 18, 1906.

11. Phelon, 48.

12. Kate Carew, *New York Journal-American*, April 24, 1910.

13. Idah McGlone Gibson, "Christy Mathewson as Seen by a Woman," *Chicago Day Book*, October 5, 1912.

14. Christy Mathewson, "My Life So Far," *Baseball* magazine, December 1914, 53.

15. "Matty's Boyhood," *Literary Digest*, June 6, 1914, 2.

16. Ibid.

17. "New Plays and Old Favorites," *New York Tribune*, October 19, 1913.

18. Bozeman Bulger, *New York Sun*, February 18, 1921.

19. Arthur Daley, "Matty the Great," *New York Times*, August 26, 1957.

20. Lawrence S. Ritter, *The Glory of Their Times* (New York: Macmillan, 1966), 260.

21. Leigh Montville, *The Big Bam: The Life and Times of Babe Ruth* (New York: Doubleday, 2006), 47.

22. Streeter, 115.

23. *New York Times*, May 3, 1910.

24. Ibid.

25. Jimmy Breslin, *Damon Runyon: A Life* (New York: Dell, 1991), 81.

26. Jonathan Eig, *Luckiest Man: The Life and Death of Lou Gehrig* (New York: Simon & Schuster, 2005), 14.

27. Ibid., 30.

28. John J. McGraw, *My Thirty Years in Baseball* (New York: Boni and Liveright, 1923), 98.

12. HIGH SPIKES FOR THE CHIEF (1911)

1. Jane Mathewson letter, courtesy of Betty Cook.

2. John J. McGraw, *My Thirty Years in Baseball* (New York: Boni and Liveright, 1923), 197.

3. Christy Mathewson, *Pitching in a Pinch* (New York: Grosset & Dunlap, 1912), 211.

4. Jimmy Breslin, *Damon Runyon: A Life* (New York: Dell, 1991), 125.

5. Ibid., 226

6. Ibid., 81.

7. David von Drehle, *Triangle: The Fire that Changed America* (New York: Grove Press, 2004), 265.

8. Frank Graham, *McGraw of the Giants* (New York: Putnam, 1944), 3.

9. Lawrence S. Ritter, *The Glory of Their Times* (New York: Macmillan, 1966), 131.

10. Ibid.

11. McGraw, 198.

12. Charles Fountain, *Sportswriter* (New York: Oxford University Press, 1993), 120.

13. Mathewson, 237.

14. Ibid., 233.

15. *Fulton* (Missouri) *County News*, April 20, 1911.

16. Fred Lieb, *Baseball as I Have Known It* (New York: Grosset & Dunlap, 1977), 81.

17. McGraw, 200.

18. Ibid.

19. Anthony J. Connor, *Baseball for the Love of It* (New York: Macmillan, 1982), 174.

20. Mathewson, 244.

21. Ritter, 101.

22. Ibid., 173.

23. Ibid., 173.

24. *New York Times*, "Giants Champions," October 15, 1905.

25. Ibid.

26. Michael Hartley, *Christy Mathewson: A Biography* (Jefferson, N.C.: McFarland, 2004), 48.

27. John Howard Harris, *Thirty Years as President of Bucknell* (Washington, D.C.: Roberts, 1926), 195.

28. Ibid., 495.

29. Harris, 399.

30. Blanche Sindall McGraw, *The Real McGraw* (New York: McKay, 1953), 237.

31. Ibid.

13. A FATEFUL DAY AT FENWAY (1912)

1. Daniel Okrent and Harris Lewine, *The Ultimate Baseball Book* (Boston: Houghton Mifflin, 1979), 87.

2. *New York Times*, October 6, 1912.

3. Mike Vaccarro, *The First Fall Classic: The Red Sox, the Giants, and the Cast of Players, Pugs, and Politicos Who Reinvented the World Series in 1912* (New York: Doubleday, 2009), 63.

4. Ibid., 223.

5. Ibid., 169.

6. Henry F. Pringle, *Theodore Roosevelt: A Biography* (New York: Harcourt, Brace, & World, 1956), 399.

7. Vaccarro, 218.

8. Okrent and Lewine, 75.

9. Ibid., 237.

10. Lawrence S. Ritter, *The Glory of Their Times* (New York: Macmillan, 1966), 110.

11. Ibid., 183.

12. Vaccarro, 259.

13. T. H. Murnane, *Boston Globe*, October 17, 1912.

14. Vaccarro, 265.

15. Ritter, 262.

16. Vaccarro, 264.

17. Ibid., 262.

18. Ibid.

19. *New York Times*, October 17, 1912.

20. Christy Mathewson, "Why We Lost Three Straight Championships," *Everybody's* magazine, October, 1941, 21.

21. Tom Simon, ed., *Deadball Stars of the National League* (Washington, D.C.: Brasseys, 2004), 65.

22. "Fred Snodgrass, 86, Dead, Ball Player Muffed 1912 Fly." *New York Times*, April 6, 1974.

23. Fred Lieb, *Baseball as I Have Known It* (New York: Grosset & Dunlap, 1977), 102.

24. John J. McGraw, *My Thirty Years in Baseball* (New York: Boni and Liveright, 1923), 168.

25. Ritter, 165.

26. Okrent and Lewine, 75.

27. Ritter, 182.

28. Philip Seib, *The Player: Christy Mathewson, Baseball, and the American Century* (New York: Four Walls Eight Windows, 2003), 77.

29. Grantland Rice, "The Essential Ingredient," *Baseball* magazine, April 24, 1920, 13.

30. Okrent and Lewine, 66.

31. *Bucknellian*, October 7, 1925.

32. Ritter, 176.

33. Christy Mathewson, *Pitching in a Pinch* (New York: Grosset & Dunlap, 1912).

34. Arthur Daley, "Matty the Great," *New York Times*, August 26, 1957.

35. Max Carey, "Why Matty Lasts," *Literary Digest*, August 23, 1913.

36. Connie Mack, *My 66 Years in the Big Leagues* (Philadelphia: John C. Winston, 1950), 100.

37. McGraw, 142.

38. Arthur Daley, *Inside Baseball* (New York: Grosset & Dunlap), 43.

39. McGraw, 143.

40. Charles Fountain, *Sportswriter* (New York: Oxford University Press, 1993), 121.

41. Ibid., 120.

42. *New York Sun*, June 7, 1913.

43. Lewis Edwin Theiss, "The Complete Story of Matty's Life," *Bucknell Alumni Monthly*, November 1925, 4.

44. A. R. E. Wyant, "Soldier and Christian Gentleman," *Bucknell World*, March 1956, 3.

45. Al Stump, *Cobb: A Biography* (Chapel Hill, N.C.: Algonquin, 1996), 276.

14. PEBBLES ON A BARREN SHORE (1913)

1. "Thorpe in Baseball," *Literary Digest*, February 15, 1913, 363.

2. Ibid.

3. Ibid.

4. Daniel Okrent and Harris Lewine, *The Ultimate Baseball Book* (Boston: Houghton Mifflin, 1979), 73.

5. Frank Deford, *The Old Ball Game* (New York: Atlantic Monthly Press, 2005), 190.

6. *Christy Mathewson Memorial Stadium Rededication Program*, September 30, 1989, 27.

7. *Scranton Republican*, December 25, 1913.

8. *New York Tribune*, October 9, 1913.

9. *New York Herald*, October 12, 1913.

10. Christy Mathewson, "Why We Lost Three World's Championships," *Everybody's* magazine, October 1914, 12.

11. Ibid., 14.

12. Ibid.

13. Ibid., 15.

14. Ibid., 21.

15. THE WORLD'S LONGEST BASEBALL ADVENTURE (1913–1914)

1. *New York Herald*, October 18, 1913.

2. James E. Elfers, *The Tour to End All Tours: The Story of Major League Baseball's 1913–1914 World Tour* (Lincoln: University of Nebraska Press, 2003), 10.

3. Lawrence S. Ritter, *The Glory of Their Times* (New York: Macmillan, 1966), 35.

4. *Cincinnati Enquirer*, October 19, 1913.

5. Gus Axelson, *Chicago Daily Tribune*, October 25, 1913.

6. Ibid.

7. *Joplin Daily Globe*, October 21, 1913.

8. Ritter, 196.

9. Ibid.

10. Ibid.

11. Ibid.

12. *Chicago Daily Tribune*, November 14, 1913.

13. *San Francisco Chronicle*, November 13, 1913.

14. *San Francisco Examiner*, November 16, 1913.

15. Ray Robinson, *Matty* (New York: Oxford University Press. 1993), 164 (emphasis in original).

16. William A. Phelon, "Reminiscences of Christy Mathewson," *Baseball* magazine, December 1914, 47.

17. Christy Mathewson, "My Life So Far," *Baseball* magazine, December 1914, 63.

18. Frank G. Menke, "Christy Mathewson's Case a Puzzle," *World of Baseball*, June 17, 1916, 9.

19. Mathewson, 66.

20. "Ball Players Hit 'Em with a Gun," *American Shooter*, January 1, 1916, 44.

21. Ritter, 21.

22. Daniel Okrent and Harris Lewine, *The Ultimate Baseball Book* (Boston: Houghton Mifflin, 1979), 96.

23. Christy Mathewson, *Pitching in a Pinch* (New York: Grosset & Dunlap, 1912), 168.

24. Ibid., 172.

25. Ibid., 174.

26. Anthony J. Connor, *Baseball for the Love of It* (New York: Macmillan, 1982), 114.

27. Ibid.

28. Ritter, 20.

29. Mathewson, *Pitching in a Pinch*, 168.

30. Ritter, 25.

16. SAY IT AIN'T SO, JOE (1916)

1. *New York Times*, May 30, 1916.

2. Damon Runyon, "How New York Feels about Mathewson," *World of Baseball*, August 5, 1916, 5.

3. Frank Graham, *McGraw of the Giants* (New York: Putnam, 1944), 89.

4. Lawrence S. Ritter, *The Glory of Their Times* (New York: Macmillan, 1966), 226.

5. *Philadelphia Evening Ledger*, July 21, 1916.

6. Christy Mathewson, *Pitching in a Pinch* (New York: Grosset & Dunlap, 1912), 83–84.

7. William B. Hanna, *New York Herald*, March 12, 1921.

8. W. J. MacBeth, "Matty, Idol of Polo Grounds, Who Is Making Good as Manager of Reds," *New York Tribune*, July 15, 1917, 4.

9. "Live Topics of the National League," *Sporting Life*, March 24, 1917, 3.

10. Christy Mathewson, "My Life So Far," *Baseball* magazine, December 1914, 64.

11. John Howard Harris, *Thirty Years as President of Bucknell* (Washington, D.C.: Roberts, 1926), 87.

12. U.S. Department of Commerce, Bureau of the Census. *Historical Statistics of the United States: Colonial Times to 1970, Part 1* (Washington, D.C.: Author, 1975), 391.

13. George M. Marsden, *Fundamentalism and American Culture: The Shaping of Twentieth Century Evangelicalism 1870–1925* (New York: Oxford University Press, 1980), 130.

14. Ibid., 142.

15. Ibid.

16. H. W. Brands, *TR* (New York: Basic Books, 1998), 716.

17. W. A. Phelon, "The Month in Baseball," *Baseball* magazine, December 1918, 92.

18. Harris, 89.

19. Al Stump, *Cobb* (Chapel Hill, N.C.: Algonquin, 1996), 276.

20. Ibid.

21. *New York Evening Telegram*, August 14, 1921.

17. THE SHADOW OF GREATER DAYS (1920)

1. Jane Mathewson memories, from interview with Betty Cook.

2. John B. Foster, ed., *Spalding's Official Baseball Guide—1913* (New York: American Sports Publishing Co.), 18.

3. "He Kept the Faith," *Toledo* (Ohio) *Blade*, October 24, 1925.

4. Helena Williams, "The Come-Back of Christy Mathewson," *Journal of the Outdoor Life*, February 1924, 77.

5. Bill James, *The Bill James Historical Baseball Abstract* (New York: Villard Books, 1986), 851.

6. Bozeman Bulger, *New York Sun*, March 1, 1921.

7. "Fans Are All with Mathewson," *Boston Post*, April 11, 1921.

8. Ibid.

9. *New York Times*, December 19, 1922.

10. "The Fight of a Clean Sportsman," *Outlook*, 131, May–August 1922, 481.

11. *New York Herald-Tribune*, October 2, 1921.

12. Fred Lieb, *Baseball as I Have Known It* (New York: Grosset & Dunlap, 1977), 155.

13. Ibid., 157.

14. "Big Six Confident He Will Win Out in Fight for Life," *New York Tribune*, October 1, 1921.

15. *New York Times*, December 19, 1922.

16. Ibid.

17. Sinclair Lewis, *Babbitt* (New York: Penguin, 1996).

18. *New York Herald-Tribune*, 1923.

19. Lucian Cary, "Mathewson's Biggest Victory," *Good Housekeeping*, August 1923, 174.

20. John Howard Harris, *Thirty Years as President of Bucknell* (Washington, D.C.: Roberts, 1926), 467.

21. Andrew R. E. Wyant, "Christy Mathewson—Great Athlete, Soldier and Christian Gentleman," *Bucknell World*, March 1956, 3.

22. Ibid., xli.

23. Ibid., xxxiii.

24. Union County (PA) Planning Commission, "Historical Site Survey #19," 1976.

25. Al Stump, *Cobb* (Chapel Hill, N.C.: Algonquin, 1996), 276.

26. W. O. McGeehan, "Mathewson's Adieu Softens Funeral Grief," *New York Herald-Tribune*, October 11, 1925.

27. Ibid.

28. Daniel Okrent and Harris Lewine, *The Ultimate Baseball Book* (Boston: Houghton Mifflin, 1979), 80.

29. *New York Herald-Tribune*, October 9, 1925.

30. Lawrence S. Ritter, *The Glory of Their Times* (New York: Macmillan, 1966), 176.

31. *New York Times*, October 11, 1925.

32. John J. McGraw, "McGraw Pays His Last Tribute to Mathewson's Bier," *Savannah Press,* October 9, 1925.

33. Stump, 276.

34. "Christy Mathewson," *Youth's Companion*, November 12, 1925.

35. *New York Herald-Tribune*, October 9, 1925.

18. THE FAMILY NAME (1929)

1. *Sunbury* (PA) *Item*, April 10, 1929.

2. *Bucknell L'Agenda*, 1927, 91.

3. Interview with Anna Outwater Day, Harrisonburg, Virginia, December 2003.

4. Interview with Betty Cook, Lewisburg, Pennsylvania, January 2004.

5. *North American Newspaper Alliance*, November 27, 1930.

6. "Judge Landis Praises Christy Mathewson in Radio Speech," *Bucknellian*, June 11, 1928.

7. Cook interview.

8. *North American Newspaper Alliance*, November 27, 1930.

9. Ibid.

10. Bucknell University Archives, Letter to Alumni Secretary Al Stoughton from Christy Mathewson, Jr., July 1930.

11. Cook interview.

12. *Sunbury Item*, January 17, 1931.

13. *Philadelphia Inquirer*, November 25, 1932.

14. *Philadelphia Inquirer*, January 9, 1933.

15. Ibid.

16. *Philadelphia Public Ledger*, May 15, 1933.

17. Ibid.

18. Ibid.

19. Grantland Rice, "The Mathewson Boys," *North American Paper Alliance*, May 19, 1942.

20. J. G. Taylor Spink, "Down Memory Lane with Mrs. Christy Mathewson," *Sporting News*, April 27, 1959.

21. Frank Ross, "Mathewson Jr. Wills Victory," *New York Sun*, May 26, 1942.

22. *New York Sun*, May 25, 1942.

23. Bucknell University Special Collections/Archives, Letter to President Arnaud C. Marts from Christy Mathewson, Jr., January 30, 1944.

24. Spink.

25. Cook interview.

26. Ibid.

27. National Baseball Hall of Fame, 1955 Induction Invitation.

28. Cook interview.

29. Ibid.

30. Ibid.

31. Ibid.

32. Ibid.

33. Ibid.

34. Spink.

35. Ken Smith, "Jane Mathewson, Widow of Beloved Christy, Still Queen of Balldom," *Scrantonian*, August 7, 1966.

36. Cook interview.

37. Ibid.

38. Ibid.

39. Smith.

APPENDIX B

1. Frank Deford, *The Old Ball Game* (New York: Atlantic Monthly Press, 2005), 110.

2. Tom Simon, ed., *Deadball Stars of the National League* (Washington, D.C.: Brassey's, 2004), 56.

3. Ibid., 60.

4. Cait Murphy, *Crazy '08* (New York: Smithsonian Books, 2008).

5. Lawrence S. Ritter, *The Glory of Their Times* (New York: Macmillan, 1966), 184.

6. *Escondido* (CA) *Daily Times Advocate*, March 25, 1989.

7. Arthur Fletcher scrapbook, property of Jean McCasland.

8. Ibid.

9. Ibid.

10. Ritter, 183.

11. Betty Cook interview.

12. Blanche Sindall McGraw, *The Real McGraw* (New York: McKay, 1953), 190.

BIBLIOGRAPHY

BOOKS

Allen, Frederick Lewis. *Only Yesterday: An Informal History of the Nineteen-Twenties.* New York: Harper & Row, 1964.

Allen, Lee. *The National League Story.* New York: Hill & Wang, 1961.

Armstrong, O. K., and Marjorie Armstrong. *The Baptists in America.* New York: Doubleday, 1979.

Asinof, Eliot. *Eight Men Out: The Black Sox and the 1919 World Series.* New York: Holt, 2000.

Blum, John M., and Bruce Catton. *The National Experience: A History of the United States.* New York: Harcourt, Brace & World, 1968.

Brands, H. W. *TR: The Last Romantic.* New York: Basic Books, 1998.

Breslin, Jimmy. *Damon Runyon: A Life.* New York: Dell, 1991.

Buford, Kate. *Native American Son: The Life and Sporting Legend of Jim Thorpe.* Lincoln, Neb.: Bison Books, 2012.

Churchill, Allen. *Remember When.* New York: Golden Press, 1967.

Claudy, C. H., and Christy Mathewson. *The Battle of Base-Ball.* New York: Century, 1912.

Collier, Peter, and David Horowitz. *The Roosevelts: An American Saga.* New York: Simon & Schuster, 1994.

Connor, Anthony J. *Baseball for the Love of It: Hall of Famers Tell It Like It Was.* New York: Macmillan, 1982.

Daley, Arthur. *Inside Baseball: A Half Century of the National Pastime.* New York: Grosset & Dunlap, 1950.

Danzig, Allison. *Oh, How They Played the Game: The Early Days of Football and the Heroes Who Made It Great.* New York: Macmillan, 1971.

Deford, Frank. *The Old Ball Game: How John McGraw, Christy Mathewson, and the New York Giants Created Modern Baseball.* New York: Atlantic Monthly Press, 2005.

Durso, Joseph. *The Days of Mr. McGraw.* Englewood Cliffs, N.J.: Prentice-Hall, 1969.

Eig, Jonathan. *Luckiest Man: The Life and Death of Lou Gehrig.* New York: Simon & Schuster, 2005.

Elfers, James E. *The Tour to End All Tours: The Story of Major League Baseball's 1913–1914 World Tour.* Lincoln: University of Nebraska Press, 2003.

Evans, Elizabeth. *Ring Lardner.* New York: Ungar, 1979.

Fleming, G. H. *The Unforgettable Season.* New York: Penguin, 1981.

Foster, John B. *Spalding's Official Baseball Guide—1913.* New York: American Sports Publishing Co., 1913.

Fountain, Charles. *Sportswriter: The Life and Times of Grantland Rice*. New York: Oxford University Press, 1993.

Frommer, Harvey. *Shoeless Joe and Ragtime Baseball*. Dallas: Taylor, 1992.

Gonzalez, Justo L. *The Story of Christianity, Volume II: The Reformation to the Present Day*. New York: HarperCollins, 2010.

Graham, Frank. *McGraw of the Giants*. New York: Putnam, 1944.

Graham, Frank. *The New York Giants*. New York: Putnam, 1952.

Grayson, Harry. *They Played the Game*. New York: Barnes, 1945.

Harris, John Howard. *Thirty Years as President of Bucknell*. Washington, D.C.: Roberts, 1926.

Hart, David Bentley. *The Story of Christianity: An Illustrated History of 2000 Years of the Christian Faith*. London: Quercus, 1975.

Hartley, Michael. *Christy Mathewson: A Biography*. Jefferson, N.C.: McFarland, 2004.

Higgs, Robert J. *God in the Stadium: Sports & Religion in America*. Lexington: University Press of Kentucky, 1995.

Honig, Donald. *Baseball America: The Heroes of the Game and the Times of Their Glory*. New York: Galahad, 1993.

Honig, Donald. *The Greatest Pitchers of All Time*. New York: Crown, 1988.

James, Bill. *The Bill James Historical Baseball Abstract*. New York: Villard, 1986.

Jennings, Peter, and Todd Brewster. *The Century*. New York: Doubleday, 1998.

Kahn, Roger. *The Head Game: Baseball Seen from the Pitcher's Mound*. San Diego: Harcourt, 2000.

Keller, Jane Eblen. *Adirondack Wilderness: A Story of Man and Nature*. Syracuse, N.Y.: Syracuse University Press, 1980.

Leventhal, Josh, ed. *Baseball . . . The Perfect Game: An All-Star Anthology Celebrating the Game's Greatest Players, Teams, and Moments*. Stillwater, Minn.: Voyageur Press, 2005.

Lieb, Fred. *Baseball as I Have Known It*. New York: Grosset & Dunlap, 1977.

Lieb, Frederick G. *The Pittsburgh Pirates*. New York: Putnam, 1948.

Lord, Walter. *The Good Years, from 1900 to the First World War*. New York: Harper, 1960.

Mack, Connie. *My 66 Years in the Big Leagues*. Philadelphia: John C. Winston, 1950.

Mack, Connie. "The Bad Old Days." In *The American Story: The Drama and Adventure of Our Country since 1728 as told by the Saturday Evening Post*. Indianapolis: Curtis, 1975.

Marsden, George M. *Fundamentalism and American Culture: The Shaping of Twentieth Century Evangelicalism 1870–1925*. New York: Oxford University Press, 1980.

Mathewson, Christy. *Catcher Craig*. New York: Dodd, Mead, 1915.

Mathewson, Christy. *First Base Faulkner*. New York: Dodd, Mead, 1916.

Mathewson, Christy. *Pitcher Pollock*. New York: Dodd, Mead, 1914.

Mathewson, Christy. *Pitching in a Pinch*. New York: Grosset & Dunlap, 1912.

Mathewson, Christy. *Second Base Sloan*. New York: Dodd, Mead, 1917.

Mathewson, Christy. *Won in the Ninth*. New York: Bodmer, 1910.

May, Ernest R. *The Life History of the United States: The Progressive Era 1901–1917*. New York: Time-Life Books, 1974.

Mayer, Ronald A. *Christy Mathewson: A Game-by-Game Profile of a Legendary Pitcher*. Jefferson, N.C.: McFarland, 1993.

McGerr, Michael. *A Fierce Discontent: The Rise and Fall of the Progressive Movement in America*. New York: Oxford University Press, 2005.

McGraw, Blanche Sindall. *The Real McGraw*. New York: McKay, 1953.

McGraw, John J. *My Thirty Years in Baseball*. New York: Boni and Liveright, 1923.

Montville, Leigh. *The Big Bam: The Life and Times of Babe Ruth*. New York: Doubleday, 2006.

Morison, Samuel Eliot. *The Oxford History of the American People*. New York: Oxford University Press, 1965.

Murphy, Cait. *Crazy '08: How a Cast of Cranks, Rogues, Boneheads, and Magnates Created the Greatest Year in Baseball History*. New York: Smithsonian Books, 2007.

Nemec, David. *The Baseball Chronicle: Year-by-Year History of Major League Baseball*. Lincolnwood, Ill.: Publications International, 2004.

Okrent, Daniel, and Harris Lewine. *The Ultimate Baseball Book*. Boston: Houghton Mifflin, 1979.

Peale, Norman Vincent. *This Incredible Century*. Pawling, N.Y.: Peale Center for Christian Living, 1991.

Petersen, William J., and Randy Petersen. *100 Christian Books that Changed the Century*. Grand Rapids, Mich.: Fleming H. Revell, 2000.

Phillips, David R., and Lawrence Kart. *That Old Ball Game: Rare Photographs from Baseball's Glorious Past*. Chicago: Henry Regnery, 1975.

Pringle, Henry F. *Theodore Roosevelt: A Biography*. New York: Harcourt, Brace, & World, 1956.

Ritter, Lawrence S. *The Glory of Their Times: The Story of the Early Days of Baseball Told by the Men Who Played It*. New York: Macmillan, 1966.

Robinson, Ray. *Matty: An American Hero*. New York: Oxford University Press, 1993.

Rosenburg, John M. *The Story of Baseball*. New York: Random House, 1973.

Rushin, Steve. *The 34-Ton Bat: The Story of Baseball as Told Through Bobbleheads, Cracker Jacks, Jockstraps, Eye Black, and 375 Other Strange and Unforgettable Objects*. New York: Little, Brown, 2013.

Schoor, Gene. *Christy Mathewson: Baseball's Greatest Pitcher*. New York: Julian Messner, 1953.

Seib, Philip. *The Player: Christy Mathewson, Baseball, and the American Century*. New York: Four Walls Eight Windows, 2003.

Simon, Tom, ed. *Deadball Stars of the National League*. Washington, D.C.: Brasseys, 2004.

Smith, Robert. *Heroes of Baseball*. New York: World, 1952.

Spalding, A. G. *America's National Game*. New York: American Sports Publishing, 1911.

Stark, Benton. *The Year They Called Off the World Series*. Garden City Park, N.Y.: Avery, 1991.

Still, Bayard. *Mirror for Gotham: New York as Seen by Contemporaries*. New York: Fordham University Press, 1999.

Stout, Glenn. *Fenway 1912: The Birth of a Ballpark, a Championship Season, and Fenway's Remarkable First Year*. New York: Houghton Mifflin Harcourt, 2011.

Streeter, Robert E., ed. *Bucknell Now & Then: A Sesquicentennial Miscellany*. Dallas: Taylor, 1995.

Stump, Al. *Cobb: A Biography*. Chapel Hill, N.C.: Algonquin, 1996.

Swift, Tom. *Chief Bender's Burden*. Lincoln, Neb.: Bison Books, 2010.

Theiss, Lewis Edwin. *Centennial History of Bucknell University: 1846–1946*. Williamsport, Penn.: Grit Publishing, 1946.

Tindall, George B., and David E. Shi. *America: A Narrative History*. New York: Norton, 1984.

Vaccarro, Mike. *The First Fall Classic: The Red Sox, the Giants, and the Cast of Players, Pugs, and Politicos Who Reinvented the World Series in 1912*. New York: Doubleday, 2009.

Ward, Geoffrey C., and Ken Burns. *Baseball: An Illustrated History*. New York: Knopf, 1994.

Wheeler, John. *I've Got News for You*. New York: Dutton, 1961.

Whittingham, Richard. *Rites of Autumn: The Story of College Football*. New York: Free Press, 2001.

MAGAZINES

"Ball Players Hit 'Em With a Gun." *American Shooter*, January 1, 1916.

Carey, Max. "Why Matty Lasts." *Literary Digest*, August 23, 1913.

Cary, Lucian. "Mathewson's Biggest Victory." *Good Housekeeping*, August 1923.

Casey, Harry J. "Famous Bone-Head Plays." *Baseball*, January 1914.

"Christy Mathewson." *Youth's Companion*, November 12, 1925.

Daniel, Harry. "Christy Mathewson." *Chicago Inter-Ocean*, September 11, 1910.

Daniel, Harry. "Three-Fingered Mordecai Brown, Wizard of Flying Curves." *Chicago Inter-Ocean*, August 21, 1910.

"The Fight of a Clean Sportsman." *Outlook*, 131, May–August 1922.

Fullerton, Hugh. "Close Decisions." *American*, May 1911.

Hartt, Rollin Lynde. "The National Game." *Atlantic Monthly*, August 1908.

Hopper, James. "Training with the Giants." *Everybody's*, June 1909.

Irwin, Will. "The Deciding Game." *Collier's*, October 21, 1908.

Klem, William, and William Slocum. "Jousting with McGraw." *Collier's*, April 7, 1951.

Lardner, Ring. "The Greatest of 'Em All." *American*, June 1915.

Lardner, Ring. "Matty." *American*, August 1915.

Mathewson, Christy. "Why We Lost Three Straight Championships." *Everybody's*, October 1941.

Mathewson, Christy. "My Life So Far." *Baseball*, December 1914.

"Mathewson's Folks." *Baseball*, December 1914.

"Matty's Boyhood." *Literary Digest*, June 6, 1914.

Menke, Frank G. "Christy Mathewson's Case a Puzzle." *World of Baseball*, June 17, 1916.

Phelon, William A. "Reminiscences of Christy Mathewson." *Baseball*, December 1914.

Phelon, William A. "The Month in Baseball." *Baseball*, December 1918.

Rice, Grantland. "The Essential Ingredient." *Baseball*, April 1920.

Runyon, Damon. "How New York Feels about Mathewson." *World of Baseball*, August 5, 1916.

Spink, J. G. Taylor. "Down Memory Lane with Mrs. Christy Mathewson." *Sporting News*. *Sporting Life*, August 22, 1908.

Theiss, Lewis Edwin. "The Complete Story of Matty's Life." *Bucknell Alumni Monthly*, November 1925.

"Thorpe in Baseball," *Literary Digest*, February 15, 1913.

Williams, Helena. "The Come-Back of Christy Mathewson." *Journal of the Outdoor Life*, February 1924.

Wyant, A. R. E. "Christy Mathewson: Athlete, Soldier and Christian Gentleman," *Bucknell World*, March 1956.

NEWSPAPERS

Boston Globe, October 17, 1912.

Chicago Daily Tribune, June 14, 1905.

Chicago Daily Tribune, October 25, 1913.

Chicago Daily Tribune, November 14, 1913.

Chicago Day Book, October 5, 1912.

Cincinnati Enquirer, October 19, 1913.

El Paso Herald, November 12, 1909.

Fulton County (PA) *News*, April 13, 1911.

Fulton County (PA) *News*, April 20, 1911.

Honesdale (PA) *Citizen*, July 5, 1912.

Lewisburg Journal, March 7, 1903.

Los Angeles Sun, March 10, 1907.

New York Evening Telegram, August 14, 1921.

New York Evening World, October 9, 1901.

New York Evening World, October 1, 1904.

New York Evening World, October 14, 1905.

New York Herald, May 5, 1908.

New York Herald, October 12, 1913.

New York Herald, October 18, 1913.
New York Herald-Tribune, October 2, 1921.
New York Herald-Tribune, October 9, 1925.
New York Herald-Tribune, October 11, 1925.
New York Sun, September 24, 1908.
New York Sun, May 25, 1942.
New York Times, October 5, 1899.
New York Times, December 31, 1899.
New York Times, April 18, 1902.
New York Times, May 22, 1902.
New York Times, July 3, 1902.
New York Times, September 1, 1903.
New York Times, October 15, 1905.
New York Times, September 24, 1908.
New York Times, May 3, 1910.
New York Times, October 6, 1912.
New York Times, October 17, 1912.
New York Times, April 6, 1914.
New York Times, May 30, 1916.
New York Times, October 11, 1925.
New York Times, August 26, 1957.
New York Tribune, June 18, 1906.
New York Tribune, October 19, 1913.
New York Tribune, July 15, 1917.
Philadelphia Evening Ledger, July 21, 1916.
Philadelphia Inquirer, April 30, 1905.
Philadelphia Inquirer, November 25, 1932.
Philadelphia Public Ledger, May 15, 1933.
San Francisco Chronicle, November 13, 1913.
San Francisco Examiner, November 16, 1913.
Scranton Republican, December 25, 1913.
Scrantonian, August 7, 1967.
St. Louis Daily-Globe Democrat, July 16, 1901.
St. Louis Star, July 6, 1902.
St. Louis Star-Times, April 25, 1932.
Sunbury (PA) *Item*, April 10, 1929.
Sunbury (PA) *Item*, January 17, 1931.
Toledo (Ohio) *Blade*, October 24, 1925.
Washington Times, October 9, 1908.

MISCELLANEOUS

1901 Bucknell L'Agenda (university yearbook).
1902 Bucknell L'Agenda (university yearbook).
1927 Bucknell L'Agenda (university yearbook).
Bucknell University Archives. Letter to President Arnaud C. Marts from Christy Mathewson, Jr., January 30, 1944.
Bucknell University Archives. Letter to Alumni Secretary Al Stoughton from Christy Mathewson, Jr., July 1930.
Interview with Anna Outwater Day. Harrisonburg, Virginia, December 2003.
Interview with Betty Cook. Lewisburg, Pennsylvania, January 2004.
Library of Congress. *Baseball's World Series 1903–1910*.
National Baseball Hall of Fame. 1955 Induction Invitation.

Union County (PA) Planning Commission. Historical Site Survey #19, 1976.

U.S. Department of Commerce, Bureau of the Census. *Historical Statistics of the United States: Colonial Times to 1970, Part 1*. Washington, D.C.: Author, 1975.

INDEX

ABOUT THE AUTHOR

Bob Gaines was born into a naval family in 1945 and was raised in California, Rhode Island, and Virginia, with an obsession since childhood for recording his stray thoughts into hundreds of notebooks. After graduating from San Diego State, Bob became an award-winning sportswriter and columnist for the largest daily newspaper in North San Diego County, soon noted for both his humor and ability to portray the depth and compassion of his subjects. In the early 1990s, Bob became director of development communications at Bucknell University in Lewisburg, Pennsylvania, where a century earlier Christy Mathewson had been an undergraduate. Having taken early retirement from Bucknell to focus on writing, Bob now lives in southwest Virginia where he is an active member of Highlands Fellowship and watches his son—a future pastor—play football at Emory & Henry College.